STRATEGIC OUTSOURCING

A Structured Approach to Outsourcing Decisions and Initiatives

Maurice F. Greaver II

AMACOM
American Management Association
New York • Atlanta • Boston • Chicago • Kansas City •
San Francisco • Washington, D.C. • Brussels • Mexico City • Tokyo • Toronto

Library of Congress Cataloging-in-Publication Data

Greaver, Maurice F.
    Strategic outsourcing / Maurice F. Greaver II.
        p.   cm.
    Includes bibliographical references and index.
    ISBN 0-8144-0434-0
    1. Industrial procurement.   2. Make-or-buy decisions.
    3. Contracting out.   4. Strategic management.   I. Title.
    HD39.5.G735   1998
658.7'2—dc21   98-48605
                                                    CIP

Printing number

20 19 18 17 16 15 14 13 12 11

This book is dedicated to my family:
my wife, **Lee,**
daughters, **Catherine** and **Lauren,**
and son, **Bradley**

Table of Contents

Preface

Today's fast-changing environment, with its premium on knowledge, flexibility, and performance, is causing organizations to rethink their paradigms. A paradigm is "a set of rules or regulations (written or unwritten) that does two things: (1) it establishes or defines boundaries, and (2) it tells how to behave inside of the boundaries in order to be successful."[1] Organizations are questioning whether the traditional paradigm of "owning" the factors of production is the best way to achieve competitive advantage. The outsourcing concept of moving activities out of the organization to where the experts (and their resources) exist, as opposed to owning all of the resources, flies in the face of hundreds of years of tradition and experience.

To embrace this concept takes great courage. As the American humorist Josh Billings observed, "True courage is the knowledge of right and the determination to do it. False courage is a willingness to do what is wrong because others say it is right." True courage is looking for the highest value-added resources, irrespective of where they are, to meet the organization's needs. False courage is continuing to rely on internal resources because doing otherwise would bring exposure to criticism and unpopularity among the employees.

Outsourcing is a management tool that evokes great emotion. Upon hearing about the outsourcing concept, most employees hate it and whoever supports it. They fear they will lose their jobs. It may tug at your heartstrings to think of employees possibly losing their jobs, but is that an overriding consideration? Not in today's fiercely competitive environment. Outsourcing can provide employees with better training, development, and career opportunities.

If you believe in the essence of capitalism, in the free flow of resources to those who can most effectively manage those resources, then you will embrace outsourcing. The celebrated economist Joseph

---

[1]Joel Arthur Barker, *Future Edge, Discovering the New Paradigms of Success* (New York: Morrow, 1992), page 32.

Schumpeter once described capitalism as a process of creative destruction. Capital movement introduces new products and services, and old ones die. New employee skill sets are born, and old ones die. If you were a buggy whip manufacturer in the early 1900s, you probably hated the horseless carriage and the Henry Fords of that era. Henry Ford once said, "The highest use of capital is not to make more money, but to make money do more for the betterment of life." The car has made our lives better, and while its invention no doubt created hardship for buggy whip manufacturers and their employees, they adjusted. Today's employees are better trained and can adjust as well. Outsourcing can improve products, services, and our lives.

Managers are provided with funds to purchase resources to operate. Far too many think there is no cost for such funds and the resources they purchase. There is a cost. Managers are employed to make difficult decisions, providing a benefit to those who provided the funds, and they are accountable for the results. The American business philosopher and author Peter Drucker said, "Decision making is the specific executive task." In the corporate world this means not just serving customers and earning a profit, but also returning a fair yield to shareholders on their investment funds and adding shareholder value. (Managers in government have an equal obligation to taxpayers, and managers of nonprofit organizations have an equal obligation to their constituencies. It may not be measured financially, but the objective is the same.)

In order to add shareholder value, managers must earn consistently more than their cost of capital[2] (for example, 12 percent). Otherwise, the funds were invested unwisely. For example, why would the organization approve a capital expenditure for a new piece of equipment unless the investment would produce at least 12 percent over time? If it would not, the organization would have been better off investing in another asset that would, paying down their debt, buying back their stock, and so on. The recent focus on profits and shareholder value, led by institutional investors, puts tremendous pressure on management teams who fail to do this. As Harry Jack Gray, former chairman of United Technologies, said, "I use the words profit and capitalism proudly. Because when business is healthy, all of society is healthy."

---

[2]Each organization's cost of capital will be different, depending on their mix of debt and equity instruments and the costs of each instrument.

This performance-driven environment motivates managers to continually evaluate the resources purchased to ensure that they are the highest value added available.[3] Those resources include people, facilities, equipment, technologies, and networks (not computer networks, but the organization's value chain of suppliers, their suppliers, customers, their customers, distribution systems, consultants, and so on). Outsourcing providers are a form of supplier. If the providers can deliver the highest value added, they should be a resource of choice.

The only secret in business is *there is no secret*. Business requires consistent high-quality decision making by leaders, not luck. Football coach Joe Paterno said, "You have to perform at a consistently higher level than others. That's the true mark of a professional. Professionalism has nothing to do with getting paid for your services." Outsourcing is not a secret formula for success, not a magic wand for vaporizing problems, and not a management fad. It is just a management tool—not "the tool" but a newer tool, which is not well understood. In a capable executive's toolbox, it coexists with tools such as benchmarking, reengineering, restructuring, and activity-based cost management. Each tool has its function (its highest and best use), and outsourcing is enjoying wider usage today.

Audience and Approach

This book is directed at the readers who work for organizations that may need outsourcing services, as opposed to firms that provide them. The organizations undertake outsourcing initiatives less frequently than do providers who deal with them daily. For this reason, providers have developed sophisticated methodologies, sales techniques, contracts, and so on. Accordingly, this book should help the organization in leveling the outsourcing playing field.

This book is intended to serve as a guide for organization executives, managers, and outsourcing team members who are exploring outsourcing. It is a how-to manual, setting forth the various issues to be addressed in an outsourcing initiative, and suggests a method for addressing them. The

---

[3]Each organization's definition of highest value-added resources will be different, depending on their needs; however, it will likely be expressed in some form of costs and benefits (see reasons to outsource).

method assumes that the organization wants to undertake the challenge of studying outsourcing, using outside consultants as advisers only. Obviously consultants could be more actively involved by either participating as team members, leading the initiative, or actually performing the team's various activities on a turnkey basis.

This book addresses the more complex outsourcing initiatives involving large-scale functions and processes in which significant monetary assets are transferred to the provider and have several years of contract duration. These initiatives should be strategically driven, and the issues and methodologies described here should be addressed by the organization. Be careful not to be lured into shortcuts by time pressures or providers suggesting sole-source solutions and quick implementation.

On the other hand, if the organization is looking to outsource smaller nonstrategic areas, component parts, or individual activities to providers with whom it is familiar, or for periods of less than a year, the methodology described here would be overkill. Certainly shortcuts can be made judiciously, but many of the issues would be the same and this book could serve as a guide in such situations—although with a condensed methodology and the use of fewer resources in less time.

The methods outlined in this book derive from my experience as a corporate chief financial officer who outsourced a number of functions to providers, as a provider who has delivered outsource services to organizations, and as an outsourcing consultant to organizations who were exploring outsourcing. The book also benefits from the experiences of my associates in the outsourcing field and from the many participants in the outsourcing seminars I have led.

This book is not intended to be an academic treatise with many research studies and statistics. In my experience, most business managers prefer a more pragmatic, straightforward approach. Accordingly, the evidence is primarily anecdotal, representing the best practices that my associates and I have observed.

Use of Terms

I have tried to use generic words in order to avoid confusion. Some words might have several definitions, so I have chosen to highlight below the context in which the words are being used:

Provider:	Strategic partner, supplier, vendor
Organization:	Corporation, company, governmental agency, association
Factors of production:	People, facilities, equipment, technologies
Reasons to outsource:	Reasons, benefits, justifications, value

Unions

This book does not address the outsourcing issues if a union is involved. Clearly, the existence of a union complicates an outsourcing initiative significantly, but for many readers this issue is not relevant. While the list of issues is lengthy, it is important to understand that if a union is involved, outside advisers become even more necessary and the cycle time for the initiative should be extended.

Maurice F. Greaver II can be contacted at:
P.O. Box 468
Centreville, VA
(703) 830-9216
www.greaver.com
mgreaver@greaver.com

Acknowledgments

I would first like to thank the many friends and associates who assisted in my development as a CPA, professional services provider, business executive, strategic thinker and writer. Of special note here are Joseph G. Seck, Jr., Albert W. Gard III, Sidney L. Monroe, Frank A. Bruni, Daniel A. Bailey, Ruben D. Nava, Boh A. Dickey, Richard B. Shultz, Richard J. Ruggieri, Gary D. Mallery, Robert W. Crandall, Mark S. Lorenzetti, James G. Bond, Mary S. Russell, Emerson Beyer, and Stacy Jackson.

Secondly, I would like to thank those who have contributed to this book and to those who supported my research in outsourcing. Of special note are Allen J. Klein, Dorsey P. Wittig, James R. Horein, Matthew O. Hughes, J. Edward Coleman, Brian T. Kelleher, Steve Perna, Dan Bauer, Kathy Boyle, Michael P. McCracken, Lori Lyon, David Dawson, Jim Butterfield, Jenny Clarke, Richard R. Cappe, Joseph W. Lennon, Eric R. Greenberg, Carol Canzoneri, Anthony Lipnicki, Robert E. Zahler, Stephen J. Sheahan, James R. Emshoff, Ph.D., Ron R. Stratton, Kersi F. Munshi, and Ricky Waller.

Many thanks go to the unique talents and extra efforts of my editors, Ray O'Connell, Kate Pferdner, Shelly Wert, and Joseph Gustaitus.

Part One

Overview of Strategic Outsourcing

Chapter 1
Overview of Strategic Outsourcing

What Is Outsourcing?

Outsourcing is the act of transferring some of an organization's recurring internal activities and decision rights to outside providers, as set forth in a contract. Because the activities are *recurring* and a contract is used, outsourcing goes beyond the use of consultants. As a matter of practice, not only are the activities transferred, but the factors of production and decision rights often are, too. *Factors of production* are the resources that make the activities occur and include people, facilities, equipment, technology, and other assets. *Decision rights* are the responsibilities for making decisions over certain elements of the activities transferred.

Outsourcing Reasons and Benefits Sought

There are many "top five reasons to outsource" surveys floating around at any one time, each giving somewhat different results. This is not surprising. The populations surveyed vary, and how one ranks the reasons to outsource often depends on which chair one sits in. If CEOs are surveyed, the results are different from those of CFOs, and their results are different from those of CIOs and others. Just as the probability of another person's suit of clothes fitting you exactly is remote, so too is the probability of another organization's reasons to outsource fitting yours equally remote. What is critical is that you understand your reasons for considering outsourcing and the benefits you seek.

A list of twenty examples of reasons to outsource and the benefits sought (hereafter referred to as reasons) are given here:

Organizationally Driven Reasons

- Enhance effectiveness by focusing on what you do best.
- Increase flexibility to meet changing business conditions, demand for products and services, and technologies.
- Transform the organization.
- Increase product and service value, customer satisfaction, and shareholder value.

Improvement-Driven Reasons

- Improve operating performance.[1]
- Obtain expertise, skills, and technologies that would not otherwise be available.
- Improve management and control.
- Improve risk management.
- Acquire innovative ideas.
- Improve credibility and image by associating with superior providers.

Financially Driven Reasons

- Reduce investments in assets and free up these resources for other purposes.
- Generate cash by transferring assets to the provider.

Revenue-Driven Reasons

- Gain market access and business opportunities through the provider's network.
- Accelerate expansion by tapping into the provider's developed capacity, processes, and systems.

---

[1]Improved performance can relate to many different areas, such as higher quality, increased productivity, shorter cycle times, higher utilization, increased outputs, and greater profits.

- Expand sales and production capacity during periods when such expansion could not be financed.
- Commercially exploit the existing skills.

Cost-Driven Reasons

- Reduce costs through superior provider performance and the provider's lower cost structure.
- Turn fixed costs into variable costs.

Employee-Driven Reasons

- Give employees a stronger career path.
- Increase commitment and energy in noncore areas.

While this list is not exhaustive, it should provide food for thought. A description of one of these reasons is presented at the end of each chapter (each location is listed at Appendix 1). The outsourcing reasons are many, and by using the methodology presented here, are attainable. Outsourcing is a powerful tool when used appropriately. As French poet, novelist, and dramatist Victor Hugo put it, "Nothing in the world is so powerful as an idea whose time has come."

Levels of Outsourcing

In manufacturing, component parts or subassemblies (groups of parts) are outsourced to providers to be made. In other operations, outsourcing can occur at the following *activity levels*:

- Individual
- Functional
- Process

Outsourcing of *individual* activities involves moving specific positions out of the organization. This could be the management position of a poorly performing function, or technical positions (for example, an information systems auditor or a competitive intelligence analyst) that are difficult to fill when turnover occurs. Before you begin a search for such positions, outsourcing should be considered.

Organizations have typically been structured on a *functional cost center basis*, with each function having specialized knowledge and responsibilities.

Processes are how the products or services actually flow through the organization. When we link similar activities to create an output for the customers' benefit, we have a process. An organization can have many functions, but the processes generally number no more than twelve to fifteen.

Each organization determines its own processes. In Exhibit 1.1, for example, the processes noted represent six of Michael Porter's nine generic "value chain" processes, as outlined in his book, *Competitive Advantage*. The functions noted represent a few of the typical functions in a manufacturing company. The Xs represent points in each process where the functions add value to the process.

To better understand outsourcing at the individual, functional, and process activity levels, let's explore several examples. At the *individual activity level*, a person may not be able to perform certain activities at the desired performance level, and accordingly, the organization (functions, processes, etc.) suffers. For example, the payroll clerk may not be able to process payroll changes, checks, tax returns, and make the necessary accounting entries on time. This may occur for a variety of reasons, such as the organization's growth and hiring demands, cumbersome software, and/or incompetence. As a result, employees are not paid on time (affecting morale and productivity), employee changes are not entered into the system timely (hurting payroll accuracy and human resource statistics), and the monthly accounting records cannot be closed on time (delaying the distribution of financial statements). The controller is unhappy—and unpopular.

Exhibit 1.1   Processes and Functions

Processes	Purchasing	Receiving	Accounts Payable	Inventory Control	Inventory Distribution
Inbound logistics	X	X		X	X
Operations				X	X
Procurement	X	X	X		
Technology development	X	X	X	X	X
Human resources management	X	X	X	X	X
Infrastructure			X		

The controller investigates and concludes that the payroll clerk is competent and that one employee cannot perform all of these activities because of the continuing hiring surge. With the remaining accounting staff operating above capacity, the controller decides to bring in payroll providers to bid on the check processing and tax compliance activities. If successful, the controller outsources these activities and is now able to redeploy any excess payroll clerk time to assist the accounting staff.

Changing the previous example slightly, at the *functional level* the chief financial officer, to whom the controller and accounting function report, may be concerned that the payroll-related problems are symptoms of a bigger problem. After consulting with others, the CFO may conclude that the controller and the accounting staff are technically weak and their skills have become obsolete. The CFO decides that proposals should be sought from firms that provide accounting services. If successful, the CFO outsources the accounting function's activities and improves the quality of the accounting function's services.

At the *process level*, changing the previous example slightly again, when the CFO approaches the CEO to discuss the possible outsourcing of the accounting function, the CEO offers another solution. He suggests that what really exists is a companywide weakness in supporting administrative processes, including human resources, technology development, and infrastructure (such as legal and accounting). The organization has maintained a very low cost structure, which is admirable; but as a result, there have been few technological innovations (due to capital budget restrictions) and very little staff training and development. This has led to process stagnation, productivity deterioration, and key employee defections.

The CEO and CFO recognize that the restrictive capital and cost structures will not likely change soon, yet technological innovation and human resource development are critical to long-term success. They decide to approach the senior management team, and subsequently the board of directors, with a proposal to outsource the infrastructure, human resources, and technology development processes over the next five years.

This can be a politically charged initiative, because it will cut across the organization, affecting many functions (and fiefdoms). It can also be complicated and require the organization to work with large, sophisticated providers (as prime contractors) who can marshal significant resources (including subcontractors) to meet the wide range of needs. If successful, the CEO outsources three entire processes, resulting in improved performance, technological innovation, and employee development, without increasing capital requirements and costs.

What Is Strategic Outsourcing?

In the first two examples, the outsourcing decisions were driven by a tactical, problem-solving mentality. In the first, outsourcing solved the payroll processing problems. In the second, outsourcing solved the skills problems. In the third, it was driven by both tactical and strategic issues in which outsourcing solved the process stagnation, productivity deterioration, and key employee defection problems, looking at long-term issues. Accordingly, the outsourcing initiative becomes strategic when it is aligned with the organization's long-term strategies, and when the typical outsourcing benefits will emerge over several years, and when the results, either positive or negative, will be significant to the organization.

Strategic outsourcing takes outsourcing to a higher level by asking fundamental questions about outsourcing's relevance to the organization and its:

- Vision of its future
- Current and future core competencies
- Current and future structure
- Current and future costs
- Current and future performance
- Current and future competitive advantages

In a 1997 survey of CEOs by *Chief Executive* magazine[2] and Andersen Consulting, 382 CEOs responded. One of the questions asked if their approach to outsourcing was strategic, tactical, or both, with the following results:

Strategic	50%
Tactical	47
Both	3
Total	100%

[2]"View From the Top—Raise High the Roof Beam," *Chief Executive*, April 1997, page 67.

These results were confirmed in a 1997 survey by KMPG Peat Marwick[3] of senior-level executives in large companies across the United States, in which 189 questionnaires were completed and returned. One of the statements made was that outsourcing is a strategic tool, and asked respondents to react, with the following results:

Agree strongly	29%
Agree somewhat	60
Subtotal—Strategic	89
Disagree somewhat	3
Disagree strongly	1
Other	3
Total	100%

Outsourcing can be implemented within one year. Generally, the outsourcing of component parts and individual and functional activities can be completed within six months, but processes can take often take longer. Though it may take several years for all of the benefits to emerge, some should become apparent almost immediately.

The cost of an outsourcing mistake can be significant and difficult to reverse. Marriage provides a useful analogy. Like marriage, outsourcing is much easier to consummate (improperly) than it is to terminate, and recover from, if done poorly.

Picture the trauma of a failed information system outsourcing contract. Your computers, software and all of the technical specialists were transferred to the provider at inception. Now in the fifth year of a ten-year contract, both you and the provider want to terminate the contract (the best of termination circumstances). But your former personnel, who are still employed by the provider, are comfortable in their new roles and don't want to return to the organization. Either a new provider must be selected, or all of the computer equipment, software, computer center, and so on, must be replaced, and personnel must be hired and trained. Can you realistically recover from this anytime soon—and without significant costs?

Of greater risk is the possibility that a core competence is embedded in the activities or factors of production that are transferred. Core competencies may be unknowingly transferred, or the knowledge that will

---

[3]"KPMG Survey: Companies Increasingly Look to Outsourcing for Competitive Advantage," *KPMG Peat Marwick LLP*, 1997, page 6.

provide the foundation for future core competencies may not be well understood and be transferred. As a result, the organization can surrender future opportunities for competitive advantage and the related profit, without recognizing its loss, from which it cannot easily recover. In our previous example, if technology development was expected to be a future core competency, the CEO and CFO may have made a serious mistake in outsourcing technology, instead of investing in it.

Outsourcing is a strategic decision, requiring proactive, professional decision-making. As American corporate executive Leonard Stern once said, "Without risks we're all caretakers, and you can get a caretaker for very little money. . . . A leader has to have the vision that will let him take 2 and 2 and make 5." This book provides an appropriate strategic decision making methodology for outsourcing. Hereafter, "strategic outsourcing" will be referred to as "outsourcing."

Outsourcing History

Outsourcing is a term invented by the information systems trade press in the late 1980s. It was coined to describe the growing trend of large companies transferring their information systems to providers. These services, however, can be traced back to at least World War II, when systems facilities management services were provided to the U. S. federal government.

Outsourcing is similar to subcontracting, joint venturing, and strategic partnering concepts, which date back hundreds of years. It has been a common practice:

- For farmers to hire groups of migrant workers to supplement the farmer's staff at harvest time
- For construction companies to subcontract elements of subsystem construction (electrical and plumbing, for example)
- For the government to contract for the production of military equipment with contractors who are strategically partnered, and for those contractors to subcontract the components

What sets outsourcing apart from these similar concepts is the fact that "internal" activities are being transferred out. This may not necessarily be the case with subcontracting and joint venturing.

For many years, manufacturers, in the automobile industry have made *component parts* that were unique and supported their product differentiation. As these components became commodities, the auto manufacturers would outsource the components to providers. This practice has expanded to subassemblies.

In recent years, many other *functions* in all industries have been actively outsourced, including the following:

- Payroll
- Pension administration
- Information systems and technology
- Telecommunications
- Document processing (mailroom, copiers, and so on)
- Accounting
- Tax compliance
- Internal audit
- Materials/supplies inventory stocking and distribution
- Facilities management and maintenance
- Food service
- Janitorial services
- Management services (construction, hotels, and the like)

Outsourcing of entire *processes* has not been prevalent. Yet recently inbound and outbound logistics (such as shipping and tracking) have frequently been outsourced. Trucking companies in particular, such as Roadway, Ryder and Schneider National, have aggressively marketed their logistics services and assumed responsibility for many internal logistics processes, including such things as drivers, trucks, and loading docks.

Outsourcing Trends

In his book, *The Age of Unreason*, noted London Business School professor and consultant Charles Handy predicts that "less than half of the workforce in the industrialized world will be in 'proper' full-time jobs in organizations by the beginning of the twenty-first century." He then goes on to describe his idea of the shamrock organization, in which each leaf of the shamrock represents elements of the organization's workforce:

> The first leaf of the shamrock represents the core workers, what I prefer to call the professional core because it is increasingly made up of qualified professionals, technicians, and managers. These are the people who are essential to the organization. . . .

If the core is smaller, who then does the work? Increasingly, it is contracted out to the organizations I call the second leaf of the shamrock. . . . All nonessential work, work which could be done by someone else, is therefore contracted out to people who make a specialty of it, and who should, in theory, be able to do it better for less cost. . . . The third leaf of the shamrock is the flexible labor force, all those part-time workers and temporary workers who are the fastest growing part of the employment scene. . . . The fourth leaf? There is one other category of subcontracting which needs to be mentioned. It is the growing practice of getting the customer to do the work.[4]

The traditional workforce of full-time workers is changing. Thirty or forty years ago, a person might well spend a career working for one or two firms. Today, people easily work for five or ten. Women have entered the workforce as the economy's service sector has expanded. Organizations have "downsized," with entire layers of middle managers stripped away. Computers now allow many people to work effectively from home. Imagine the flexibility that will be created when video conferencing technologies are perfected!

What changes have occurred so that outsourcing is now embraced as an important restructuring tool? Here are some of them:

- Large organizational size is no longer a competitive advantage.
- Small, agile niche competitors can now change industries and cost structures overnight.
- Competitive pressures are more severe in a global economy.
- Product and service cycle times have reduced dramatically, and time based competition demands quicker response.
- Investors and analysts demand a focused management that delivers.
- Bottom line performance, growth, and size are no longer predictors of future profits.
- Significant operating and financial performance improvements are critical to success, and long term survival.

[4]Charles Handy, *The Age of Unreason* (Boston: Harvard Business School Press, 1991), pages 31, 90–93, 101.

- Supplies of technical specialists are reasonably plentiful, thus employing them internally is unnecessary to their availability.
- Cutting edge technology and knowledge are now recognized as competitive weapons but are expensive to acquire and successful results are often elusive when implemented internally.

The nature of shareholders worldwide has also changed in the past decade. In the United States, for example, institutional investors such as pension funds and mutual funds now own almost half of the shares of publicly traded companies. These investors, unlike individuals, have the clout to influence corporate executives to create shareholder value. If companies fail to consistently deliver economic value added, institutional investors pressure boards of directors to make management changes. Accordingly, executives are searching for tools that can help them meet these new challenges. Outsourcing is just such a tool.

Historically, outsourcing was used when organizations could not perform, perhaps due to incompetence, lack of capacity, financial pressures, or technological failure. Now outsourcing is being used to restructure organizations that have been quite successful. These organizations now recognize that management's undivided attention on building core competencies and serving customer needs is critical. Anything that distracts from this focus will be considered for outsourcing.

In the past, the most significant outsourcing involved component parts manufacturing and information systems. But today fast changing technical staff functions (such as accounting, tax compliance, and pension administration) that require substantial systems investment, support, and expertise, are being outsourced more and more. Organizations are reluctant to invest in and maintain cutting-edge technology and technical specialists internally, when they know that similar assets exist externally, and were developed with others' investment and risk.

The trend in larger organizations is to outsource entire processes. This will be done with strategic relationships and the transfer of significant decision rights. The providers will have large, sophisticated operations providing value-added services at a level incomprehensible even fifteen years ago. The outsourcing begins with processes furthest from the core and then moves toward it. It is unlikely that operating processes or management positions will ever be outsourced. Another trend, involving large diversified companies, is to outsource global functions and processes to large providers with stronger global presence and expertise. For example, the centralized internal audit function for a U.S.-based company that seeks a global presence can be outsourced to one of the large auditing firms with operations throughout the world.

For smaller and midsize organizations, outsourcing of individual activities is growing. While this may have started with short-term replacements when open positions occurred (rent-a-CFO, for example), these arrangements make sense over the longer term for technical positions whose needs are recurring but are not needed on a full-time, permanent basis. This could include senior positions (CFO, CIO, CMO, etc.) or midlevel technical positions, such as project managers, programmers, and merger/acquisition analysts. These positions will not be outsourced to large providers, but to small providers of one to ten persons. This is where the very capable, but downsized middle managers, who worked for large organizations, could end up working.

A longer-term prediction involves organizations whose necessary core competencies or anticipated future core competencies have weakened or are nonexistent. While these areas are not being outsourced right now, such organizations will begin to outsource them over the next decade to superior providers for a period of time. This may sound like heresy, but is necessary in order to cut the learning curve on building these core competencies, after which time, they can be insourced and invested in heavily. This is not dissimilar to the way that Japanese companies built core competencies during the decades following World War II, by forming joint ventures (an outsourcing cousin) and signing licensing agreements with superior companies.

Outsourcing Growth

Outsourcing is expected to grow at double-digit rates over the coming decade. In a 1996 survey by KPMG Peat Marwick LLP of Fortune 500 CEOs, 94 percent of them said that they outsource and many predicted a marked increase. It found that 86 percent expected to outsource additional processes over the next five years.[5] In a 1997 survey by KPMG Peat Marwick, "G2 Research predicts that by the year 2000, the worldwide

[5]CEO Briefing "Outsourcing's Inexorable Growth," *Investors Business Daily*, October 24, 1996, page A3.

market for such services will approach $282 billion, with a growth rate of 20 percent."[6]

In a 1996 survey by AMA Research (a division of the American Management Association), in which thirty-seven activities were listed and sent to managers in the purchasing, administrative, and financial functions in AMA member companies, there were 619 respondents, with the following results:

- 94 percent of the respondent firms outsource at least one listed activity, and the average number of activities outsourced is nine.
- Outsourcing is growing most rapidly in accounting and finance activities, where it has doubled in the past three years. Other important growth areas: information systems (a 40 percent increase since 1994) and marketing (a 35 percent increase).[7]

According to information retrieved from Dun & Bradstreet's information database, the number of outsource providers increased 65 percent between 1989 and 1994.[8] Why is this happening? In addition to the reasons already explained, many providers found that their traditional markets and related revenues had flattened out or dropped during the recession. Outsourcing gave providers a growing market to exploit.

For example, from the 1960s to the 1980s the largest accounting firms willingly relinquished audit work (fees) to "internal audit" functions within their clientele. In the past few years those same firms have aggressively sought to recapture that audit work by providing outsourcing services. Outsourcing contracts often run for a period of years (as long as ten), and can represent tens of millions of dollars in value, with the typical information systems contracts running into the hundreds of millions and higher.

[6]"KPMG Survey: Companies Increasingly Look to Outsourcing for Competitive Advantage," *KPMG Peat Marwick LLP*, 1997, page 11.

[7]Eric Rolfe Greenberg and Carol Canzoneri, "Outsourcing: The AMA Survey," *AMA Research Reports*, 1997. (Note: This survey is printed in its entirety in Appendix 3.)

[8]Newswatch—Industry Focus, "Outsourcing Is Everywhere," *CFO Magazine*, December 1994, page 23.

Another Reason to Outsource:
Obtain Expertise, Skills, and Technologies
That Would Not Otherwise Be Available

In a fast-evolving market where new technologies are emerging, the knowledge and skills of individuals are very limited. The technologies themselves may be proprietary and not available on the open market. If organizations can attract the knowledge and skills base or technologies, they have an advantage.

Not every organization will be able to attract this knowledge and skills base. In fact, some organizations couldn't attract these individuals at even a healthy compensation premium, due to an unattractive reputation, physical location, lines of reporting, and so on. What do these organizations do to stay competitive? Similarly, other organizations may be able to acquire the individuals but not the technology. What do these companies do to stay competitive?

Outsourcing allows these organizations to obtain the knowledge skills base or technology. The provider can and has attrracted the base because the provider's current and future core competencies match that of the knowledge skills base. The provider is attractive as a long-term employer because the provider can offer a career track and higher future compensation for successful performance. The provider has the technology and is willing to effectively rent it long term, at a price, if it can deliver the service.

Chapter 2

Methodology

The Seven Steps to Successful Outsourcing

The following are the suggested steps to successful outsourcing:

1. Planning initiatives
2. Exploring strategic implications
3. Analyzing costs/performance
4. Selecting providers
5. Negotiating terms
6. Transitioning resources
7. Managing relationships

These steps represent section headings in this book and are summarized in this chapter (see Exhibit 2.1). The steps can and should be modified to fit the specific organization and outsourcing situation. On the other hand, caution should be exercised when those wishing to begin outsourcing immediately encourage significant shortcuts. As the British philosopher Alfred North Whitehead put it, "Seek simplicity and distrust it." It takes time to implement an outsourcing initiative, and longer to do it right.

While the steps are listed in their approximate chronological order, many of them are interrelated and should run somewhat parallel. This is important because:

- There is constant learning, testing, and adjustment to the project as it progresses. The value of this new information would be lost for the earlier steps if the steps were rigidly followed sequentially.

Exhibit 2.1   Seven Steps to Successful Outsourcing

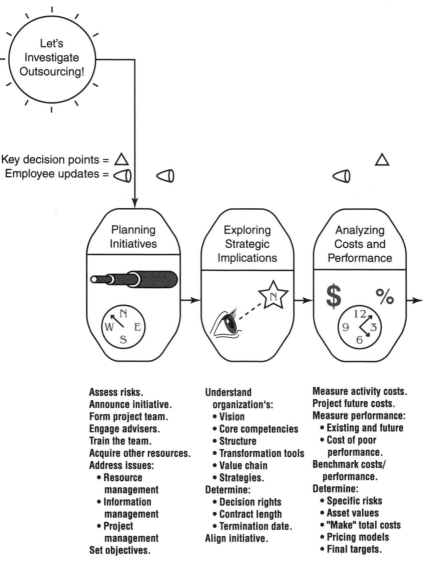

Let's Investigate Outsourcing!

Key decision points = △
Employee updates = ◁

Planning Initiatives

Exploring Strategic Implications

Analyzing Costs and Performance

Assess risks.
Announce initiative.
Form project team.
Engage advisers.
Train the team.
Acquire other resources.
Address issues:
• Resource
management
• Information
management
• Project
management
Set objectives.

Understand
organization's:
• Vision
• Core competencies
• Structure
• Transformation tools
• Value chain
• Strategies.
Determine:
• Decision rights
• Contract length
• Termination date.
Align initiative.

Measure activity costs.
Project future costs.
Measure performance:
• Existing and future
• Cost of poor
performance.
Benchmark costs/
performance.
Determine:
• Specific risks
• Asset values
• "Make" total costs
• Pricing models
• Final targets.

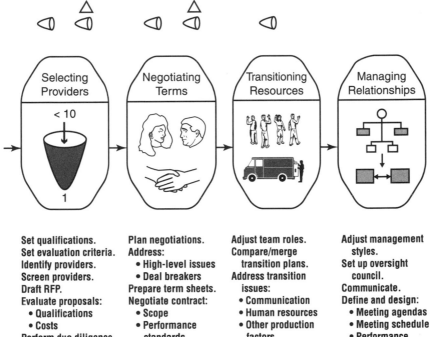

Selecting Providers	Negotiating Terms	Transitioning Resources	Managing Relationships
Set qualifications.	Plan negotiations.	Adjust team roles.	Adjust management
Set evaluation criteria.	Address:	Compare/merge	styles.
Identify providers.	• High-level issues	transition plans.	Set up oversight
Screen providers.	• Deal breakers	Address transition	council.
Draft RFP.	Prepare term sheets.	issues:	Communicate.
Evaluate proposals:	Negotiate contract:	• Communication	Define and design:
• Qualifications	• Scope	• Human resources	• Meeting agendas
• Costs	• Performance	• Other production	• Meeting schedule
Perform due diligence.	standards	factors.	• Performance
Determine:	• Pricing	Meet with employees:	reports.
• "Buy" total costs	schedules	• Organization	Perform oversight role.
• Short-list providers	• Terms and	• Provider.	Confront poor
• Finalist provider	conditions.	Make offers/termination.	performance.
• Review with senior	Announce	Provide counseling.	Solve problems.
management.	relationship.	Physically move.	Build the relationship.

Outsourcing Success at JLG Industries

JLG Industries (JLG) is one of the world's leading manufacturers, distributors, and international marketers of mobile aerial work platforms. Sales are made principally to independent distributors, who rent and sell the products to a broad customer base, which includes users in the industrial, commercial, and construction markets. Headquartered in McConnellsburg, Pennsylvania, JLG has two additional manufacturing facilities in Bedford, Pennsylvania, and sales and service locations in Scotland and Australia.

Paraphrasing their 1996 annual report,

> Another initiative in achieving operating excellence is . . . strategic outsourcing . . . to manage our manufactured components that may be more efficiently and economically sourced from outside vendors. This initiative is aimed at achieving ongoing cost reductions, improving quality, and adding capacity, while allowing us to better utilize our employees and concentrate our resources on fewer and more important areas of our manufacturing processes.

At JLG, they have made outsourcing a process rather than a discrete event. The strategic corporate outsourcing department's goal in to contribute to JLG's strategic profitable growth by focusing on noncore manufacturing competencies and noncore processes that are available outside of JLG at a better value. JLG achieves profitable growth by gaining competitive advantage, including optimizing performance, quality, and cost through strategic alliances with providers having world-class expertise that deliver value, reliability, speed, and innovation, and which can support their international expansion. They have been outsourcing for more than ten years, with their outsourcing volume growth matching the overall business growth. A major evolution has been their production departments recognizing that the provider base is more efficient at performing JLG's noncore competencies, resulting in requests to outsource the work.

JLG outsources for many reasons:

- To improve the business focus of meeting the customer's needs, by concentrating on the broader business issues (the "what" of the business) while having operational details (the "how" of the business) assumed by outside experts.
- To gain access to world-class capabilities; expertise and excellence come from specialization.
- To share risks on the basis of the provider making capital investment decisions on the behalf of multiple clients.
- To become more flexible, more dynamic, and better able to change to meet changing opportunities.
- To redirect resources to more strategic activities that provide a greater return in serving the customer. Instead of acquiring resources through capital expenditures, they contract for them on an "as used," operational expense basis.
- To improve the value chain by migrating to higher integrated parts (outsource complete parts, subassemblies, kits, painted components) and more process-integrated and value-focused providers.

- To reduce or control operating costs.
- To gain additional capacity.

In the make or buy decision, JLG uses the following summary criteria:

CUSTOMER VIEW OF FUNCTION:	■ *Outsource/buy:* Customers concerned with outcome; functions not visible. ■ *In-house make:* Customers concerned with the process; functions are the key differentiator.
WORLD-CLASS ABILITY:	■ *Outsource/buy:* Resources not available. ■ *In-house make:* Resources and capabilities exist to continue or achieve world-class performance.
CAPABILITIES AND PHYSICAL ASSETS TO PERFORM FUNCTIONS:	■ *Outsource/buy:* Available on the market from qualified providers. ■ *In-house/make:* Requires specialized capabilities and assets: few qualified, independent providers.
PERFORMED CAPABILITY VS. ALTERNATIVE SOURCES:	■ *Outsource/buy:* External providers are clearly more competent. ■ *In-house make:* Leadership position exists.
TIME AND COST REQUIRED TO CLOSE PERFORMANCE GAP:	■ *Outsource/buy:* Significant capital and resources required to improve the gap. ■ *In-house make:* Internal source has clearly competitive cost advantage; improvement rate is high.

JLG's outsourcing strategy involves:

- Building trust with providers by providing them with JLG's strategy, thereby encouraging them to make capital investments to improve their processes and reduce JLG's cost
- Continuing to reduce lead time and increase delivery frequency to support the journey toward synchronous flow manufacturing
- Optimizing the supply chain by exploiting the core competency of procurement to a sustainable competitive advantage
- Encouraging providers to suggest product redesign to optimize their processes and ultimately reduce their sale price

There are many success stories. One involves their use of the JIT II, a concept where JLG's provider has an employee on-site. This in-plant representative, with access to JLG's MRP system, orders and maintains their company's inventory. The initial JIT II providers, Olympic Steel, Inc., and Marmon/Keystone Corporation, were to perform this in-plant activity only for raw material. Currently, Olympic Steel and Marmon/Keystone deliver more than 50,000 value-added parts per month on a five-times-per-week basis.

In summary, JLG Industries has a strategic outsourcing plan, and they work closely with their providers to cost-effectively deliver parts to their assembly lines.

- If there is not continuous referral to the early steps, it's possible for the project's purpose (reasons to outsource) to blur and wander on to undesired purposes.
- Running in parallel reduces overall project cycle time, getting to a go/no go decision quickly, which is very important to overall project success—delays can kill such a project.

Exhibit 2.2 shows a somewhat staggered start/finish line, emphasizing parallel tracks.

It might be valuable to assign different team members to lead each of the phases of the initiative. This would encourage the earliest start for each phase and also train the team members in elements of project management, so that some of them could assume the project leader roles on the subsequent outsourcing initiatives.

Planning Initiatives

As with any significant new initiative, planning activities, including project management issues, are important. Typically, cross-functional teams are formed to study and implement outsourcing initiatives, so team member and leader selection come into play. The project team assesses the risks and the resources, information, and management skills needed to mitigate those risks. Team objectives, deliverables, and timetables should be set and management "buy-in" must be achieved.

Exhibit 2.2   Staggered Start/Finish for the Methodology Phases

Methodology Phases	Start	Outsourcing Initiative Cycle Time	Finish
Planning outsourcing initiatives		————————————	
Exploring strategic implications		————————————	
Analyzing costs/ performance		————————————	
Selecting vendors		————————————	
Negotiating terms		————————————	
Transitioning resources		————————————	
Managing relationships		————————————	

Because the outsourcing providers are not only experts in their fields but also experts in negotiating contracts, organizations often involve outside advisers to level the playing field. These advisers can include:

- Outsourcing consultants to help the team work effectively and efficiently in the shortest cycle time
- Lawyers experienced in negotiating and drawing up outsourcing contracts
- CPAs experienced in analyzing costs using sophisticated tools such as activity-based costing
- Other specialists, depending on the situation

How the organization announces the outsourcing initiative to its employees must be planned and well executed. Since employees inevitably learn of the initiative as soon as it is decided, it is better to make an announcement that outsourcing will be explored. Otherwise, employees will generally assume the worst, without having the facts (including the benefits to them), and morale will plummet. Employees must also be kept informed about the initiative's progress.

Exploring Strategic Implications

Outsourcing can be a powerful strategic tool. To harness its power, however, involves asking fundamental questions regarding outsourcing's relevance to the organization's:

- Vision of its future
- Current and future structures
- Current and future core competencies
- Current and future costs
- Current and future performance
- Current and future competitive advantages

By exploring the answers to these questions, the project team is better able to understand how outsourcing can fit within the organization's strategies, and how its implementation will affect those strategies. For example, an organization might have strategies to reduce costs (to remain competitive) and introduce employee-driven, self-directed work teams (to improve morale). While on the surface outsourcing would be a logical tool to achieve cost reduction, it would probably also appear to employees to be dangerous (it might, for example, foster job insecurity). As a result, an outsourcing initiative might discourage the type of employee support necessary for team building. By exploring these strategic implications, executives can evaluate the probabilities of outsourcing's success and how to implement it more effectively.

Outsourcing is an effective restructuring transformation tool, and the project team learns how it fits with other transformation tools that may also be used by the organization. Further, any transformation initiative will need to confront issues, such as resistance, caused by change. The project team will plan for overcoming such resistance, especially in emotionally charged environments involving outsourcing employees.

Analyzing Costs and Performance

In the traditional, financially driven make or buy decision, the project team studies the existing costs of the activities (such as functions and processes) to be outsourced and compares them to the providers' proposals for the costs of outsourcing those activities. Unfortunately, most organizations capture costs on a cost element basis (such as salaries, benefits, rent, and depreciation) as opposed to an activity basis. The outsourcing project team, however, conducts activity-based analyses in order to understand the costs of the activities that might be outsourced and those that are staying. To this are added the cost of invested capital and the estimated costs of poor performance.

Further, having gathered activity-based costs for existing activities, the team makes reasonable projections of future costs for these activities. It estimates which costs do not disappear with outsourcing and what new costs will be incurred as a result of outsourcing. These costs must be added to the provider's pricing. Finally, there are financial benefits resulting from outsourcing that are other than cost-related. These are estimated and used in the make or buy decision.

Current performance is likewise measured and analyzed. Performance improvement is often a reason for outsourcing, so a baseline is set against which to measure improvement. Further, the project team estimates the financial impact of the internal unit's poor performance. And finally, future performance is projected, given anticipated changes in business and other conditions. But even if performance improvement is not a goal, understanding existing performance is fundamental to setting provider performance standards and monitoring their performance.

The project team addresses and sets a value on the assets that may be transferred to the provider as a result of outsourcing. The various alternative provider-pricing models are considered to decide which best fits the organization's outsourcing situation.

Selecting Providers

The project team lists the criteria for a "qualified" provider based on the reasons to outsource. Potential providers are identified and preliminary investigations are made to determine their qualifications and confirm their interest in the transaction. Their qualifications are then compared to the criteria, and a decision is made on whether they should be invited to propose.

Requests for proposals (RFPs) are prepared and delivered to the targeted providers' list. The RFP must be highly structured if the proposals are to be comparable and responsive. The RFP may include:

- Reasons to outsource
- Outsourcing scope—service specifications
- Provider qualifications
- Pricing models preferred
- Performance measures
- Requests for innovative ideas
- Notice of bidders' communications/meetings

When the proposals are returned, they are evaluated and compared to the other proposals and to the organization's expectations (as set forth in the RFP). This is an evaluation of both qualifications and cost. Due diligence should be performed, such as reference checking, output testing, and site visits. Then further discussions are held with the providers on the short list, who then make formal presentations. Finally, a prime provider candidate is selected and negotiations can be planned.

Negotiating Terms

Negotiations do not begin until the following have occurred:

- The project team (or its delegate) is prepared to negotiate.
- The negotiation strategy has been planned.

- The provider has completed its sales process.
- The ground rules for the negotiation have been set.

The negotiations begin with a term sheet, which is used to convert the RFP and resulting proposal into an informal contract summary. To do this, the parties negotiate the terms and reach final agreement on the major issues. It will include specific terms for the:

- Scope of services
- Factors of production
- Performance standards
- Transition provisions
- Management and control
- Pricing, including for changes in the business, scope and volume
- Termination provisions

The term sheet leads to detailed negotiations, which enables the lawyers to draft a contract document. This brings more specificity still and introduces the legal language necessary to reach an enforceable agreement.

Transitioning Resources

When the deal is done, it is time to begin the transition. The human resources issues are carefully addressed, and with sensitivity. When in doubt, two words to remember are: overcommunication and overcompensation. These have been valuable employees and they deserve respect. How these employees are treated on their way out will go a long way in determining how the remaining employees, who were not outsourced, view not only outsourcing but also the organization as a whole. Their reaction will affect future outsourcing initiatives.

The other factors of production, such as equipment, facilities, software, and third-party agreements, may then be transferred to the provider. This is easier if the provider is coming on to your site, or more difficult, if the factors must be relocated.

Managing Relationships

When the provider's services begin, one type of management ends (such as managing the production factors) and another begins (such as managing provider relationships). A key to building the new relationship is how both parties will monitor performance, evaluate the results, and resolve problems.

Periodic reporting, meetings, and audits will have been agreed to in the contract. Although this is important, the relationship should be built on trust and commitment to success. This is a partnership of shared commitment. Together it stands (succeeds), while separately it falls (fails).

Relationships are formed by people, not by the contract. And these people will be tested when unforeseen problems arise, employee feelings are hurt, and perceptions of unfair advantages emerge. It is a new type of management that demands new skills. Accordingly, the best persons to manage the provider relationship may not be the technical specialists who headed the function or process that was outsourced.

As the contract approaches its end, the relationship team considers whether to extend it, renegotiate it, or conduct a new competition. The team decides whether to follow the original methodology or a streamlined process for this exercise.

Inhibitors to Outsourcing

As discussions about outsourcing are held, the following inhibitors are likely to emerge and will need to be addressed before the initiative can gain much energy:

- Uncertainty
- Loss of control
- Loss of core competencies
- Employee unhappiness
- Difficulty in reversing
- Risks of failure

Feelings of uncertainty will range from wondering what outsourcing is all about, to doubts about whether qualified providers exist, to questioning whether the providers will deliver what they promise. Providing a description of the initiative and the methodology to be followed should relieve those feelings of uncertainty. It must be emphasized that nothing will be done without a review of the facts and appropriate due diligence of the promises.

Management may question whether it wants to relinquish control, generally in the form of decision rights, over the activities to be outsourced. Historically, management teams have followed a command-and-control approach, so outsourcing goes against their management paradigms. Fortunately, respected business leaders, including Jack Welch, Tom Peters, and others, have shown that big isn't always better and that control, through owning all of the decision rights or factors of production, isn't necessarily productive. Partnering with more capable, focused organizations can work better.

There will also be concern that outsourcing may cause a loss of core competencies or a hollowing out of the organization's ability to compete. The outsourcing initiative, therefore, focuses on aligning its objectives with the organization's strategies. In particular, it addresses the risk of losing core competencies through a test of the outsourcing targets, to determine that they are not current or future core competencies. In most organizations, the number of outsourcing targets is high, so the initial targets should easily steer clear of any strategic conflicts.

Any analysis of employees' views on outsourcing will initially conclude that outsourcing is a mistake. The biggest employee concern is job security. But how much security do employees really have compared to what they think they have? Ask them to think back over the last fifteen to twenty years of organizational restructuring, including the periods of mergers, acquisitions, buyouts, downsizings, and reengineerings, and observe how poorly employees have fared. American essayist and lecturer Helen Keller once said, "Security is mostly superstition. It does not exist in nature."

Realistically, an employee's skills are that employee's security. As Harold Geneen, former chief executive officer of ITT, once put it, "In the business world, everyone is paid in two coins: cash and experience. Take the experience first; the cash will come later." Outsourcing better aligns employees' special knowledge and skills with the provider's core competencies, and as their new employer, the provider can offer a better career path, supported by stronger training and development.

Outsourcing can be reversed, but it is difficult. It is also unusual, if the outsourcing decision was originally made for the correct reasons. Reversing the decision means bringing the outsourced activities back in house.

An organization that begins outsourcing is like a traveler taking an airplane trip. Travelers could drive their cars to their destinations, but they choose to outsource the transportation to the airline. Only something major (for example, discovering a fear of flying) will prompt a reversal of the decision. If the plane experiences problems on take-off, it returns to the airport. But most people don't get off the plane and into their cars; they wait for the next plane. If they become unhappy with the air carrier, they don't stop flying; they simply change air carriers. There are options to reversing the outsourcing decision, such as changing or adding providers.

Are all outsourcing initiatives successful? Of course there have been outsourcing failures. There is risk. The organization's managers may be asking, "Why should we take these risks?" In the words of the great skier Jean-Claude Killy, "To win you have to risk loss." In today's fast-changing environment, staying the same is riskier than outsourcing. If a function or process isn't performing well, they are a drag on the organization. The risk of an outsourcing failure is greatly lessened when a thorough methodology such as the one described in this book is followed. This methodology helps mitigate your risks.

The New Provider Relationships

Today, most organizations recognize the value of strong, close relationships with a few high quality providers. This was not always the case. In past decades, in the old organization/provider relationship, the organization (customer):

- Viewed the provider as a necessary evil, and certainly with little trust.
- Controlled the provider economically by spreading small orders among many providers.
- Communicated with providers as little as possible, and when they did, it was confrontational.
- Continually pressured providers to lower their prices.
- Would switch providers for any price decrease.
- Refused to measure the beneficial ways in which providers could perform (to add value), but focused only on the negative measures of provider failure.
- Recognized little value in sharing important information on forecasts, scheduling, etc. with providers, forcing larger inventory stocks and long lead times.
- Saw no value in tapping into the providers' creativity or core competencies for product/service design or total cost reduction.

The methodology described in this book may have the appearance of the organization putting the providers through the traditional proposal process. But deeper review of the details reveals that this methodology is actually focused on:

- Building a sound, trusting relationship that can become strategic
- Increasing the volume of business with fewer providers, when they perform well
- Sharing the control and the decision rights with providers
- Increasing reliance on the providers, tying the two businesses, and their future success, closely together
- Holding frequent communication and on-site meetings with providers to solve problems and design better ways of operating
- Encouraging providers to also outsource to strengthen their supply chain
- Recognizing that low price is generally not the only, or even the best, determinate of provider selection
- Exploring ways to measure providers' contributions to success, not just failures
- Encouraging the sharing of information and systems wherever possible
- Rewarding the provider for input of all kinds, not just related to their service
- Sharing the gains made from outsourcing
- Overcoming the "not invented here, thus it's no good" attitude

The relationship starts with the first communication (generally the request for proposal) and builds from there. If the organization is to receive maximum benefit, the project team should understand how to nurture the relationship and not revert to the old adversarial style. Outsourcing done well is a partnership that benefits both organizations.

Another Reason to Outsource:
Increase Flexibility to Meet Changing Business Conditions, Demand for Products/Services, and Technologies

Ian Wilson, former Chairman of General Electric, once said, "No amount of sophistication is going to allay the fact that all your knowledge is about the past and all your decisions are about the future." Think back ten years, about your industry, and your niche in it:

- Who were the players?
- What were seen then as the opportunities for, and threats to, each of these organizations?
- Did unanticipated new competitors arrive in the market?
- Are today's products or services the same?
- How did you and your customers operate?
- Is customer demand the same as then (or even last month or last year)?
- Did your suppliers change or did their operating methods change?
- What new technologies have emerged and what is their impact?
- Did unanticipated new laws or regulations appear?
- Did industry paradigms shift?

What has been your track record for predicting the future? Weren't there many changes you didn't foresee? Unless you leapfrogged ahead in market share and profitability during the past ten years, then you didn't see the future more clearly than your competitors and potential competitors. If they didn't leapfrog you, then they were no more prescient than you were. So, if you agree that the future is foggy, how can you gain a competitive advantage? By being quicker to adjust when the fog burns off. In a football game, it is often the team that makes the better on-field and halftime adjustments that wins.

Outsourcing allows us to change our business quickly, to meet new conditions because:

- We are not invested in the existing resources, our provider is.
- Our providers' core competencies allow them to stay on the cutting edge (of our noncore areas), thus making it possible to take quick shifts in stride.
- We can add new provider capacity when demand surges and reduce provider capacity when demand slackens, with little cost to us.
- We can add providers with new technologies that best match our needs as they emerge, without the up-front risk and investment.

Outsourcing provides the flexibility to be able to react to an uncertain future.

Part Two

Planning Initiatives

Chapter 3

Project Management and Champions

Risk Assessment

Any new program, product, service, or project has risks, and an outsourcing initiative is no different. The risks can be divided into three types:

- Risks inherent in any project
- General risks that would be present in most outsourcing projects
- Specific risks that would confront the specific organization, people, resources, and providers involved

Inherent risks are not discussed in this book, but could be explored further with project or risk management texts. Many chapters in this book deal with the general risks. A process for analyzing specific risks is covered in the discussion of performance standards in Chapter 11. These specific risks are not further discussed because there would be endless possibilities depending on the situation. Nevertheless, because it is often the specific risks that threaten a project, this area needs a lot of attention from the project team.

There is a myth that risks can be transferred completely, to the provider or anyone else. This is not true. Some of the risks can be transferred to the provider, but not all. The organization, for example, that outsources its outbound logistics in a fixed-price contract to a transportation company may have transferred much of the financial risk to the provider. But what if the provider is unable to perform satisfactorily and customers are lost? While contractual liquidated damages may salve the wounds, the risks were real. Contractual damages are unlikely to compensate for a loss of business reputation, customers, and revenues. Controls beyond the contractual control remedy, such as managing the relationship and monitoring the providers' performance, must be in place to mitigate these risks.

The senior management and project team must manage the general risks in a way that doesn't jeopardize the launching of the initiative or the organization's long-term business. Typically, an outsourcing consultant gets involved with senior management early in their discussions about outsourcing, to review the opportunities and the risks. Examples of the general risks might include the following:

Risks Relating to Project Design[1]

- Senior management does not support the initiative.
- Powerful antioutsourcing forces defeat the initiative.
- Employees react very negatively to the outsourcing initiative.
- The project team leader and members are poorly chosen.
- The outsourcing initiative's scope is not clearly articulated.

Risks Relating to Managing the Project[2]

- A comprehensive outsourcing initiative methodology is not followed.
- The project team doesn't have the necessary outsourcing expertise.
- The outsourcing initiative is not well aligned with the organization's strategies.
- The promised resources are not available as needed.
- The requisite information (costs and performance, for example) is either not available or poorly analyzed.
- The best providers are either not identified or don't respond to the RFP.
- The RFP is poorly prepared, so the proposals are not responsive or comparable.
- The proposals are not properly evaluated and the best provider is not selected.
- There is insufficient support when problems arise.
- The initiative is poorly managed.

[1]Discussed later in this chapter.

[2]See further details in this and the next three sections of this book.

Risks Relating to the Transition to the Provider's Services[3]

- The project handoff (knowledge gained during the early phases of the initiative) to the relationship manager is poorly handled, the transition is poorly planned, or both.
- Employees resist the changes.
- The provider experiences transition or start-up problems or both.
- Technical problems cause delays or missed deliverables.
- The organization fails to let go.

Risks Relating to Managing the Provider's Services[4]

- The provider does not perform (initially) as promised.
- The performance standards and measures are confusing or don't appropriately assess performance.
- The organization's key input providers do not cooperate.
- Problem-solving exercises fail.
- The relationship does not grow, but deteriorates.

As General George Patton of World War II fame once said, "Take calculated risks. That is quite different from being rash." Risks are managed by developing controls for each risk, to mitigate its possible impact. Examples of these controls for the project design risks follow.

Senior Management Acceptance and Support

Because outsourcing involves a number of strategic issues, as well as significant risks and rewards, senior management's clear and unequivocal stated support is a prerequisite. The best ways to demonstrate that support are:

- Formally announcing and expressing support for the initiative — and providing a timetable for its completion
- Articulating how outsourcing fits into the organization's vision and strategies
- Assigning a senior manager as the project champion (sponsor)

[3]See further details in Part Seven.

[4]See further details in Part Eight.

- Taking the time to choose an excellent project team and getting commitment for their time from the team members' superiors
- Periodically briefing senior management (by the project leader and the project champion) to retain their support

The project champion's primary roles are to guide the team, to ensure that the necessary resources are made available, to keep the project team on track (for example, adequate controls are in place), and to keep senior management informed (as to scope, objectives, risks, and so on). The project champion is also one of the key decision-makers on outsourcing. In a 1997 survey of CEOs by *Chief Executive* magazine and Andersen Consulting, 382 CEOs responded. One of the questions asked related to who was making the decisions on outsourcing, with the following results:

Senior Management/CIO	51%
CEO	30
CFO	7
Middle Management	8
Other	4
Total	100%

The project champion also provides top level cover, just as fighter planes protect bomber squadrons, when the inevitable obstacles arise. When this occurs, the project champion must act swiftly to eliminate the obstacles. But it is a pressure pot position, as a champion for change. As American actress and director Eva le Gallienne put it, "Innovators are inevitably controversial." It is effective if the project champion suggests that one of his or her areas be included in the list of outsourcing targets. In this way, the project champion is not perceived as suggesting that outsourcing is a good management tool "for the other executives' areas."

Powerful Opposing Forces

Any change management tool will find resistance, owing to the fact that human beings don't readily accept change well. Outsourcing will quickly bring out the employees' emotions. It is not popular with all employee groups, and especially those who have built fiefdoms and fear a loss of power. Count on managers who consider their areas vulnerable to outsourcing to oppose it.

Further, their superiors may also sense a loss of power, so don't expect their support either. As former U.S. Secretary of State Henry Kissinger once said, "Power is the ultimate aphrodisiac." A good rule of thumb is that executives will not outsource their own positions or the positions of those who report directly to them. For executives to seriously consider outsourcing, the area would have to be at least two levels below them. The project team can expect to hear many excuses about why outsourcing will not work. Examples of these excuses are included in Appendix 2.

The project team must understand how to manage change in order to overcome the resistance. The British novelist and historian H. G. Wells put it best, "What on earth would a man do with himself if something didn't stand in his way?" An outsourcing initiative can be killed through delay and other tactics. This is discussed further in Chapter 8.

There will also be a group of employees who don't fear a loss of power as much as a loss of comfort. They could lose their jobs or their jobs could remain unchanged while their friends' jobs are put at risk. In addition, their duties or their employer could change. They may be forced to relocate in order to keep their jobs and leave family and friends. Understanding their stress level over the unknown and learning how to deal with it is an important project team goal.

Employee Announcements

Before choosing the project team and advisers, a word of caution. If the organization has not already done so, this is probably its last chance to inform the employees of the outsourcing initiative before word leaks out. Choosing a team, holding meetings, taking employees out of their normal duties, engaging advisers, and similar activities will almost certainly make the initiative common knowledge.

If they don't know what is happening, people can react very negatively to outsourcing. Julius Caesar said, "As a rule, what is out of sight disturbs men's minds more." It is better to stay ahead of the employee morale curve by keeping them informed and maintaining a positive perspective. If word leaks out before a formal announcement, employees invariably jump to the worst possible conclusion—they and their friends will lose their jobs, will be unemployed forever, will lose their life savings and their families . . . and die poor and alone. This is an unlikely scenario, but one that is embraced. Such pessimism can lead to deteriorating moral performance, or worse, unnecessary employee turnover.

Even in the best of situations, with intelligent employees appropriately informed and providers who will likely want to hire the employees, there will be stress. In most cases, the organization can explain why outsourcing should be explored and indicate that this is only a test to determine if outsourcing is a viable tool. Employees deserve to be told this. Further, the organization can promise that as soon as it knows more, it will keep the employees informed.

There are logical times to update the employees. For example:

■ When the project plans have been completed (share the plan)
■ When the costs and performance analyses are ready to begin (their assistance may be needed)
■ When the requests for proposals have been prepared (so a provider employee doesn't unofficially communicate to an organization employee)
■ When the short list candidates have been selected, to begin due diligence (a significant event—outsourcing is progressing)
■ When the contract has been completed (to bring closure, this is a significant event—focus on what terms affect the employees, such as severance and other benefits)
■ When the transition begins (for an orderly, effective change in the existing employer/employee relationship)
■ At any point when the initiative is put on hold or has been canceled

It is obvious that updates are designed to announce a significant development and to prepare the employees for the next stage. The goal is to avoid surprises or unofficial communications (like rumors) which could trigger stress and discontent. (This subject will be addressed further in Chapter 19.)

Choosing the Project Leader

The outsourcing project leader role is complex and challenging. It runs from managing the project, the team, and the individual team members to gathering technical support, facilitating discussions, and drawing out consensus to drafting reports, making presentations, and convincing nonbelievers. All this must be dealt with while often being given fuzzy authority, tight deadlines, limited resources, and sometimes unrealistic management expectations. And in addition, it involves leading a project with strategic implications and significant employee issues. While this may look like a job for Superman or Wonder Woman, it is doable, especially with advisers available, and it can be a tremendous career booster when it is completed successfully. Showing the ability to lead such a project should be recognized and rewarded by the CEO, the project champion, and others.

Perhaps the most critical step in the outsourcing initiative is the choice of the project leader. As American entrepreneur H. Ross Perot put it, "Eagles don't flock, you have to find them one at a time." While support from senior management can overcome many obstacles, a weak project leader almost always dooms the outsourcing initiative.

This is no position for someone who is worn out or on the way out, or equally bad, someone who is untested.

What characteristics and skills should a project leader possess? Look for the following:

- Successful project management experience in the organization, with strong facilitation and consensus-building skills
- An understanding of the benefits of outsourcing, acceptance of it as a sound management tool, and the drive to implement it
- A reputation as someone who is results-oriented and risk-conscious
- An understanding of the organization's culture and how to get things done in it
- Strong decision making skills
- Excellent communication and presentation skills
- The ability to remain objective in the face of pressure from those who resist change and try to defeat outsourcing

These characteristics can probably be summarized in one word—leader. Look for the up-and-coming leaders in the organization, and you will quickly narrow down the list of potential project leaders.

If the outsourcing initiative will be the organization's first transformation project (or the first in some time), then either the project champion or project leader should have several additional battle-tested traits:

- A commitment to change and a willingness to lead the way in their own spheres of control ("we will show you—we will change first")
- An ability to recognize and relinquish old paradigms while searching for new paradigms to solve new problems
- The skill to connect the overall vision to the daily change activities for those involved in the initiative

The assumption has been made in this book that the organization has decided to perform the outsourcing initiative largely without assistance. Obviously, a consulting firm specializing in outsourcing could perform and complete the project, either in its entirety (although this is not recommended) or in part. If this approach were to be taken, the project champion role remains the same. The consulting firm would provide the project leader and team.

Choosing the Project Team

Choosing team members is a critical step in successful outsourcing. The provider will bring its best and brightest to the negotiating table. Should the organization put forth any less? Since outsourcing demands time—which is appropriate, given the risks and rewards—the team concept allows the project leader to share the workload.

The project leader should have significant input into the choice of the team members. What characteristics and skills should outsourcing team members possess? Look for the following:

- Motivation to participate
- A record of delivering on promises
- Strong communication skills
- An ability to think creatively and strategically
- Solid performance evaluations
- Relevant specialization within the organization
- Breadth of experience from outside the organization

The team members should be objective, and they should represent a cross-section of the organization's functions. Because they will have to live with the results, representatives of the potentially outsourced areas' internal customers should be included on the project team. Because it would be difficult for them to be objective, it is preferable that team members do not come from the areas that will likely be considered for outsourcing. They will become more actively involved later in the initiative, as part of the relationship team. Having said that, the project team should have access to, and the full cooperation of, the individuals in the areas to be considered for outsourcing.

Representation on the team by the legal and human resources functions if they exist in the organization (or in their absence, by an adviser) is important, since there are significant legal and human resources issues in outsourcing. Also, because certain outsourcing phases are similar, in part, to purchasing, researching, costing, and negotiating, having individuals with these skills on the team would be helpful. Support from the information systems area is generally needed as well.

Team members should be available part-time at the beginning of the project, but should be available full time for a period of days, then weeks, as the project moves through the stages of analyzing costs and performance, selecting providers, and negotiating terms phases. Their commitment of the time to participate in the project, not just be involved in it, is critical. There is an old saying, "Involvement in this context differs from commitment, in the same sense that a pig's and chicken's roles differ in one's breakfast of ham and eggs. The chicken was involved—the pig was committed." The project team will generally wrap up its work at the same time as the contract signing. After that, a relationship team will manage both the transition of the production factors to the provider and the ongoing relationship.

Project Management Issues

The initiative's scope must be clearly articulated in order to avoid a number of potential problems, including the following examples:

- If the objectives are not well understood, the project team could miss senior management's objectives entirely by taking too broad a scope or too narrow a scope.
- The project team may attempt more than can be realistically accomplished.
- The project team could end up overanalyzing the population of targets, without reaching definitive conclusions.
- The project team may unnecessarily avoid potentially sensitive areas (such as certain positions or sacred cow functions) if they are not given specific instructions that they can target any appropriate area.

The project leader will prepare for and then lead the team through a discussion, in which they will address a number of project management issues, including the project's scope. These topics are discussed in the next two chapters.

Another Reason to Outsource:
Improve Operating Performance

Performance measures are an integral part of today's management role. Examples of these measures include:

- Productivity (inputs ÷ outputs, for example, number of hours ÷ number of widgets made)
- Quality (waste and rework, for example, number or cost of warranty claims)
- Timeliness (meeting deadlines, for example, number of on-time shipments)
- Cycle time (elapsed time from start to finish, for example, number of rings to answer the telephone)
- Utilization (hours worked ÷ standard number of hours, for example, number of hours performing a specific activity this week ÷ 40 hours)
- Creativity (innovation, for example, number of products successfully introduced)
- Outputs (number of items completed, for example, number of characters data entered)

Because the providers' survival depends on superior performance in a narrow business scope, they are highly motivated to achieve it. This motivation is surrounded with a superior package of resources, such as on-point core competencies, cutting-edge technologies, state of the art equipment, experienced management and well-trained, motivated personnel. Together, this makes a provider's probability of improving your operating performance in noncore areas very high.

Does this mean that there are not highly motivated individuals, functions, or processes within organizations? Of course not. But unless they are working in the organization's core areas, they probably do not have the rest of the resource package. (If the whole package is there in a noncore area, then the organization either doesn't understand its core competencies or its resource allocation process is poorly managed, or both.)

Noncore area managers simply do not get the resources necessary to build top-flight functions or processes. They may do more with what they have, but their "more" generally isn't as good as the niche specialists, who can apply a superior resource package to achieve superior performance.

Outsourcing allows organizations to capture the providers' superior resource package for their noncore areas, thereby allowing them to improve their performance.

Chapter 4

Outside Advisers

The Need for Outside Advisers

Some organizations have outsourcing experience and may have less need for outside advisers. But many find it necessary to bring in help. Their reasons may include the following:

- To help manage risks
- To level the playing field with provider expertise
- To assist the project manager in focusing on outsourcing issues
- To act as a paradigm buster (challenge established thinking)
- To offer independent observations on the outsourcing environment

First, outsourcing initiatives have risks and experienced consultants can help manage them. As discussed in Chapter 1, the strategic implications and economic costs of an outsourcing error can be significant. Scope, performance, provider relations, and pricing are just a few of the issues that must be comprehensively addressed, if the organization's objectives for outsourcing are to be achieved. Senior management may bring in the outside advisers to discuss procedures and their implications. The project team may bring in the outside advisers to address key issues in detail, or help the project manager manage the project.

Second, in many cases the lack of outside advisers gives the provider an unfair advantage. This is because outsource providers are experienced and negotiate outsourcing agreements frequently, but most organizations do not. As a result, the playing field is not level. The use of outside advisers tends to level it. These advisers have significant experience in outsourcing and in negotiating outsourcing agreements, and thus can deal with the providers on an equal footing.

Third, while project leaders should have project management experience, they are unlikely to have much outsourcing experience. Further, team members are often assigned to the project team on a part-time basis, while continuing to juggle all or part of their normal duties. Accordingly, the project team may find that an experienced outsourcing project manager (adviser), whose only focus is on the initiative's success, can be instrumental in keeping the team properly focused on outsourcing issues.

Fourth, the project team may need assistance in addressing the ways in which the organization's paradigms will affect the outsourcing initiative. Paradigms are often unwritten and unrecognized, having become deeply ingrained in the organization's culture. Frequently, the paradigms must be exposed and challenged before any effort to change can make progress, because the paradigms tend to limit the organization and team members' thinking as to what options are possible. The outsource adviser, being an outsider, can more easily see the paradigms, and being independent, can more easily challenge them.

Fifth, the project team members bring to the team their baggage, bias, and attitudes toward the organization and its politics, processes, and people. An outsourcing initiative has a number of highly politicized elements, involving such things as human resource adjustments, turf battles, and empire destruction. Accordingly, the project team may find that an independent observer is helpful in decision making, including recognizing the underlying political issues, being objective in dealing with people's biases and attitudes, and overcoming the inevitable gamesmanship associated with such projects. This is discussed later in this chapter under "Overcoming Resistance."

Decision Making

For each of the preceding reasons to bring in outside advisers, there are several common themes: (1) management assistance, (2) outsourcing expertise, and (3) independent observation. A lack of resources and skills often leads to poor decision making, which in turn leads to poor results. Outsourcing advisers have lived through many outsourcing initiatives and have gained insights into what works and what doesn't. Poor decision making doesn't work. Poor decisions at the beginning of an outsourcing initiative have a way of compounding into later problems. The outsourcing adviser can help the project team avoid the decision traps that can doom outsourcing projects.

Here is a summary of ten common decision traps:

1. *Plunging in.* Beginning to gather information and reach conclusions without first taking a few minutes to think about the crux of the issue you're facing or think through how you believe decisions like this one should be made.
2. *Frame blindness.* Setting out to solve the wrong problem because you have created a mental framework for your decision with little thought, that causes you to overlook the best options or lose sight of important objectives.
3. *Lack of frame control.* Failing to define the problem in more ways than one or being unduly influenced by the frames of others.
4. *Overconfidence in your judgment.* Failing to collect key information because you are too sure of your assumptions and opinions.
5. *Shortsighted shortcuts.* Relying inappropriately on "rules of thumb," such as implicitly trusting the most readily available information or anchoring on convenient facts.
6. *Shooting from the hip.* Believing you can keep straight in your head all the information you've discovered, and therefore "winging it" rather than following a systematic procedure when making the final choice.
7. *Group failure.* Assuming that with many smart people involved, good choices will follow automatically and therefore failing to manage the group decision-making process.
8. *Fooling yourself about feedback.* Failing to interpret the evidence from past outcomes for what it really says, either because you are protecting your ego or are tricked by hindsight.
9. *Not keeping track.* Assuming that experience will make its lessons available automatically and therefore failing to keep systematic records to track the results of your decisions and failing to analyze these results in ways that reveal their key lessons.

10. *Failure to audit your decision process.* Failing to create an organized approach to understanding your own decision making, so you remain constantly exposed to all the above mistakes.[1]

The project champion and outside advisers serve as the team's coaches. As such, they make sure that (1) the team's quarterback (project leader) and players are in the best position to succeed, (2) that the right plays (project plans) have been called, and (3) that they are ready for the probable blitzes and stunts of the defense (powerful opposing forces).

Potential Adviser Roles

In addition to the general assistance previously outlined, outsource advisers can play many specific roles, including:

- Senior management's guide (in the early stages)
- Outsourcing trainer
- Project facilitator
- Project plan reviewer
- Employee communications editor
- Existing and projected costs analyzer (for example, an activity-based costing expert)
- Cost and performance benchmark analyzer
- Project researcher (for example, identifying potential providers)
- Request for proposal drafter
- Contract negotiator
- Contract drafter
- Human resources transition counselor
- Provider performance reviewer
- Dispute arbiter

Typically, these outsource advisory professionals might include lawyers, certified public accountants, change management professionals, human resource professionals, and technical specialists with expertise in the

---

[1]From *Decision Traps* by J. Edward Russo and Paul J. H. Schoemaker. Copyright © 1989 by J. Edward Russo and Paul J. H. Schoemaker. Used by permission of Doubleday, a division of Bantam Doubleday Dell Publishing Group, Inc., pages xvi–xviii.

areas being outsourced. As the British essayist William Hazlitt once said, "Men of genius do not excel in any profession because they labor in it, but they labor in it because they excel."

The adviser's expertise can be drawn upon over the entire project or during specific phases of it. But, if the advisers are to be used during specific phases, they should be involved in the planning phase as well. This allows their input at the start, so that later project rework can be avoided. The value of their involvement in the planning will far outweigh the costs.

Outsourcing Training

In order for the team to operate effectively, each member needs to have a sound grounding in outsourcing concepts. Further, each member needs to understand the overall outsourcing initiative process. While books such as this provide valuable guidance and serve as an ongoing reference resource, it is not as effective as a one-day or two-day seminar to launch a project.

First, people learn information in different ways. For example, some learn by:

- Reading
- Listening
- Debating (talking and interacting)
- Observing
- Doing (hands on work)
- Systematically experiencing (taking one step at a time)
- Seeing the big picture (through use of metaphors, case histories, and the like)

Obviously, a book provides only one learning style: reading. Seminars are designed to provide for the needs of all of the learning styles.

Second, training seminars give the team a common learning experience and reference point. This can be particularly important when tackling somewhat controversial subjects, such as outsourcing. In the many outsourcing seminars I have taught, I have observed that at the beginning at least 25 percent of the participants don't believe outsourcing is an appropriate tool (because they don't understand it) and another 25 percent are doubters. A team in which at least 50 percent of the members may at least have doubts will not be effective. That is why it is crucial to confront these issues before undertaking an outsourcing initiative.

Outsourcing Adviser Skill Sets

Generalist outsourcing advisers have a broad knowledge and experience of all facets of outsourcing. They are not typically what American news reporter and commentator Eric Sevareid implied when he defined a consultant as "any ordinary guy more than fifty miles from home." Ideally, this broad knowledge and experience would include having previously been involved on both sides of outsourcing transactions, as both executives doing the outsourcing and as providers performing services, as well as serving as consultants to organizations that are outsourcing. This breadth of experience allows the consultant to understand the motivations and probable actions of each party in the transaction, so as to identify potential problems early, before they converge.

In addition to this breadth of experience, these individuals should also have the following:

- Well-developed strategic thinking skills
- Sound decision-making knowledge
- Keen observation skills
- Excellent problem-solving experience
- Good communication skills, especially listening skills
- Effective training abilities (so there is a transfer of knowledge)
- Strong outsourcing project management and risk management experience
- Change management expertise, especially in confronting resistance
- Good blend of technical skills and people management skills
- Strong results orientation

The following sections in this chapter describe the outsourcing specialists that can be brought in to handle or advise on specific elements of the initiative. The generalist adviser often has at least one of these specialties and has a working knowledge of the rest of them.

Lawyers

Outsourcing initiatives involve long-term contracts, negotiation, and risk management activities that corporate lawyers concentrate on. All lawyers are not created equal. There are corporate lawyers who deal with a wide variety of legal issues, and then there are lawyers who specialize in outsourcing, handling many such transactions each year. The provider will have the second type of lawyer. Which type do you want? Lefty Rosenthal once observed, "The difference between an amateur and a professional is the difference between a general practitioner and a heart specialist. The only similarity is that they're both called doctors." Which one do you want doing your open-heart surgery (outsourcing)?

If there is no in-house legal counsel, then the outsourcing consultant can assist the team in finding an external outsourcing counsel. If the organization does have in-house legal counsel, then the ideal team is a combination of in-house legal counsel and an external legal counsel with outsourcing expertise.

It is important to involve the lawyers early on in the outsourcing initiative. The relationship's structure and the fundamental terms that affect the parties' contractual rights are often settled early and not during the formal contract negotiations. Accordingly, if the lawyer does not become involved early, the lawyer's value is limited to preparing the contract and negotiating its language. By their nature, lawyers will not be limited, and issues that may be raised by them at the eleventh hour, when the provider thought all issues had been settled, should be addressed and resolved right away. It saves a lot of time, frustration, and fees to involve them early on. Just as important, it reduces the chance of a rift in the provider relationship, just when it looked like it was blossoming.

Other Specialists

Depending on the team members' skills and the availability of additional resources within the organization, the use of other specialists as resources may be helpful.

■ Certified public accountants with experience in activity-based costing techniques can be invaluable in identifying the costs of activities to be outsourced and the financial analysis in the make or buy decision.

■ Benchmarking specialists can be helpful in benchmarking the internal unit's costs and performance against competitors and other world-class organizations having similar units.

■ Change management (transformation) specialists can be helpful in recognizing the risks associated with studying and implementing a transformation tool such as outsourcing and in assisting in creating an environment in which such an initiative can be successful.

■ Human resources specialists can be helpful in dealing with the ever-present challenges that an outsourcing initiative will present to employees.

■ Technical experts can be helpful in complex activities, functions, or processes, for example, in which the providers are proposing the adoption of technologies not previously used by the organization.

Consider the risks involved in an outsourcing initiative, and consider the use of outside advisers as an integral part of your risk management and controls.

Overcoming Resistance

In most transformation projects there is resistance to change. Being an independent observer who is unbiased, the outside adviser can help the project team prepare for the resisters and overcome their objections. Resisters generally make up only a small part, perhaps 10 to 20 percent, of the population of employees.

Their resistance will be active or passive. Active resistance is much easier to deal with because the project team can see it and hear it. Yet it is confrontational, and can be "in your face." The project team must be brave in facing these verbal assaults. As American business executive Herman W. Steinkraus put it, "The desire to remain popular has influenced too many decisions."

Passive resistance is the more dangerous resistance, because the project team doesn't even know it exists. But it is a mistake to assume that silence is acquiescence. As the American humorist Josh Billings once said, "Silence is one of the hardest arguments to refute." In fact, the project team must assume there are passive resisters and expose the resistance. Resisters must be converted over time, and the earlier the better.

The resisters do not usually oppose the transformation project 100 percent, but only a small percentage of the project's elements. Accordingly, the project team tries to expose not only the resisters, but also the key elements of resistance. If these elements are not essential to the project's goals, they may become negotiating points offered to overcome the resistance.

The project team needs to prepare for those who resist change by devising a confrontation strategy. In so doing, they should determine in which circumstances they will play the following roles:

- Heavyweight fighter
- Bantamweight fighter
- Wrestler
- Priest

The heavyweight's approach is to stand in the middle of the ring, go toe to toe with the resister, and slug it out. After all, given that it has senior management's blessing and full support, the project team is the 400-pound gorilla. The fact that senior management announces the initiative is effectively either a request for employee support or an invitation into the ring. There may be employees who attempt to undermine the outsourcing initiative through any means available, including applying pressure, withholding information, playing politics, threatening, delaying decisions, or sabotage (the initiative or the related factors of production). These activities must be met head on, toe to toe. Accordingly, using the heavyweight fighter approach makes sense and can lead to a fairly quick, but bloody, victory.

Swift action by the project champion, eliminating such obstacles, will also send a strong message to those who would throw up future ones—this is not acceptable! As Andrew Jackson said, "Take time to deliberate, but when the time for action arrives, stop thinking and go in." The organization deserves a fair and objective test of its outsourcing initiative. Unfortunately, most resisters recognize their lack of support and refuse to come to the center of the ring. Most prefer to choose their battles and locations.

For example, resisters might choose to enter the ring only when the project team has opened itself to attack or faltered with a misstep, such as a poor communication or an inaccurate analysis. In this way, the resister hopes to gain support by arguing that this problem is indicative of outsourcing's overall weakness. When this happens, the project team plays the bantamweight fighter's role and counter punches with short jabs, slowly wearing down the resister. This is a much slower, but less bloody, fight, in which stamina is important.

Then there are times when, after some initial success, the resister mounts an offensive. Then the project team will play the wrestler's role. As soon as the resister overextends, and goes too far (and they invariably do), the project team uses leverage and the opponent's momentum to topple the resister. There may be several rounds of grappling before the resister is pinned, so patience is important. This is also a slow, but generally bloodless, fight in which aggressiveness is the resister's undoing.

Most often, the opponent refuses to fight, but they also refuse to change. This is passive resistance. Now the project team must play the priest's role. In effect, the priest must seek out the resisters, listen to and understand their concerns, isolate the differences of opinion, and convince them to accept the changes. This is done by involving the resisters in the process, providing them with information, asking them to participate in the debate at key meetings, and showing them what's in it for them. As the humorist Will Rogers put it, "People's minds are changed through observation and not through argument."

If there are points that can be negotiated away in order to gain the resisters' support, that should be done. At the same time, they must understand that the change is not optional, only inevitable. This can be a slow process, so it must be started early. Because it is without a fight, it has no long-term injuries and generally the resistance leaders can lead the resistance group's conversion, so they don't lose face and don't bear a grudge.

Another Reason to Outsource: Reduce Costs Through Superior Provider Performance and the Provider's Lower Cost Structure

A common question that managers raise about outsourcing is how can we expect to reduce costs by outsourcing if the provider must perform the same activities and earn a profit?

It's a good point—if the provider performed the same activities in the same way that the organization did, the provider could not reduce costs, much less make a profit.

But the provider will apply a superior package of resources, such as on-point core competencies, cutting edge technologies, state of the art equipment, experienced management, and well-trained, motivated personnel. For these reasons, the provider

performs better, doing things, faster and more efficiently with fewer resources.

The providers also have very different cost structures from the internal unit. Because, for example,
the provider has larger scale, it may have greater purchasing power and obtain discounts not available to
the internal unit. It also has the ability to spread its
overhead over more activity units (other clients' work,
for example), so its per unit overhead costs are lower.
When we think of the internal unit's employee costs,
we recognize that these costs include salaries and
benefits (taxes, insurance, retirement, parking, cafeteria, and so on). What may not be recognized is that
there are significant overhead costs associated with
employees, such as:

- Work space, including telephone and computer
- Supervision (the time spent by supervisors on
  activities related to an employee or employee
  group, including direct supervision, monitoring
  results, periodic evaluations, meetings)
- Training, including any travel-related expense
- Technology used by the employee
- Top management time spent reviewing such
  things as the unit's annual business plans, budgets, and issues

When these overhead costs are added in, we can
see that fully loaded employee costs can be 100 percent or more of the employees' salary. Sending it to
providers who can reduce it will result in savings.

Outsourcing allows us reduce our costs because
the provider operates differently (often very differently) and achieves overall lower costs. While this is
an excellent reason to outsource, it is only one of
many, and it is often overrated when compared to the
other reasons.

Chapter 5

Setting Objectives

Organizational Objectives

When tapped for an important project by senior management, some loyal and hardworking employees would plunge right in with enthusiasm. Be careful!

Before plunging in, there are a number of questions that the project team should explore with senior management through discussions, surveys, and other means of information gathering in order to frame the project and its objectives, for example:

- What problems does senior management hope to solve?
- How painful are these problems?
- If these problems were to continue, what would be the strategic implications?
- Why is the organization considering outsourcing?
- What other options were considered?
- Why was outsourcing chosen?
- How was this decision made?
- Who are the project's supporters and doubters?
- What results does the organization hope the project can achieve?
- How does it hope to achieve the desired results?
- What are the critical means for achieving the desired results?
- How do the results of this initiative affect other decisions?
- What are the obstacles to achieving the desired results?
- What are the consequences if the initiative fails?

PROVIDER: Morrison Knudsen Corporation

CUSTOMER: Tektronix, Inc.

SCOPE: Facility maintenance, facility engi-
                       neering, construction manage-
                       ment, and support services

LOCATION: Beaverton and Wilsonville, Oregon
                       manufacturing plants: 29 build-
                       ings, 4 million square feet, 500
                       acres

REASONS   Textronix' reasons to outsource
TO   included focusing on its core
OUTSOURCE: businesses, sustaining reliable
                       facilities services, improving the
                       quality of the services, reducing the
                       costs associated with these ser-
                       vices, and retaining key skills/
                       experience.

CONTRACT:
    Duration: 1994–1999
    Amount: $90,000,000
    Pricing: Cost-plus and fixed-fee

Headquartered in Portland, Oregon, Tektronix is a worldwide supplier of electronics and systems in the areas of tests and measurement, television systems, and computer graphics. The company has approximately 10,000 employees worldwide. As a result of this outsourcing initiative, approximately 100 Tektronix employees became Morrison Knudsen employees, and approximately 30 Tektronix employees were terminated.

Morrison Knudsen is an international engineering, construction, environmental, and mining company headquartered in Boise, Idaho. The company has approximately 8,500 employees worldwide. Its operations, maintenance, and logistics division serves clients worldwide, such as Anheuser-Busch, Siemens, Exxon, General Motors, IBM, DuPont, and the U.S. Navy.

At the Tektronix plants, Morrison Knudsen is responsible for the management and delivery of all facilities services, systems, equipment, and programs associated with the building interiors and exteriors, grounds (above and below), roadways, parking lots, air quality, and the environment. These responsibilities include all the activities associated with support for facilities management functions, such as the procurement of goods and services. The facilities services and programs are separated into seven functional categories:

- Major maintenance
- Planning
- Engineering and construction
- Process operations
- Site maintenance
- Administrative services
- Emergency response team
- Corporate food services

Morrison Knudsen also operates the central utilities plants, maintains the electrical, plumbing and HVAC systems, and provides dock services, move coordination, furniture/asset management, the operation of six cafeterias, and custodial support. The contract includes maintenance of 500 acres of landscaped grounds. Whenever there is a major renovation or expansion, a Morrison Knudsen team of architects, engineers, designers, and space planners is responsible for getting the project finished. That includes planning, design, and project management services.

The results of the outsourcing initiative have included:

> - An initial cost savings of 15 percent resulting from maintenance labor force reductions and improved management and operating techniques
> - Ongoing savings of at least 10 percent
> - Reduction of energy costs by more than $1 million annually through better management
> - Major capital improvement programs designed and installed by Morrison Knudsen, for savings of 15 percent plus

- How will the organization know if the desired results have been achieved?
- Who are the ultimate decision makers?

There is an expression that "the only dumb questions are the ones that should have been asked, but were not." The project team is digging itself a very deep hole if it doesn't get senior management to answer these and similar questions.

It is so easy for a team to take its marching orders and start hurrying toward its objective. But just as a ship, if its course is set incorrectly by just a few degrees at the beginning of its voyage, can miss its island destination by thousands of miles, so can a project team miss their mark. Indeed, the team must push back at the project champion to be sure it has all of the information to develop its project plan document.

Outsourcing Targets

Generally, when senior management decides to consider outsourcing, it has thought through many of the questions set forth above and has good answers to them. It also has specific outsourcing targets in mind and should share its objectives with the project team.

Perhaps a particular area has been underperforming for years and despite management changes hasn't improved. It may want to move that area out to a provider. Direction is important. If senior management sincerely wants outsourcing to happen, then it should pose the challenge as follows: "Make it happen, or prove why it cannot be done!"

For each of the target areas, the project team should look at the levels and scope of outsourcing, and the type of provider that best fits with senior management's desires. This will provide a better understanding of the way the initiative's objectives should be designed. Now it's time to get more specific about the targets suggested by senior management:

- What are its initial targets for outsourcing?
- Why have these targets been chosen?
- How does it evaluate the effectiveness of these targeted areas?
- What activities do these targeted areas perform?
- Are there priorities to this list of targets?
- At what activity levels do the targets perform?
- Does it want to outsource all or parts of these targeted areas?
- What type of provider is it interested in working with?

Outsourcing can occur at the following *activity levels*:

- Component parts
- Individual
- Functional
- Process

In manufacturing, *component parts* or subassemblies (groups of parts) are outsourced to providers to be made. When Chrysler outsources the production of auto seats, tires, and brake linings, it is outsourcing component parts. This level of outsourcing has become commonplace in transferring manufacturing costs from higher-cost areas such as urban U.S. locations to lower-cost areas such as rural U.S. or international locations.

At the *individual* level, activities of individual workers or managers are outsourced to a provider. When an organization outsources a key technical position, such as benchmarking specialist, this is an example of individual activity outsourcing. Such an arrangement makes sense in the long term for technical positions that are needed regularly, but not on a full-time, permanent basis. This level of outsourcing is also becoming more common when the activities are at management levels and the organization is unhappy with the manager's performance but is not ready to outsource the entire function.

At the *functional* level, organizations outsource the activities of a function that involves specialized knowledge and responsibility. In recent years, organizations have increasingly outsourced the following functions:

- Information systems
- Telecommunications
- Accounting
- Tax compliance
- Internal audit
- Human resources

Processes are the way in which products or services actually flow through the organization. Outsourcing of entire processes has not been prevalent, but in recent years inbound and outbound logistics have become more frequently outsourced. For example, if a manufacturer decides to outsource its loading docks and its trucks and drivers, it is outsourcing its logistics processes.

Outsourcing initiatives can have different *scope objectives*, as follows:

- Total outsourcing
- Selective outsourcing

With *total* outsourcing, all of the activities are outsourced. This is the easiest way to outsource in the sense that accountabilities are clearer—if, for example, human resources function formerly performed specific activities resulting in specific outputs, then the provider will do the same thing, only better, for example, less expensively.

But there are times when the organization may not want to outsource all the activities of an individual, a function, or a process. In that case it turns to *selective* outsourcing. Perhaps the organization only wants to outsource the administration, recruiting, and training activities of the human resources function. Setting the scope, price, and performance measures for selective outsourcing can be more challenging than for total outsourcing.

Outsourcing Initiative Plan Objectives

At this point the project team has received the answers to a number of broad questions about the organization's strategy, including the reasons to outsource that interest senior management.[1] (These answers will be further explored and tested in the section on "Exploring Strategic Implications.")

[1]Organizations that are familiar with ISO 9000 standards should also refer to the guidelines for quality in project management.

Given this information, the project team must:

- Set the project's objectives, including:
  - ▲ Resource management issues
  - ▲ Information management issues
  - ▲ Project management issues
- Set the criteria for evaluating the project's success

In setting the project's objectives, the direction given by senior management must be considered first. This direction can range from a fairly general approach, such as "to run a fair and objective test to see if outsourcing is a tool we should use," to a more direct and specific approach, such as "to either outsource these target areas or prove why it cannot be done." The project team should either follow senior management's direction or offer an alternative.

In order to set the final objectives, the project leader should lead the team through a discussion of the issues. These issues are similar to any project, and the following is a checklist of questions and issues to consider:

Resource Management

- *Material.* What supplies, software, etc. are needed?
- *Equipment.* What computers, furniture, etc. are needed?
- *Money.* What budget is necessary for expenses, adviser fees, etc.?
- *Time.* What are the deadlines and time investments to meet them?
- *People.* Who will support the team (employees, advisers)?
- *Information.* What information is necessary?
- *Activity.* What activities must be performed and by whom?
- *Methods.* Are there unique ways of performing these activities?
- *Processes.* Are there overall processes for such a project?
- *Results.* What are the deliverables? What will they look like?

Information Management

- *Baselines.* What are the expectations and success factors?
- *Schedules.* How will activities be scheduled?
- *Budgets.* How will we budget our time and money over the project?
- *Forecasts.* What forecasts are necessary?
- *Estimates.* What estimates should be made in comparison to using hard data?
- *Data collection.* What data must be collected?
- *Risks.* What could cause the project to fail?

- *Reporting.* How often should we report our progress, and to whom?
- *Analysis.* What analysis work must be performed?
- *Rebaselining.* When and under what conditions do we adjust the expectations and success factors?

Project Management

- *Organizing.* How will the team be organized?
- *Planning.* Who will plan the activities, assignments, deadlines, etc.?
- *Specifying.* How detailed will the plan be?
- *Contracting.* Will advisers or outside support personnel be used?
- *Assigning.* How will we assign activities to team members?
- *Prohibiting.* What rules do we want to protect the team?
- *Monitoring.* How will we evaluate our progress?
- *Accepting.* How will we determine consensus?
- *Changing.* How will we determine when changes are needed?
- *Analysis.* What analysis work must be performed?[2]

(This book gives advice on an overall process for an outsourcing initiative and on specific resource management, information management, and project management issues associated with outsourcing. Beyond this and the previous chapter, it does not further address general project management issues and the risks inherent with any project. For further guidance on the art of resource management, information management, and project management, consulting other books is encouraged.)

The project team should then challenge those objectives with several questions:

- What obstacles are likely to be faced?
- Given the organization's environment, how realistic are the objectives?
- Are the resources available to achieve the objectives?
- Is the necessary information available?
- Can this project be effectively managed?
- Has the critical path[3] for the project been identified?
- Is management ready for the launch of this initiative?

---

[2]Adapted from Robert D. Gilbreath, *Winning at Project Management* (New York: Wiley, 1986), page 93.

[3]As indicated in Chapter 2, the different phases for the project can and generally should run more in parallel than strictly sequentially.

Bringing this project team together on these issues requires a combination of:

- Strong consensus building
- Smooth facilitation of discussions
- Sound decision making
- Respect for teammates
- Political savvy
- Courage
- Discipline
- Objectivity

The team will undoubtedly be frustrated during this phase. The project leader is establishing his or her leadership position. The team is coming together with many different agendas, including some that are personal. The opposition will be trying to influence the planning to mitigate any effect on their fiefdoms. In fact, the project champion may need to actively participate and intercede to reach a consensus. Outsourcing consultants can be helpful during this period as well.

It is important here to reach consensus and move out as a team. As the old Chinese proverb says, "A journey of a thousand miles begins with a single step." The team should be able to condense its plan (it might also be referred to as a charter or mission statement) into a written paragraph for each of the following:

- Overall objectives—what is the team trying to do (including specific targets)?
- Why is the initiative being undertaken (reasons to outsource)?
- Who will be involved, and what are their time commitments?
- When will the project be completed (with a possible list of interim milestones[4])?
- What will be delivered at the end and to whom?
- How will the team proceed?

This document will be consulted in each of the regular update meetings, when the team comes together to evaluate their progress and perhaps

---

[4]Logical interim milestones for the project team to report back to senior management would be at the conclusion of the analysis of costs/performance of the internal unit (see Chapter 11), when potential providers have been identified (see Chapter 13), and when the term sheet negotiations have been completed (see Chapter 18).

adjust the plan. Publilius Syrus, first-century Latin writer of mimes, wrote, "It is a bad plan that admits of no modification." Additionally, the meetings should include a discussion of members' observations about the ways in which the organization and the opposition are reacting. Remember, where there is smoke, there is usually a fire. The team might consider adjusting its method of communication. The project team might explore if there any adjustments that are necessary to communications.

Criteria for Evaluating Outsourcing Success

Just as each key activity in the organization should have performance measures, so should the project activities have measurements for success. The team should identify the criteria by which its progress should be measured. Good criteria to start with are finishing on time, finishing within the budget, and meeting the objectives.

In an outsourcing initiative, there are other criteria that might also be considered:

- Given the potential improvements in performance, cost savings, and other things (see also Appendix 1, "Reasons to Outsource"), consider setting related goals to achieve specific improvement levels.
- Given the importance of team members (who are often assigned only part-time) meeting their commitments, consider setting some individual measures for participation and delivery.
- Given the potentially damaging employee reaction to the initiative, consider an employee complaint and/or turnover factor to motivate the team to be sensitive and talk favorably about the initiative.
- Given that the initiative could start a long-term relationship with one or more providers, consider developing a survey so each provider can evaluate how fairly the team ran the competition.

The project leader and project champion should periodically evaluate these criteria and share the results with the team at the update meetings (which should occur weekly or biweekly), and, as appropriate, with senior management.

Management Acceptance of the Plan

The project team should return to senior management and present its project plan document and review its details in order to get a reaction to the plan, to make any adjustments necessary, and to get approval to move forward. Further, the conclusions may need approval from the board of directors (for example, outsourcing an internal audit would probably require audit committee approval).

In this meeting, if the project team has not already done so, the seven-step methodology should be described. This will give senior management a better understanding of the project team's framework and, ideally, make it more comfortable with the initiative. Reassurance is important because senior management will then be more likely to support the project team if things go awry and/or will help break down resistance. As Charles E. Wilson, former Chairman of General Motors, once said, "No plan can prevent a stupid person from doing the wrong thing in the wrong place at the wrong time—but a good plan should keep a concentration from forming." Communication with senior management will also help them understand why the project will take as long as it will.

With approval to move forward secured, the project team should think through the issues discussed in Part Three of this book in order to confirm that senior management's outsourcing intentions don't conflict with other strategies. By exploring these questions, the team will be better able to understand how outsourcing can best fit within the organization's strategies—and how it will affect those strategies.

This is also a good time to update the employees. The project team might share the project plan in summary form. It might explain the reasons the organization is considering outsourcing and the project team's specific objective. It might indicate the areas in which employees can contribute information. It might ask a series of generic questions, asking employees to think about their answers and respond to the project team. Wherever possible, the employees should be involved.

Another Reason to Outsource: Enhance Effectiveness by Focusing on What You Do Best

Each organization has two or three core competencies (special knowledge or skill sets—see Chapter 7) that allow it to compete effectively. One of the keys to customer satisfaction and superior performance is to focus on the core competencies by:

- Understanding them, in their current state, and how they must be developed to sustain their value
- Investing in them, through capital infusion and continuous improvement
- Testing them with customers, potential customers, suppliers, and so on, to determine that they remain on the cutting edge
- Using them to develop new generations of products or services that will attract customers and create competitive advantages

Any organization has limited resources, and those resources should concentrate on the core competencies. It also has many competencies that are not core, which unfortunately create a drag on the limited resources. How many people can you effectively manage?

This is not to suggest that noncore competencies are unimportant, or that their employees are not honest, hard working, and valuable. It does suggest, however, that organizations can lose focus and resources by trying to address noncore issues and competencies. Noncore competencies take up time, energy, and work space, all of which cost money. Worse yet, management loses sight of what is really important—satisfying customers by exploiting the organization's core competencies.

Outsourcing allows the organization to unburden itself of the activities related to noncore competencies by moving them to organizations that can perform them better. Even if costs remain the same, this is an excellent reason to outsource, because outsourcing will let management concentrate on the core competencies.

Part Three

Exploring Strategic Implications

Chapter 6
Organizational Structure

Overview

Outsourcing challenges many of the ways in which organizations have traditionally been structured. For example, large size, vertical integration, and functional organizational structures have long been accepted as foundations for business success—and for good reasons.

But those reasons have largely disappeared, and recently CEOs have begun to reconsider these structures, philosophies, and rules. As the Chinese philosopher Confucius once said, "Only the wisest and stupidest of men never change."

Unfortunately, for employees who have been grounded in these philosophies and have based their careers on operating within such rules, many are finding it very difficult to understand and accept the new rules. They should be thinking more like Sir Henry Bessemer, a British engineer, who discovered a new method of producing steel. Bessemer said, "I had an immense advantage over many others dealing with the problem inasmuch as I had no fixed ideas derived from long-established practice to control and bias my mind, and did not suffer from the general belief that whatever is, is right."

Exhibit 6.1 describes the traditional organizational structure, made up of functional silos.

The new model is a customer-focused, process-driven organization. Exhibit 6.2 describes the newer organizational process structure, in which all the employees understand their roles and how they contribute to customer satisfaction.

How the organization is structured should be closely tied to its vision of the future.

Exhibit 6.1   Functional Silos

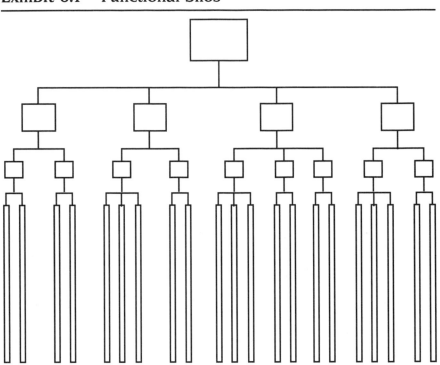

Exhibit 6.2   Process-Driven Organization

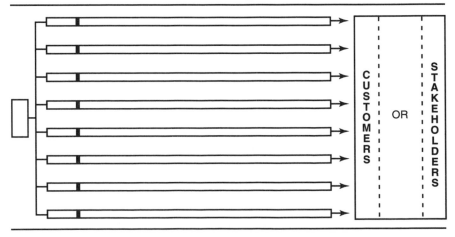

The Vision

One of senior management's most important jobs is to articulate its vision of the organization at a point in the future. This vision is developed by the leadership and is articulated widely throughout the organization, giving a realistic, inspiring, and detailed description of the destination that the organization is aiming for. It provides the North Star that guides the organization to its destination and prevents it from going off course.

The vision is a word picture of what the organization will look like and what its products, services, markets, and customers will be. It describes what core competencies will be necessary, describes how the organization will distribute its products and services, and specifies how it will interact with customers. It outlines the future organizational structure, culture, and style and describes the future performance objectives (such as quality, productivity, and cycle time) and financial condition.

It should be the leadership's objective to clearly set forth the vision so that all employees understand the strategies to achieve it and how their activities and functions fit into it (see Exhibit 6.3). If the vision is inspiring, they will reorganize their activities to help achieve it. Together, leadership and motivated employees can make incredible progress.

Few organizations have recognized how powerful a vision can be in energizing employees to achieve it. Once employees understand the vision, they are empowered to implement it. Jack Welch, CEO of General Electric and generally regarded as one of the premier CEOs of the twentieth century, said about GE's emergence as one of the world's most competitive companies, "You can express a vision to a broad number of people. . . . You can implement it and together you can all win. . . . That's what a good leader does."[1]

If the organization's leadership has effectively articulated the vision, and the vision includes alternative sourcing concepts (such as a focus on core competencies and outsourcing for the rest of the activities), then the project team can more effectively align its outsourcing objectives with the organization's strategies.

Employees will also understand the bigger picture: where the organization is going, and why outsourcing is a tool contributing to achieving

---

[1]Noel M. Tichy and Stratford Sherman, *Control Your Own Destiny or Someone Else Will* (New York: Doubleday, 1993), pages 339, 340.

Exhibit 6.3   Strategic Organizational Alignment

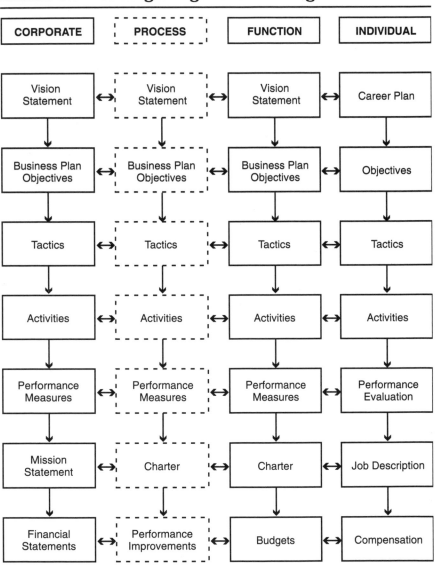

the vision. If outsourcing is not a part of the organization's vision, then those who try to defeat the outsourcing initiative will have some ammunition to do so. In that case, the CEO's support for the initiative must be evident early and often.

A well-understood vision also helps employees understand change—why resources have been concentrated on core competencies. Otherwise, even if their activities, functions, and processes aren't immediately outsourced, they experience frustration as they watch their staff downsized and benefits such as training, travel, and new technologies become restricted. In a customer-focused, process-driven organization, the focus is on how to best meet the customers needs by drawing upon the organization's core competencies, not on maintaining the status quo.

Size and Vertical Integration

From the 1950s to the 1970s, Wall Street rewarded large, vertically integrated, and diversified companies that had strong revenue growth. ITT Corporation, under Harold Geneen's leadership, is a good example of such a company. ITT prospered because of Geneen's ability to acquire thousands of companies, manage them as a portfolio, and control their operations. Wall Street rewarded ITT with ever increasing stock values, which made subsequent acquisitions ever cheaper.

Geneen was a brilliant manager—for his time. After a glorious run of 58 consecutive quarters of showing a growth rate of more than 10 percent, its sheer size doomed ITT, and it was taken apart by Geneen's successor.

Size and vertical integration were once an advantage, but this is changing. In his book, *Liberation Management*, Tom Peters explained why:

> Given the importance of reliable supplies of raw material such as iron and oil in yesterday's economy, and general uncertainty due to limited communications capabilities (no electronic data interchange) and transportation, having everything under your direct control—under your roof, if possible—made some sense. No more.
>
> For one thing, lumpy raw material is yielding to ephemeral brainpower as the source of most value added. And brainpower, unlike an oil field or coal deposit, is fickle—dispersed, ever changing. Also, thanks to the new technologies that provide the ability to communicate and coordinate in a virtually error-free, paperless way (courtesy EDI, and favorite outfits as different as GM and Wal-Mart), companies can have their cake (reliability) and eat it too (take advantage of others who are

more effective at a special task). In the end, though, there's one paramount force: innovation and flexibility, today's imperatives, are ipso facto at odds with owning all the resources.

Amidst all this, old ideas about size must be scuttled. "New big," which can be very big indeed, is "network big." That is, size measured by market power, say, is a function of the firm's extended family of fleeting and semipermanent cohorts, not so much a matter of what it owns and directly controls.[2]

By their very nature, large size and structure stifle creativity and entrepreneurship. The controls necessary to manage these behemoths make employee empowerment difficult at best. Look at how MCI and Sprint have become real competitors for AT&T in just a few decades, by out-innovating and out-marketing AT&T. Seeing this, AT&T decided to break itself into a more manageable organization. Robert Allen, AT&T's chairman and CEO, said, "The complexity of trying to manage these different businesses began to overwhelm the advantages of integration." Other organizations, such as GM, Sears, Kodak and Marriott, have done the same thing.

Wall Street now generally frowns on large size, diversity, and vertical integration, and rewards profitable, focused, innovative companies. As the English economist Ernst F. Schumacher put it, "Any intelligent fool can make things bigger, more complex, and more violent. It takes a touch of genius—and a lot of courage—to move in the opposite direction."

General Electric, under Jack Welch, is a good example of such courage. While GE is large, it has prospered because of Welch's ability to continually redirect resources to profitable lines of business, focusing the company on what it does best (where it is number one or number two in the market) while getting rid of the rest. He has dramatically shrunk the company in size and diversity while dramatically increasing its earnings, market position, and stock value.

At today's speed of change, owning (or employing) factors of production for areas other than core competencies can be very risky. The disadvantages of this "owning" approach are many, including:

■ *Slower to change.* Fast, agile competitors can change industries overnight. It takes months for large organizations to recognize the need and much longer to make the change.

[2]From *Liberation Management* by Tom Peters. Copyright © 1992 by Excel/a California Limited Partnership. Reprinted by permission of Alfred A. Knopf Inc., page 305.

- *Higher investment.* "Owning" means putting it on the balance sheet, (investing in assets), or income statement (investing in training).[3]
- *Poor investment yield.* New technologies can quickly render equipment and trained employees obsolete in a competitive marketplace.
- *Fixed costs.* Costs are relatively fixed and sunk over the short term.
- *Higher total costs.* The devil is in the overhead and inferior performance.
- *Management hardships.* Behemoth organizations are more difficult to manage well, and they distract from the core competencies.
- *Less innovation.* "Owning" reduces the opportunities to interact with providers who are cutting-edge innovators.
- *Staid culture.* Paradigms become stuck in concrete if not frequently challenged by outsiders.

Outsourcing is a relatively new tool, gaining acceptance as a method for mitigating some of these risks. It forces change, and forces organizations to come to grips with outdated business practices and why they should be challenged. As Peters put it in *Liberation Management*:

Success in the marketplace today is directly proportional to the knowledge that an organization can bring to bear, how fast it can bring that knowledge to bear, and the rate at which it accumulates knowledge. Market power mostly derives from one's skill at bringing together the best network of insiders and "outsiders"—to take advantage of a fleeting (a few years at most) opportunity. The ability to bring knowledge to bear fast is, in turn, largely a function of:

- the reach of the firm's "network," including insiders and outsiders of any size, from anywhere
- the density of the network, meaning (1) the variety of the network partners brought to bear on the particular project and (2) the intensity of the relationships one has that can be called upon at a moment's notice
- the network's flexibility and skill at reconfiguring

---

[3]When using the newer overall corporate performance measures, such as economic value added, making higher investments on the balance sheet forces managers to recognize that they must earn a return on those investments equal to their cost of capital before they can begin to add shareholder value.

By definition, such networks include but are not limited to: (1) suppliers, (2) supplier's suppliers, (3) distributors, (4) franchisees, (5) other middlemen, (6) customers, (7) customer's customers, and other specialized resources such as university professors and consultants.[4]

Outsourcing providers are an integral part of the "suppliers" within this network. Accordingly, outsourcing will play a significant role in changing how organizations achieve competitive advantage and ultimate success.

Functional Hierarchy Structures

Organizations have traditionally structured employees on a functional basis, with each function having specialized knowledge and responsibilities. These might include the following examples:

- Marketing
- Sales
- Purchasing
- Operations (may be split into several functions)
- Legal
- Finance

Years ago, employers preferred a liberal arts education, and so there were only a handful of quality university business education programs. Also, few people attended college, so most people entered the workforce with little skills. The "function" was where young untrained workers learned their specialized skills. Expertise was found in the top functional leaders, and it was acquired through on-the-job training, not dissimilar to the apprenticeship programs for young craftsman. Today college graduates with specialized business degrees, even MBAs, are plentiful. Yet, there have been only minor changes in the functional organizational structure. Instead of a training focus, functions have become more technically focussed as business transactions became more complex. Hiring and managing capable specialists is more important, but that creates still more problems.

[4]Peters, *Liberation Management*, page 310.

In the past several decades each function has been further broken down into specialties. For example, the marketing function might now include departments in market research, advertising, public relations, and customer satisfaction measurement. But each subdivision brings bureaucracy and overhead.

Each function requires specialized education and experience. It is unlikely that the sales function would seek accounting graduates or the purchasing function would want law school graduates. In today's more complex business world, these specially trained people then do specialized activities and tasks, honing their expertise. After a while, their reason for working is to become the best sales rep or purchasing agent, hoping to rise to the top of their function.

A number of problems arise in these functionally driven organizations:

- Functional bosses become the focus.
- Functional growth is encouraged.
- Larger functions become liabilities.
- Resources are not appropriately allocated.
- Costs increase as overhead swells.
- The customer gets lost.

What is created in functionally driven organizations are silos of functional specialists, each talking their own language, addressing their own issues, producing their own outputs, and delivering their own reports. Their objectives become focused on impressing their bosses with their specialized expertise. After all, the functional bosses train them, evaluate their performance, increase their compensation, and recommend their promotions.

Occasionally, a turf battle erupts between the specialist silo functions over whose responsibility a particular matter is. Then these become missile silos for warfare. But why is functional growth important? Because the larger the function (the greater its span of control and the deeper its expertise), the more compensation, power, and prestige its top specialists will get. It seems to make sense from the point of view of risk management—more functional specialists create room for subspecialists, hence there is less likelihood of error.

But the larger the function, the slower it operates, and this becomes a liability. As technical reviews occur, each piece of information is analyzed, screened, and retained. Because information is one of the most powerful commodities in an organizations, it is often only released when it is needed to support specific decisions with which the function agrees. If the information doesn't quite fit their desires, but must be released nevertheless, then the proverbial spin is put on it. The information so necessary to run the organization may be distributed too little, too late, and too spun to do much good.

Further, the allocation of resources becomes a problem. When budgets need to be approved, who knows enough to challenge a specialist on the needs of the specialist's function? Instead of resources flowing to needs, they flow to those with the best track records or to managers who are politically more powerful. They continue to build strengths, whereas others with real needs are left out in the cold. This is how overhead becomes bloated. The excesses are well hidden, and only become apparent when a thorough analysis is done, by consultants or in a free market test (request for proposals in an outsourcing initiative). During the 1980s, the theory on how to eliminate this ever-increasing overhead was to downsize the organization and remove entire layers of middle management. This did reduce costs and speed up information and decisions. Unfortunately, it did not create customer-directed behavior or a focus on core competencies.

Finally, the most significant problem is that the customer frequently gets lost in the organization's functional focus. The functions don't talk or listen to each other, except at the most senior management level, much less talk or listen to the customer. Customer satisfaction must be the number one objective of every employee, and other functional objectives distract from this. But an organization can recapture a customer focus—by changing from a functional structure to a process structure.

Process Structures

With the recognition of problems relating to functional hierarchies, many organizations are moving solely to a process structure or in tandem with a functional organization (creating what is often referred to as matrix management). Processes are how the products or services flow through the organization. When we link similar activities to create an output for the customers' benefit, we have a process. An organization can have many functions, but the processes generally number no more than twelve to fifteen.

Instead of employees being part of a somewhat isolated functional silo, they become a value-adding contributor within several customer-focused chains of activities, or processes (see Exhibit 6.4). Employees now understand how they contribute to customer satisfaction. More importantly, the customer's voice is heard, from the ultimate customer through the internal customers and finally to the service providers. This accelerates decision making and improves decision quality.

Along with such a process restructuring comes the identification of the many nonvalue-adding and supporting activities that are performed in an organization. These are activities that don't contribute anything or contribute only to overhead bloat and which should be eliminated or reduced. Although most organizations follow a differentiated products/services strategy—as opposed to the low-cost provider strategy (that focuses on achieving the lowest costs in the market)—lower costs can be achieved, which can create competitive advantage, allowing greater investment in those areas that support the differentiated products/services.

By outsourcing noncore processes, organizations can reduce the number of processes it must directly manage and invest in, enabling it to invest heavily in the remaining core processes. The remaining processes, functions, and capabilities should be outsourced (see Exhibit 6.5).

Outsourcing can become effective more quickly once the process focused restructuring has occurred. First, the major cultural transformation

Exhibit 6.4   Contributions of Functions and Individuals to the Processes

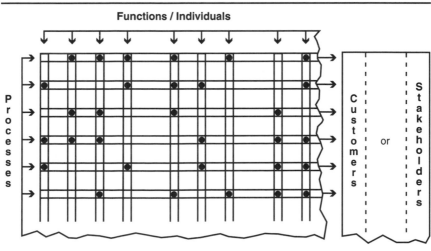

Exhibit 6.5   Core Process Focus

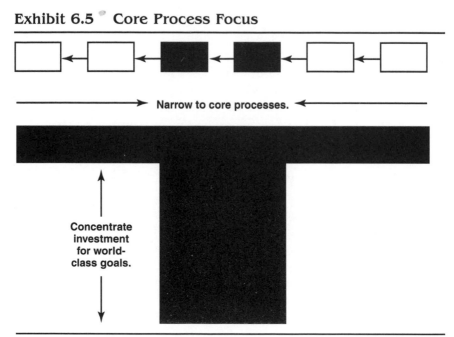

Narrow to core processes.

Concentrate
investment
for world-
class goals.

Source: James R. Emshoff, Ph.D., Strategic Outsourcing Seminar (New York: American Management Association, 1994).

issues—including resistance to changes away from a functional focus—have already been addressed. This reduces employee stress. Second, the concept of adding value can now be the focus. This reduces management resistance to finding the best value-added contributors regardless of their association with the organization—they can be employees or outside providers. Third, if the barriers between functions have been eliminated (or at least lowered), then the barriers between employees and providers can be lowered as well.

Another Reason to Outsource:
Transform the Organization

Unless there is serious trouble causing bottom line deterioration, most organizations proactively change very little from year to year. Transformation is painful. Organizations generally don't embrace transformation tools such as reengineering, TQM, activity-based cost management, and restructuring (including outsourcing) until faced with a crisis. But that's a mistake. As Noel M. Tichy and Stratford Sherman have explained:

> Jack Welch turned over more rocks than his predecessor. His philosophy of 'changing before you have to' led him to attack potential problems before obvious symptoms of trouble appeared. . . . A corporate culture is the sum of the norms, beliefs, and values that define appropriate behavior. . . . How do you change corporate culture? Welch has started the process by orchestrating a corporation wide dialogue of ideas. . . . Welch always has seen the revolutionary process as endless, simply because the world beyond the corporation never stops changing. . . . The revolutionary process is agonizing for employees, and many were deeply shaken by the experience. But Welch upset his employees for a reason: he could not create new order without tearing down the old.[5]

Outsourcing is a restructuring transformation tool that can be used to create a dialogue about change.

[5]Tichy and Sherman, *Control Your Own Destiny*, pages 30–32, 68–69.

You should attack potential problems before obvious symptoms of trouble appear. Look at your noncore competency areas. Look at the initial reasons to outsource and start there. For example, if cost reduction and poor performance are issues, which noncore areas have high costs and are also performing poorly? Begin a dialogue. The answers won't be a secret or a surprise to the employees, because they have a pretty good idea who the targets should be. Then institute an outsourcing initiative with a broader objective in mind — organizational transformation.

Chapter 7

Determining Core Competencies

What Core Competencies Are

Organizations compete for customers, revenue, and market share with products and services that meet customers' needs. Core competencies are the innovative combinations of knowledge, special skills, proprietary technologies, information, and unique operating methods that provide the product or the service that customers value and want to buy. When a process driven structure, focused on the customer, can access core competencies, then a powerful strategic force is unleashed.

Organizations have many capabilities and competencies; however, only a few of these are combined and integrated in such a way that they can be considered core competencies. If the competencies do not create products or services that the customers see as exceptionally different they are probably not core. If the competencies are fleeting, easily imitated, or belong to a few individuals who could leave, then they are probably not core.

Most of the remaining capabilities are important to the business's survival, but not to its ultimate success. These are either essential or supporting capabilities (such as processing the payroll, shipping the products, filing the tax return), but not core, and should be considered for outsourcing. Finally, there may be a group of capabilities that are considered nonvalue added. These should not be outsourced, but eliminated.

PROVIDER: APAC Teleservices, Inc.

CUSTOMER: Farmers Insurance Group
                  (Farmers)

SCOPE: Call center support

LOCATION: Cedar Rapids, Iowa

REASONS TO   Farmers' reasons to outsource
OUTSOURCE: included focusing on their core
                  competencies, extending their
                  after-hours and catastrophe
                  claims services (National Catas-
                  trophe Center) and establishing
                  a virtual direct marketing and
                  processing operation for its
                  personal-lines (Farmers Direct).

CONTRACT:
  Duration: 1996–1999
  Amount: $10,000,000
  Pricing: Fixed price

Farmers, headquartered in Los Angeles, California, is one of the largest property casualty insurers in
the United States, providing auto, home, commercial,
and life insurance policies. The company has approximately 17,000 employees.

APAC, headquartered in Deerfield, Illinois, has
25,000 employees. APAC provides customer optimi-
zation services for many corporations, including leaders in insurance, financial services, communications,
and other industries. It operates ninety call centers
for these clients.

APAC handles inbound telephone calls from
Farmers' policyholders twenty-four hours a day, 365
days a year, routed calls from Farmers' 190 claims
offices from 4:00 P.M. EST to 7:30 P.M. PST on week-
days, and for all hours on weekends and holidays. The
types of calls handled include:

- Taking claims for auto and property damage
- Answering questions on pending claims status
- Escalating serious claims (those involving injury or serious damage) to claim representatives or adjusters through nationwide paging
- Arranging tow truck services, glass replacement, and emergency services for policyholders
- Identifying claimants' concerns and messaging branch claims personnel with daily reports

In addition, APAC handles inbound and outbound direct marketing telephone calls. When Farmers wants to expand into new markets, it solicits business through advertisement or direct mail campaigns. APAC receives calls from (or returns calls to) prospective policyholders and prequalifies the prospect. If a sale is possible, the prospect is passed to a licensed agent (also an APAC employee) to quote and sell the product. If a sale occurs, APAC binds the coverage by processing the initial premium payment using VISA, MasterCard, or a one-time debit to a checking account. If the prospect only wants information, then APAC forwards the necessary addressee information to Farmers' fulfillment provider. All of the foregoing is managed through contact management systems, which interface with Farmers' systems daily.

As a result of this outsourcing initiative, APAC has:

- Launched the National Catastrophe Center and Farmers Direct.
- Handled fifty-seven catastrophes in fifteen months with a claimant satisfaction rating of 96 percent.

- Answered 95 percent of the calls since program inception within twenty seconds.
- Improved the call handling by 18 percent.
- Reduced the average after call handling time by
  17 percent in three months.
- Sold over 25,000 insurance policies.
- Streamlined training to increase employee
  retention while reducing classroom time by 30
  percent.

Exploiting Core Competencies

Knowledge, skills, technologies, operating methods, and information are
found throughout the organization in small pockets, sometimes hidden or
misunderstood, and often under-appreciated. This is because the combinations that will benefit the organization (like the combination to a lock),
have not been discovered. Management, like a safecracker, must discover
the combinations, through innovative thought and application, to create
core competencies (see Exhibit 7.1). As German poet and dramatist Johann
Wolfgang von Goethe put it, "Knowing is not enough; we must apply.
Willing is not enough; we must do."

Then management enhances the core competencies through investment and determines how to better integrate them into the processes.
Further, management must search for ways to make these valuable assets
available across the entire organization in order to improve existing products and services.

Customer perceptions are crucial to understanding the combination.
Core competencies are what sets the organization's products and services
apart from the competitors similar offerings. Sometimes an organization
doesn't recognize its core competencies because it doesn't understand its
customers' perceptions. It may believe that its core competencies are x and
y, only to learn by talking with customers that the attributes they value
don't relate to x at all. The attributes related to y would be valued, but this

Exhibit 7.1   Turning Core Competencies Into Value

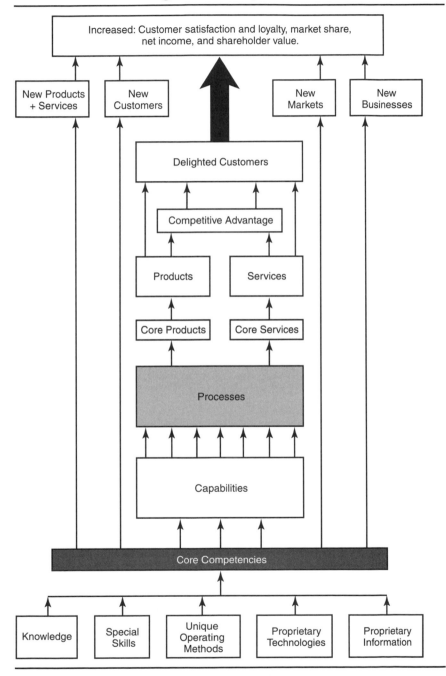

is not considered something the organization does well. The organization didn't know it, but its customers were attracted by attributes related to a hidden core competency z.

All competencies are dynamic. Like muscles, they must be fed and exercised. They either strengthen because they are nurtured, or they deteriorate because they are ignored. It can take years of focus, investments and continuous improvement to build, but failure to do so can severely restrict future growth.

Continuing the muscle analogy, a person may like hiking and thus develop strong leg muscles; but a sudden passion for kayaking will demand an increase in upper body strength. So too, industries change, requiring management to adjust its core competencies. Over time, core competencies tend to have less impact as new competitors or technologies develop. For example, core competencies can be rendered useless by new competitors who introduce a new technology (such as digital watch technology) and make existing technology (mainspring watch technology) obsolete. Sound strategy involves understanding in which core competencies to invest (and how much), to maintain competitive advantage, and when to acquire and develop different core competencies in order to create future competitive advantage.

Reasons to Identify Core Competencies

Typically, organizations see their possibilities for competitive advantage in marketing terms by comparing their marketing position and strategy (e.g., low cost vs. differentiation) in their industry and the price and performance of their offerings to their competitors. Others may see some advantage in their accumulated assets. In fact, these are only the tip of the competitive iceberg.

Smart organizations also compete for current core competencies that underlie the organization's strategies, as well as for those core competencies that will be necessary to gain future competitive advantage. This is what competitors have difficulty seeing. Sun-tzu, the fourth century B.C. Chinese military leader, said, "All men can see these tactics whereby I conquer, but what none can see is the strategy out of victory is evolved."

How fast can the organization acquire and develop these core competencies and at what cost? Their ability to do this and integrate them into the organization are what will determine their future: their ability to deliver products and services, their scope, the degree of differentiation, the costs, and the price the market will pay. This core competency competition must be a management focus.

There are many ways to acquire and develop core competencies:

- Hiring talented people
- Renting talented people (consultants, academicians, etc.)
- Executing development contracts (to share the cost of developing core competencies with, for example, suppliers or customers)
- Joint venturing (to share existing core competencies)
- Licensing (the use of core competencies)
- Acquiring or taking equity positions in organizations (who have the core competencies)

Outsourcing is not a substitute for acquiring and developing core competencies (unless the existing and anticipated future core competencies have weakened or are nonexistent, respectively), but it can be beneficial to management. By outsourcing activities that are not core:

- Management has more time to effectively focus on what is important—improving core competencies.
- Superior provider performance and lower costs bring additional resources to invest in and improve core competencies.
- Superior provider[1] expertise in noncore areas can be used to improve core competencies.

If you look at the elements of core competencies individually—such as knowledge, special skills, proprietary technologies, information, and unique operating methods—it becomes clear that providers can offer enhancements to any or all of these—the knowledge element, for example. Much has been written in recent years about the untapped potential of intellectual capital inside organizations. While this is true, it is equally true that organizations have not begun to tap the intellectual capital in its supply chain, of which providers are a part. Given the breadth of knowledge across many industries and functions, and depth of knowledge in their

---

[1]In this context, "provider" includes all providers serving the organization and the providers' networks of employees, outside experts, and providers.

specialties, one could make a strong argument that there is much greater potential for intellectual capital in the supply chain. Remember the old saying, "Two heads are better than one." With supply chains, it's more like hundreds of heads are better than one.

Finally, and perhaps more importantly, if performed poorly, an outsourcing initiative can be harmful. The organization must take great care not to outsource a core competency that is embedded in whatever is transferred to the provider. Current core competencies may be unknowingly transferred, or the knowledge that can create future core competencies may not be well understood and be transferred. The organization can suffer damages from which it cannot recover.

For example, when the U.S. electronics industry surrendered the television market, this dramatically reduced their opportunities to participate in later products that needed display screens, such as hand-held TVs, calculators, and computer monitors. This occurred because they either didn't have the core competencies or they were no longer on the cutting edge. In order to avoid such a catastrophe, the project team must understand the organization's current and future anticipated core competencies.

In discussions of outsourcing's risks, there is often the debate on whether outsourcing will "hollow out" the organization. People fear that outsourcing means giving up productive capabilities, including the factors of production, and that these are the basis of competitive advantage. This concern has merit when it applies to core competencies, but it is generally applied to any asset, capability, technology, skill, and so on that might be needed in the future. This is referred to the "pack rat" theory of managing resources—if you keep every resource that you have accumulated, you won't regret it because it will be there for you if you need it.

This argument ignores three points:

1. There is a cost to storing and maintaining these resources.
2. Outsourcing them doesn't mean they are unavailable, only that you don't "own" them.
3. There is no recognition that the provider brings any other added value to the transaction.

The project team should to be prepared for this discussion.

Examples of Core Competencies

The business press has written extensively about the core competencies of some of the higher profile companies. Here are some examples:

Company	Core Competency Example
Black and Decker	Small electric motor technology
Casio	Display systems technology
Domino's Pizza	Cycle time and logistics management
Honda	Combustion engine and drive train technology
Motorola	Portability technology
Nike	Athletic shoe research and design
Service Master	Motivational and training systems
Sony	Miniaturization technology
3M	Adhesives/coatings technology
Toys R Us	Information and distribution systems
Wal-Mart	Information sharing systems with providers and logistics skills

Nike is an excellent example of an organization that helped redefine an industry segment and reaped impressive revenue, market share, profits, and shareholder value. Thirty years ago we called them "sneakers" or "tennis shoes." They were generally made of canvas and rubber, and although they were more comfortable than dress shoes, they were only slightly so. Today, we wear athletic shoes whenever possible for their comfort and versatility.

Nike is also an excellent example of an organization committed to alternative sourcing. Nike's core competencies revolve around its understanding of athletes' footwear needs (attained through research and development), the design competencies to meet those needs, the marketing skills to deliver the message (including endorsements and advertising skills), and the logistics systems to get the shoes delivered. But Nike doesn't make the shoes! The manufacturing and most of the remaining competencies and activities are outsourced. Nike does what it does best, and outsources the rest. This is the new model.

Method of Identifying Core Competencies

Organizations often look at their successful products or services, then perhaps a key component, and reach a conclusion on their core competencies. The investigation must go deeper. It has to discover the combinations of knowledge, special skills, proprietary technologies, information, and unique operating methods that are embedded in those successful products or services. Then an analysis is done to see how these are integrated to develop a core competency.

Generally, the identification of core competencies should be beyond the scope of an outsourcing initiative. Senior management should provide this information directly or indirectly by putting certain core competency areas off limits to the outsourcing initiative, and it can be elaborated on as necessary by the project champion. In larger organizations, discovering core competencies can be time consuming and expensive (although critical). A team of senior executives, not the project team, should take on the task.

For purposes of illustration, however, let's assume that senior management doesn't know the organization's core competencies. We will use a successful ladies shirt manufacturer as an example of how to look for them. Their reason for outsourcing is cost reduction, because despite an excellent reputation and competitive pricing, they are only breaking even financially. After an in-depth analysis of the operations, the following is learned about their shirt production:

- *End product:* Ladies shirts
- *Component products:* Yarns, dyes, thread, and buttons
- *Activities involved:*
  - ▲ Designing the shirts
  - ▲ Cutting the patterns
  - ▲ Purchasing the raw materials
  - ▲ Mixing the dyes to achieve unique colors
  - ▲ Dying the yarn
  - ▲ Weaving the cloth
  - ▲ Cutting the shirt parts to specifications
  - ▲ Sewing the shirt parts
  - ▲ Sewing the shirt parts together, producing shirts
  - ▲ Packaging the shirts
  - ▲ Shipping the shirts
- *Other supporting activities:* Marketing, managing, maintaining equipment, selling, billing and collection, accounting, etc.

- *Factors of production:*
  - ▲ People with special skills
  - ▲ Facilities in which to work, laid out to achieve maximum efficiency
  - ▲ Special equipment and technologies for dying, weaving, cutting, sewing, packaging, and shipping
- *Competitive strategy:* Differentiated product

Given this information, a top-down analysis (one of several available identification methods) for potential core competencies can begin. A representative sample of customers (retailers) and their customers (consumers) can be questioned about why they bought the manufacturer's shirts (as opposed to competitors'). Follow-up questions would inquire about the shirts' qualities, fashion, price, performance, and so on. Similar questions could also be asked of suppliers, industry experts, and knowledgeable employees.

This exercise should produce a list of positive and negative attributes about the shirts. For example, the shirts might be viewed positively as having:

- Cutting-edge fashion
- Styling that accentuates the figure
- Bright, unique colors
- Colors stay bright even after repeated dry cleanings
- Eye-catching packaging

For each attribute, a root cause analysis can be performed. Its objective is to identify those core competencies (combinations of knowledge, special skills, proprietary technologies, information, and unique operating methods) that create the positive attribute. Start by asking knowledgeable employees, "Why does this positive attribute exist?" The focus should not only be on the component products and internal operations, but should also include all elements of the value chain (suppliers, their suppliers, and so on). For example, why do the shirts stay bright even after repeated dry-cleaning? Answer: "Because the special equipment we use to weave the yarn into cloth weaves the cloth tighter."

For each such answer, ask, "Why is that?" Do this successively several times for each attribute and the root cause competencies of the positive attribute should begin to appear:

Why is this equipment special?

"Well, the equipment is available in the market, but we reset the specs to a tighter weave."

Why is it the equipment and not the yarn that effects the brightness sustainability?

"The yarn does affect it, because it is the highest quality yarn and it picks up the dyes better than most yarns."

Why is it the yarn and not the dye that effects the brightness sustainability?

"The dye does affect it, because we buy only the highest quality dyes."

Why are the yarns and dyes not available to competitors?

"They are, but we use this special process we developed to dye the yarns and dry them, so our process is different."

Similar questions could also be asked of suppliers and industry experts.

Now the project team has learned that there are several combinations of factors (root causes) that affect the shirts' brightness sustainability—the knowledge of equipment specification adjustment, the quality of the yarns and dyes, and the special process for dyeing and drying yarn. If competitors could simply buy the equipment, yarns, or dyes, or easily copy the dyeing and drying process, then these factors would not be further considered possible core competency elements.

What sets the manufacturer's shirts apart from competitors in brightness sustainability is probably a combination of special knowledge and technology competencies—of the specification adjustment, how the quality of yarns and dyes affects the finished yarn, and the special process for dyeing and drying yarn. Further, these competencies do not belong to just one person, so that his or her departure loses the core competency.

The team then looks for ways in which these competencies are combined and integrated. Now core competencies possibilities should begin to appear. The shirt manufacturer understands how to integrate each of these factors, in a value-added way, into the front end of the manufacturing process (up through the "weaving the cloth" activity). Thereafter, there appears to be little value added, and this back end manufacturing may also not be cost-effective (overall high cost with a break-even result). This combination of special knowledge and front end operating methods may be a core competency.

The final test is to determine if the perceived core competencies can serve as a platform for the launch of new products, services, or markets. For example, could this core competency allow the shirt manufacturer to make ladies coats (new product), men's shirts (new market) or, moving further afield, home furnishings (draperies and bedspreads) and toys (stuffed animals and indoor tents)? Could the manufacturer redirect its attention to making component products, such as dyed yarns and cloth? Once this top-down analysis is completed for all of the attributes, then there is a list of possible core competencies that senior management can review.

If senior management agrees, the project team might consider outsourcing the back end of the manufacturing process to a low-cost producer. The project team would not consider outsourcing the core competencies that deal with the front end of the manufacturing process.

Another Reason to Outsource:
Reduce Investments in Assets, Freeing Up These Resources for Other Purposes

When they think of "investing," most managers think of using cash or debt today in order to benefit tomorrow. Generally this involves purchasing capital assets or inventories. But there are also current expenses that benefit future years, such as investments in training, other employee development programs, and transformation programs (reengineering, for example). While accounting policies require that these costs be "expensed", as opposed to "capitalized", they are nevertheless investments. Managers should continually ask:

- Are we getting a fair return on these investments?
- Should we continue to make these investments?

- What if we no longer have sufficient cash or debt capacity to make these investments?
- Could we get a fair price if we were to sell these investments?
- Could we sell these investments at any price?

Outsourcing allows you an opportunity to transfer assets and these ongoing investments to the provider, receiving either cash or lower future costs. It also eliminates the need for future investments of this type. For example, in outsourcing the outbound logistics process, you would transfer the truck fleet, loading docks, parts inventory, and other equipment to the provider for cash. You would no longer need to make investments in driver training, pension funds, and improving the process. These funds could now be used in other more pressing areas, such as investing in core competencies.

A few words of caution. Providers are not banks, nor are they benevolent uncles. If you need cash and can get it from a bank or financial markets, then you should do so, since your carrying costs will be lower. If you think that providers will pay you more than the market value for your assets, you are deceiving yourself. The provider may "allow" you more on the assets than the market value (just as a car dealer overvalues your trade-in), but you will repay the extra allowance, plus a finance charge, in your monthly outsourcing costs over the life of the contract.

Chapter 8

Restructuring

Outsourcing Related to Other Transformation Tools

In general business language, "restructuring" is often used to mean change. In the language of organizational transformation, it has a narrower definition. When an organization thinks about transforming itself in order to improve, it has a number of tools from which to choose. These tools are summarized in Exhibit 8.1.

Exhibit 8.1   Alternative Approaches to Operational Change

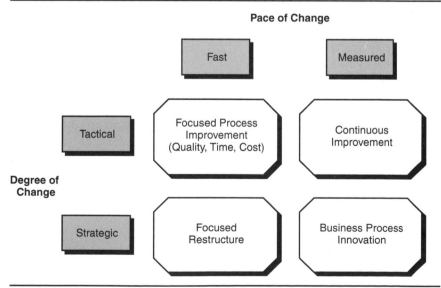

Thomas H. Davenport, "Need Radical Innovation and Continuous Improvement? Integrate Process Reengineering and TQM," *The Planning Forum* (May/June 1993), page 8.

PROVIDER: Arthur Andersen

CUSTOMER: Camp Fire Boys and Girls

SCOPE: Accounting operations, tax com-
                     pliance, and network administra-
                     tion, and financial/consulting
                     support to the local councils

LOCATION: Kansas City, Missouri

REASONS TO   Camp Fire's reasons to out-
OUTSOURCE: source included focusing on ful-
                     filling their mission to America's
                     youth, flexibility in structuring
                     the department and service
                     delivery, and improving the
                     finance and accounting opera-
                     tion's performance in providing
                     timely and accurate financial
                     information.

CONTRACT:
    Duration: 1996–1998
    Pricing: Fixed price with annual CPI
                       adjustments

Through a program of informal education, Camp
Fire provides opportunities for youth to realize their
potential and function as caring, self-directed individuals, responsible to themselves and others. As an
organization, Camp Fire seeks to improve those conditions in society that affect youth. It fulfills its purpose by developing and supporting national and
community-based programs for 670,000 participants,
in cooperation with 128 local Camp Fire councils
nationwide. Camp Fire's national headquarters, in
Kansas City, Missouri, employs twenty-six people.

Prior to outsourcing, Camp Fire management was
very concerned about the security for their existing
personnel in the accounting department, some of

whom had been with Camp Fire for many years. As a part of the outsourcing arrangement, two Camp Fire employees were reassigned to other areas, three Camp Fire employees became Arthur Andersen employees, and Arthur Andersen added three additional people to fill vacant or newly created positions.

Arthur Andersen is a global multidisciplinary professional services firm that helps clients improve their business performance through assurance and business advisery services, business consulting, economic and financial consulting, and tax services. Andersen is headquartered in Chicago and serves clients from 363 locations in seventy-eight countries. Its clients include some of the world's largest corporations, including Colgate-Palmolive, Delta Airlines, Federal Express, GTE, Hallmark, and Quaker Oats.

At Camp Fire, Arthur Andersen is responsible for all accounting operations from the director of finance level down, including financial reporting, internal reporting, budgeting, general accounting, cash accounting, fixed assets, accounts payable, accounts receivable, cost accounting, and payroll processing. In addition, they are responsible for network administration and PC support for the entire Camp Fire organization. Andersen is also responsible for federal, state, and local tax filings and management of the Government Surplus Property program for Camp Fire. During this past year, due to restructuring at Camp Fire, they also provided financial expertise, support, and assistance to the Program and Council Services Department and participated in council site visits as needed.

As a result of this outsourcing initiative, Arthur Andersen has:

- Significantly reduced accounting processing times by 65 percent.

- Customized financial and management reports to provide more accurate and meaningful information to Camp Fire management and board members.
- Developed budgeting and cash management tools to better support Camp Fire's operations.
- Implemented several technology-related improvements, including both hardware and software upgrades and standardization of technology implementation to maximize system efficiency.
- Reduced the percentage of receivables greater than sixty days by more than 30 percent.

In 1997, the account team assigned to Camp Fire's contract won Arthur Andersen's Quality Award, a firmwide award granted within the Contract Finance and Accounting Services (CFA) practice. This award is the highest CFA award available. Its purpose is to recognize an engagement team that has focused on continually exceeding the expectations of the client and achieved successful continuous improvement implementation.

In the top left quartile, focused process improvement tools, such as activity-based cost management (activity-based costing, activity-based management, or both) or focused benchmarking, bring incremental improvements to the organization. They are tactically focused on analyzing and measuring the performance of functions and processes and can be completed within months. The tools tend to be project-oriented, bottoms-up driven initiatives. The risk of failure is relatively low.

In the top right quartile, continuous improvement tools, such as total quality management or benchmarking, bring incremental improvements to the organization. They are tactically focused on analyzing processes and improving performance and can take several years to complete. These tools tend to be company-wide, bottom-up driven programs, requiring significant cultural and behavioral change. Given the high cost of training all the employees and the long time necessary for implementation, the risk of failure is higher.

In the bottom right quartile, business process innovation tools, such as reengineering, make a dramatic impact and can take several years to complete. They are strategically focused on analyzing processes and improving performance, by radically rethinking how processes operate. These tools tend to be program-oriented, top-down driven initiatives, requiring significant operational and behavioral change. Given the heavy reliance on technology as an enabler and the long time needed for implementation, the risk of failure is higher.

In recent years, reengineering has euphemistically come to mean changing the organization by whatever means. Accordingly, some believe that outsourcing is a form of reengineering. In his breakthrough *Harvard Business Review* article, Michael Hammer defined the term "reengineer" as to "use the power of modern information technology to radically redesign our business processes in order to achieve dramatic improvements in their performance."[1] In their book *Reengineering the Corporation*, Hammer and James Champy defined the term "reengineering" as "the fundamental rethinking and radical redesign of business processes to achieve dramatic improvements in critical, contemporary measures of performance, such as cost, quality, service and speed."[2]

In Chapter 1, outsourcing was defined as the moving of internal activities out of the organization. These activities can relate to individual, function, or process units. The provider may then choose to reengineer, or use other transformation tools, to improve the unit's performance. Outsourcing should not be synonymous with reengineering. There are many reasons to outsource that have nothing to do with improving performance or the use of reengineering to achieve it. There are many uses for reengineering that have nothing to do with outsourcing. Either or both together can be used as transformation tools.

[1]Michael Hammer, "Reengineering Work: Don't Automate, Obliterate," *Harvard Business Review*, July-August, 1990, page 104.

[2]Michael Hammer and James Champy, *Reengineering the Corporation* (New York: Harper-Collins, 1993), page 32.

Focused Restructuring

The bottom left quartile of Exhibit 8.1 involves focused restructuring tools, such as outsourcing or mergers and acquisitions, that make a significant impact on the organization and can be completed in months. They are project-oriented, top-down driven initiatives, which can be used to achieve a wide variety of objectives, from improving performance to maximizing asset values, to creating more effective or efficient capital structures. The risks associated with these initiatives tend to be lower than either continuous improvement or business process innovation programs because they are focused and require short cycle times. The risks are directly related to the quality of planning and to the sensitivity with which key employees are coached and comforted through the changes.

The following shows examples of restructuring tools, summarized by the types of restructuring:

Operational Restructuring

- Changing definitions of levels of authority
- Changing definitions of lines of reporting
- Changing definitions of processes, functions, position specifications
- Downsizing, removing layers of management, etc.
- Outsourcing

Asset Restructuring

- Joint venture
- Initial public offering
- Special shareholder distribution
- Acquisition
- Sale to a third party

Financial Restructuring

- Share repurchase
- Sale of minority position
- Stock merger
- Recapitalization
- Leveraged buyout

In each category, the examples are listed in ascending strategic order. The tools can be combined to meet one objective, or one tool might meet several objectives. Restructuring became a favorite tool in the 1980s, and continues today, as organizations and shareholders explore ways of improving competitiveness and maximizing shareholder value.

Transformation

If the outsourcing initiative will be an organization's first transformation project (or the first in some time), the project team should think about the challenges of implementing change. To oversimplify a complex subject, successful change is unlikely without the following elements present:

- Sufficient unhappiness with the current environment
- An enticing, attractive solution
- A probability of successfully making the change
- The capital necessary to make the change

Sufficient unhappiness may not mean the extreme—that "people are fed up and are not going to take it any more," but it's close. Unhappiness takes the form of increasing frustration, stress, performance deterioration, and perhaps even some physical pain manifesting itself. This unhappiness is somewhat widespread within a group and has passed from the murmuring stage to cries for help. The project team should ask itself if there is enough unhappiness to make a change be seriously considered.

An attractive solution for a better future beckons to people, indicating that happiness is possible (or at least much less unhappiness than the current state). The solution entices them. Henry F. Harrower said, "It is always safe to assume, not that the old way is wrong, but that there may be a better way." The solution sometimes comes in the form of a change "program," such as TQM, or the more common form of a focused improvement project, such as outsourcing, in which the potential benefits are shared with the group. The project team should think about ways in which it could present outsourcing as a solution.

The group then analyzes the probability of a successful implementation of the outsourcing solution. It might look at the decisions that must be made, the risks involved, willingness to change, the "pain of the change," and so on, to determine if they think they can solve the problem by outsourcing.

The capital necessary to make the change involves (1) the working capital for the resources necessary to make the change and (2) the emotional capital invested in old ways of thinking, or paradigms. The project team should ask itself if the investment in outsourcing will be justified.

The necessary resources include the people, enabling technologies, consultants' fees, and so on, that will be used to make the change. The emotional capital invested in old paradigms must be relinquished in much the same ways that an investment in a defunct company would be written off. This divesting is done on both a group and individual level, and is very, very difficult. Mark Twain said it best: "Habit is habit and not to be flung out of the windows by a man, but coaxed downstairs a step at a time."

What has that investment given them?

- The power to solve many important problems
- Their status among their peers as a problem solver
- Monetary remuneration (in many cases a salary based on how well they use the paradigms)
- Their title and the corner office (perhaps the result of their facility in using their paradigms)

New paradigms put everyone at great risk. The higher one's position, the greater the risk. The better you are at your paradigm, the more you have invested in it, the more you have to lose by changing paradigms.[3]

Resistance to change often then rears its ugly head when individuals discover that their old paradigms were comfortable and new paradigms bring discomfort. But as the French novelist Anotole France said, "One must never lose time in vainly regretting the past nor in complaining about the changes which cause us discomfort, for change is the very essence of life." Successful transformation projects, such as outsourcing, have other success factors, and the project team needs to:

- Get senior management acceptance.
- Set fast project cycle times because delays kill such projects.

[3]Adapted from Joel Arthur Barker, *Future Edge, Discovering the New Paradigms of Success* (New York: Morrow, 1992), page 69.

- Establish a sense of urgency and follow up on a timely basis.
- Set ambitious goals of what should and should not change.
- Fix specific problems, not the entire organization's problems.
- Communicate with employees and involve them whenever possible.
- Use small early victories to increase commitment and build momentum.

Transformation projects are irresistible targets for those who resist change. The project team needs senior management's support and that support should be made plain to the employees. Resisters will understand that their actions jeopardize their employment. In addition, information should flow freely and employees should cooperate with the team's inquires. Otherwise, the project team cannot make progress or meet its goals.

Transformation projects typically start with great fanfare and management support. Each passing day can lessen that. The projects should be launched and finished quickly. Most outsourcing projects can be completed in six months, and even the most complex ones can be completed within a year. Delays can kill a project. In fact, those resisting changes often use delay tactics, hoping enthusiasm wanes before they have to change. But as Greek philosopher Heraclitus said, "Nothing endures but change." The project team should set the project's goals for short terms and aggressively meet them.

Short projects require a sense of urgency. A six-month to twelve-month outsourcing project cannot afford to waste even a few weeks. Project team members should roll into action immediately, and issues, obstacles, and other challenges must be dealt with decisively. Results should be monitored and adjustments to the project plan should be made weekly or biweekly.

Outsourcing is a powerful transformation tool that can achieve excellent results. The project team should set ambitious goals for performance improvement, cost savings, innovation, and so on (see Appendix 1, "Other Reasons to Outsource"). Also, outsourcing directly affects the employees. There is a clear link between such a project and their continued employment, compensation, and benefits, and they know it. It must be made clear what the organization wants to change and what is off limits. This reduces the employees' stress about "waiting for the next shoe to drop."

Organizations have many problems that need solving, and for some outsourcing is the preferred tool. The project team should set focused goals to fix specific problems with a limited project scope, relating to one to three specific areas that should be considered for outsourcing. There will be opportunities to expand the scope, but the team should avoid this temptation. These additional opportunities can be covered in the next outsourcing initiative.

Transformation projects create stress, because change is stressful. The project team should communicate early and often with the employees who might be affected by the project's results. Where possible, involve employees in the discussions, ask their opinions, listen to their concerns, and reinforce the benefits for the organization and for them.

Good news must be shared. The project team should fix times for announcing beneficial results. This might include information about the existing internal area's costs and performance, competitor intelligence (from benchmarking), preliminary benefits outlined in the proposals, and so on. Don't wait six months to share the good news. The team members and management need to feel that their commitment is well founded, that progress is being made, and that success is imminent. Use these small victories to also lay a foundation for future projects.

One question that invariably arises is—should the organization try to transform its internal unit before it turns to outsourcing, or should it wait until outsourcing begins and then allow the provider to do it? For example, should the organization reengineer the unit or let the provider do it? Generally, the provider should do the transforming.

The provider has the expertise and will have to live with the results. The provider may already have the systems and processes in place, and only the transition of the internal unit needs to occur. If the organization believes that there are great cost savings available to the provider, this should be considered in negotiating the price. The organization should either strive for a lower price or negotiate a gain-sharing agreement in which the organization participates in the cost-saving benefits as they are realized. If the organization wants to undertake the transformation project, then it should do a thorough analysis of the costs and the risks.

Having said that, the outsourcing project team will do most of the work that would be done in a focused process improvement project using activity-based cost management (ABCM) tools and focused benchmarking —except for the implementation. There would be synergy operating both projects simultaneously with little extra cost, except for the ABCM implementation costs. But there would be some delay, several months at the most, in the outsourcing project during the ABCM implementation. So if performance improvement and cost savings are goals for outsourcing, if there is a belief that great savings are attainable, and there is little concern about time, running an ABCM and a focused benchmarking project prior to outsourcing would be appropriate.

Alternatives to Outsourcing to a Provider

Resistance from employees will be lessened if they understand that other outsourcing options will be explored beyond the traditional provider option. These alternatives would include:

- Selling the unit
- Setting up a joint venture
- Spinning off the unit to its employees

If the project team concludes that a function's or a process's performance is above average to exceptional and at least above desired levels, and the organization would be willing to continue using its services, alternatives should be considered. Selling the unit to a third party would keep it somewhat more intact, especially if the buyer either wasn't in that business, or wasn't as strong as the internal unit. This would also provide a financial return on the organization's investment in the unit.

A joint venture could be set up with a partner to commercially exploit the unit's special skills. The partner could be an outsource provider who does not have the internal unit's special skills or technologies, but does have the desire to enter that service niche and has the capital, marketing, distribution channels, and other infrastructure to support the venture. This option would be attractive in situations in which the unit has developed technologies that are unique but have broader market applications in which the organization is unwilling to invest.

Probably the most exciting alternative for the employees would be to spin the internal unit off on its own. This would keep it intact and provide ownership opportunities for its employees. Before communicating this outside of the project team, however, the project them must be sure this is the direction that the organization will go. As American physician and author Oliver Wendell Holmes, Sr., said, "Man's mind, stretched to a new idea, never goes back to its original dimensions." It would be very difficult to later suggest that the organization had changed its mind, and now these same employees would become employees of another provider.

In order to accomplish this, the organization would need to give the unit:

- Time to set itself up as an independent business
- Time to acquire the talent for the newly required roles (marketing, sales, accounting, etc.)
- An initial contract for the unit to provide services to the organization

Just as important, the possibility of running and owning an internal unit in the future would be a strong motivator for every manager in the organization. If this alternative could be institutionalized, every manager would be driven to achieve excellent performance (from which the organization benefits now) in hopes of ultimately being spun off.

Another Reason to Outsource: Improve Risk Management

Let's use the organization's tax function to illustrate this reason for outsourcing. During the 1960s through the 1980s, many organizations insourced their tax planning and compliance activities in order to assure access to capable tax specialists, but at a lower cost than what they were paying their CPA firm. Since then, many have found unforeseen costs and risks.

As the tax code grew larger and became more complicated, tax staffs expanded, incurring more employee and overhead costs. Many organizations, especially during economic downturns, couldn't (or wouldn't) support the annual expense of updating the tax libraries, tax software, and staff training to stay abreast of the ever-changing tax code. Because there was little chance of providing a reasonable career path for its tax staff beyond the tax function (and those positions were limited), costly turnover resulted. Perhaps the biggest risk (and potential cost) was that errors were made that missed tax savings or created tax liabilities. But you might ask, "why don't we just give the tax planning and compliance back to a CPA firm, who previously delivered such services, and let them handle these services each year?"

The answer is based on to the economics of today's professional services. The CPA firm will have tax generalists who can handle most of your tax work when you need it, and they have tax specialists who can deal with the unique issues as they arise. In order to maintain this staff "on call":

- Their billing rates must cover the staff's down-time.
- Their utilization rate (billable time) is less than if their activities could be scheduled with assurance.

Accordingly, billing rates tend to be quite high. This is good value for the high-level tax work, but can be very expensive for the more mundane and voluminous lower-level tax work.

Further, while the CPA's services could historically be terminated at will, the elimination of the ban on solicitation of clients during the 1980s allowed open competition for clients and increased the possibility of client turnover. This creates a more efficient market (lower fees), but in order to maintain profitability, the CPA firm must increase staff utilization. Therefore, the staff may only be able to invest the minimum amount of time to meet your needs, before moving on to other clients' work. As a result, the deep understanding of your *business* (as opposed to *taxes*), which might uncover tax savings, is sacrificed.

Finally, because client turnover occurs more frequently, as clients are aggressively "sold" (on lower price or differentiated service, for example), the CPA firm may be unwilling to invest for the long term in larger staffs, industry specific technologies, and training across the staff assigned to replace your tax function. They are naturally unwilling to bear the entire investment risk.

As a result of all of this, the costs and risks of providing the desired in-house level of tax services "on call" prohibit the CPA firm from being cost-effective. But what if we changed the balance of risks and rewards? What if we signed a longer-term agreement for services, so that we bear some of the risk? The costs come down and the CPA firm's willingness to invest goes up.

With outsourcing, we adjust the risk and reward formula. The CPA firm becomes an outsource provider and can better manage the risks associated with staff issues (such as compensation and benefits), technology, training, and turnover costs than we can. Given their expertise, they can also manage the error risk better than the organization can. Outsourcing highly technical functions may be worthwhile in order to reduce the risks.

Chapter 9

Aligning Outsourcing With Strategy

Overview

By this point in the process, the organization's senior management should have been able to articulate the following to the project team (see Chapter 5):

- Vision of the organization's future
- Potential targets of opportunity
- Reasons to outsource

In the three previous chapters, the project team explored the organization's:

- Vision
- Current and future organizational structures
- Current and future core competencies and competitive advantages
- Outsourcing initiative as it relates to alternative transformation tools

In this chapter the project team will explore with senior management:

- The nature of the relationship sought with the provider
- The decision rights that will be transferred to the provider
- The length of the desired contract

After this exploration is done, the project team can test the alignment of the outsourcing initiative with the organization's strategies. The project team and senior management should feel comfortable with this alignment before going any further. Anyone the project team deals with will have questions about outsourcing and may even challenge it. The project team's ability to demonstrate this alignment will go a long way toward winning cooperation and making the transition smoother.

The Provider Relationship

It is very important that the project team understands the type of provider relationship that the organization would be most comfortable with, and senior management can provide guidance. This will affect the types of providers that are asked to respond to the request for proposal (RFP), and how the scope is described in the RFP.

There are *different types of outsource provider*, as follows:

- Strategic partner
- Supplier

The strategic partner provider will approach the relationship as if it were a part owner of your business. They will not only want to perform the services requested, but also to participate in strategic planning meetings and share in the strategic decisions. They will want to marshal whatever resources are necessary to deliver those services, and will prefer a pricing model in which it is rewarded for outstanding results (pay for performance, gain sharing, or value-based fees, for example). It would be appropriate to consider paying this bonus with the organization's stock (assuming it is a corporation), in order to tie the two organizations' financial futures more closely together. This type of provider is generally a better fit for functional or process outsourcing and for areas that are closer to the core competencies, because there is generally more strategic impact at these levels. The number of providers able to operate as a strategic partner is more limited.

The supplier provider wants to deliver the requested services with a performance that at least meets the specifications. They will use an operational, tactical, or transactional approach, paying close attention to activity performance. Their role will be well defined. The supplier provider will prefer a pricing model that compensates it fairly for both its efforts and results. This type of provider is generally a better fit for component parts, individual activities, less important functional levels of outsourcing, and areas not as close to the core competencies, because there is less strategic impact at these levels. Many providers are able to operate as supplier providers.

In a 1997 survey of CEOs by *Chief Executive* magazine[1] and Andersen Consulting, 382 CEOs responded. "Those respondents who view their approach to outsourcing as strategic tend to think of their outsourcers as partners or allies and consider outsourcing a key part of their strategic planning process."

One of the questions asked was about how they viewed the provider, and the results were as follows (emphasis added in italics):

Partner/trusted adviser (*strategic*)	47%
Strategic alliance/joint venture (*strategic*)	22
Provider (*supplier*)	26
Other:	5
Total:	100%

From the CEO's perspective, it appears that strategic partners are more desired.

Assigning Decision Rights

The project team should confer with senior management on how it feels about making certain decisions as opposed to ceding control of those decisions to the provider—and under what conditions those decisions should be made. This too will affect the types of providers that are contacted to respond to the RFP, and how the scope is described in the RFP.

The decision rights can be broken down into the following categories:

- Factors of production
- Operating processes
- Management—other
- Strategic

[1]"View From the Top—Raise High the Roof Beam," *Chief Executive*, April 1997, page 67.

Decisions about factors of production relate to the resources to be deployed. Who directly manages the resources? Who evaluates, hires and fires, promotes, or transfers the employees? Who decides which equipment, technologies, and third parties will be used, whether new ones should be phased in, and when?

Decisions on operating processes relate to how work will be performed. Who directly manages the work that is done? What activities will be performed, and by whom? How will those activities be performed? Who evaluates performance and adjusts the work to improve performance?

Other management decisions relate to issues that don't involve factors of production or operating processes. Who will adjust the outsourced area based upon organizational changes (structural, locations, and volume, for example)? Who will assess the risks that come with change? Who will oversee the organizational transformation made necessary by major changes in the outsourced area?

Strategic decisions relate to the way in which long-term direction will be set. Who will assess the organization's future needs? Who will formulate strategy for the outsourced area? Who will tie that strategy to the organization's strategy? Who will investigate and evaluate emerging technologies?

Generally, the provider will control the factors of production, the operating processes, and some of the other management decisions. This is natural—given that the provider is the expert in these areas. The provider will know best how to deliver and apply a superior package of resources, such as on-point core competencies, cutting-edge technologies, state of the art equipment, experienced management, and well-trained, motivated personnel.

The organization will generally have oversight of these decisions and will control most of the management and strategic decisions. This is natural in that the organization is as knowledgeable, or more knowledgeable in these areas. Further, the organization will want to retain the knowledge of these details in order to have the flexibility to be able to change providers, if it decides it wants to.

In its oversight role, the organization, for example, may want to have final approval over

- The provider's account manager and key direct reports
- Any voluntary movement of personnel to other contracts

- Any significant changes in technology (that might too tightly lock the organization to the provider, for example)
- Any changes in the outputs (such as report formats and frequency)
- Any changes in the processes (things that could harm related organization processes, for example)

The organization is represented in the decision making by a relationship manager, who is supported by appropriate technical specialists. For large, complex transactions this would be a full-time group. For smaller, less complex transactions, the relationship manager might be dedicated full-time (to one or several contracts), and the rest of the group part-time.

Without a full-time relationship manager, the organization may not be sufficiently engaged in the relationship, in monitoring and evaluating performance, and in addressing issues. This means provider performance could suffer because the provider takes shortcuts. But more probably it would occur because problems fall through the cracks, the provider cannot get answers to questions (causing delays or inappropriate assumptions to be made), the provider's suggestions for organizational improvement (that affects its performance) are not acted on, and so on. It takes time to manage the relationship.

In the decision rights exploration, there are a number of factors to consider:

- Culture
- Reasons to outsource
- Pricing model preferred
- Contract duration preferred

What is the organization's culture for decision making? Are decisions tightly controlled and made by the organization's leadership, or is decision making diffused throughout the organization? If decisions are currently made at the top levels only, it may be difficult for the organization to cede much decision making to the provider. On the other hand, if decision making is diffused, it would be natural to cede much of the decision making to the provider.

The reasons to outsource will also be a factor in assigning decision rights. If the reasons to outsource are more strategic, the organization may want a larger share in the decision making. For example, if a reason to outsource is to increase the organization's products' or services' value or customer satisfaction, the organization may want to participate more actively in the decision making. On the other hand, if the reasons to outsource are performance or cost driven, involving the technical details of how the factors of production operate, the organization may willingly cede much of the decision making to the provider, because they have greater expertise in such details.

The desired pricing model will also affect the provider's willingness to share the decision-making. For example, if the organization wants a flat fee, most of the financial risk has been shifted to the provider and the provider will expect to be able to manage that risk, in part, through freedom of decision making. If the desired fee structure is cost plus, then the organization is bearing the major portion of the financial risk, and the provider should be willing to share more of the decision making. If the provider's fees (and thus profits) are performance based, then the provider will expect greater freedom in the decision making.

The desired contract duration is yet another factor affecting the ceding of decision rights. If the duration is short, the organization will likely want to share in the decision making, because it will have to live with those decisions if the provider does not continue after the contract expires. If the contract is longer, the organization should be willing to cede more of the decision rights.

Contract Length and Termination Date

The project team should confer with senior management on how long it wants the contract to run. This decision will affect the types of providers that are asked to respond to the RFP and how the requested contract length is described in the RFP. In the same survey of CEOs by *Chief Executive* magazine[2] and Andersen Consulting, cited above, one of the questions was about the length of outsourcing contracts, with the following results:

Less than 3 years	65%
3–5 years	26
5–7 years	6
8–10 years	3
Total	100%

[2]Ibid.

The organization is encouraged to use as short a term contract as is reasonably practical (which in certain circumstances may not be very short). The organization and the provider should enter into the relationship with a goal of making it a long-term relationship—but a contract term does not make this happen, how the parties operate does. If the relationship goes well, both parties will want to extend the contract

Longer contracts tend to be used when:

- The relationship will be more strategic (with a strategic partner provider, for example).
- The areas being outsourced are functions or processes that are closer to the core competencies.
- There are significant assets being transferred to the provider.
- There are significant investments the provider must make in order to achieve the reasons to outsource (such as performance improvement and cost reduction).

In situations like these, success cannot be achieved quickly and a short contract is impractical. If the relationship will be more strategic, it takes time for the provider to learn the organization's business, bring its vast resources to bear, and implement the strategic changes. If the outsourced functions or processes are closer to the core, it makes sense to have less organizational change and provider turnover. If there are significant assets to be transferred for cash, the provider will want enough time to earn a satisfactory return on its investment. If the provider must make significant up-front investments (start-up costs, for example), the provider will want a enough time to recoup that investment.

Shorter contracts tend to be used when:

- There are significant uncertainties involved.
- There will be a supplier relationship (not strategic).
- The areas being outsourced are component parts, individual positions activities, or functions that are clearly noncore.
- The assets being transferred are not significant.
- The provider will invest little in start-up costs.

If significant uncertainties exist, a shorter contract allows the parties to renegotiate when the fog lifts. Supplier relationships tend to operate at the operational, tactical, or transactional level; so a new provider can be brought on board without needing to repeat a long learning process. Outsourcing contracts involving noncore areas or insignificant assets can be shorter because providers are fairly interchangeable without many transition problems. If the provider will invest little in start-up costs, less time is needed to recoup those costs.

Another way of addressing this question of contract length is to consider if there is a natural life cycle to the factors of production (people, equipment, and technologies, for example) or to the processes underlying the relationship. For example, if a new information system is being suggested by the provider, and it is likely to be cutting edge for the next three to five years, why should a longer contract be signed? If the provider's services are labor intensive and the provider personnel's average years of service before turnover or promotion are three years, why should a longer contract be signed? The contract should cover a period well short of the natural life cycle, so if a change will be made in providers, the new one will be on board in time to plan the new cycle and the necessary factors of production acquisitions to meet its needs.

A final step in deciding contract length is to explore the organization's strategies to see if there is a contract length that is best aligned with those strategies. For example, if the new product strategies call for major new product launches during the next two years, followed by two years of intensive research and redesign, then outsourcing of elements of marketing or design should consider this. For example, the marketing contract should run two to three years, and the design contract should run four to five. These lengths would also give the organization time to evaluate the market's acceptance of the products, which are related to the providers' performance, prior to making a decision on renegotiating the contracts.

However, contracts should not be unreasonably short. There are outsourcing initiative costs for the organization in conducting a new competition. If the providers that you want to join the competition don't think it is real (the organization is just "kicking the tires") because you are not voicing any dissatisfaction with the existing provider, they may decide to stay out. If a provider change is made, there are:

- New transition costs, such as provider training
- Some transition disruption to operations (even in the best of circumstances)
- Harmful effects on the provider's employees (who may have been the organization's former employees)

- Time-consuming relationship building exercises
- Other costs for time and money

There is no reason to undertake these costs any more frequently than is absolutely necessary. If the right choice is made of the provider, and a sound relationship is built, there will be little need to test the market, and the existing contract can be renegotiated and extended.

The project team should also consider the annual business cycles in setting the actual date of contract termination. The contract does not have to run for a period of whole years and can end whenever it makes good business sense for it to end. Most functions and processes have volume peak and valley periods, and the contract should end in the valley period. For example, if tax compliance activities are being outsourced, the contract should end at least six months before the tax return preparation cycle begins. If the organization has a December 31 year-end, the federal and state tax return preparation cycle probably begins in February or March. Accordingly, the contact should end no later than August or September, so that if a change will be made in providers, the new provider can have a sufficient preparation period before the crunch.

Testing What Might Be Outsourced

The project team can now test the alignment of the outsourcing initiative and the original outsourcing targets against the organization's strategy and examine the strategic implications. Answering the following questions should prove enlightening:

- *Is the concept of outsourcing (or alternative sourcing) a part of the organization's vision?* If not, how will this effect the probability of a successful outsourcing initiative (for example, fair study, smooth implementation, and so on)? If not, can the organization's CEO explain to employees outsourcing's alignment with the organization's strategies in other ways?
- *Are the outsourcing targets not current or future core competencies?* If not, can the target areas be segmented to allow outsourcing of the elements that would not include the core competencies?
- *Are the reasons to outsource clearly articulated and aligned with the overall organizational strategy?* If not, how should the reasons to outsource

or strategy be redefined? If not, can the organization's CEO explain to employees the reasons to outsource in other ways?

- *Are the organization's structures (process driven, for example) conducive to smooth operations and meeting customers' needs?* If not, how will this effect the probability of a successful outsourcing initiative?
- *Are there no transformation tools that might be better at solving the problems senior management is trying to solve?* If not, how should this be communicated to senior management before further work is done on the outsourcing initiative?
- *Is the proposed type of provider relationship consistent with the organization's strategies and culture?* If not, how should the type of relationship be adjusted?
- *Is the assignment of decision rights consistent with the organization's culture, reasons to outsource, preferred pricing models, and so on?* If not, how should the decision rights assignments be adjusted?
- *Is the contract length that is being sought consistent with the type of the provider relationship sought, the levels of outsourcing, how close to the core the outsourced areas are, and so on?* If not, how should the contract length sought be adjusted?

If the answers to these questions are yes, the project team should prioritize the targets. In doing this, there are several things to be considered:

Senior Management's Original Directions

- The areas that will have the greatest impact on the reasons to outsource (for example, if cost savings is the goal, start with the area with the highest cost; if increased quality is the goal, start with the area having the most waste, rework, and errors)
- The areas that would have the greatest positive impact on customers (for example, those touching the customer)
- The areas that would have the greatest positive impact on other units within the organization (for example, those units that operate earlier in the processes)
- The areas that would be the most cooperative (those under the project champion's influence, for example)
- The areas which would have the best local providers

If the answer to any of these questions is no, then the project team should pause, answer the second question, and think about whether the outsourcing initiative should be adjusted or whether the targets are the best choices. If the outsourcing initiative is adjusted appropriately, but the targets are inappropriate, then the project team should ask:

- *Are there other areas of the organization, which are not core competencies, that should be considered outsourcing targets as well?* If yes, how should this be communicated to senior management for their consideration before further work is done on the stated targets?

The project team should advise management of its conclusions regarding strategic alignment and its planned course of action.

This is also a good time to update the employees. The project team might reemphasize how outsourcing is aligned with the organization's overall strategies. Also, in the next several chapters, the project team will be reviewing the details of the costs and performance of the areas being considered for outsourcing. At this point, the project team might identify people who will be interviewed. It might highlight the areas in which employees can contribute information. It might ask a series of generic questions, asking employees to think about their answers and respond to the project team. As always, the employees should be involved wherever possible.

Another Reason to Outsource:
Gain Market Access and Business Opportunities Through the Provider's Network

The Japanese call it *keiritsu,* a system in which companies develop interlocking partnerships with suppliers and customers. Religious people call it the "church." Children call it the "family." College students call them "fraternities" and "sororities." Other examples include the country club set, the "good old boys," the "old money establishment."

These terms all refer to the same thing—associating with those who will provide support in times of need or opportunity. These groups become powerful support mechanisms for their members. They support the group's long-term survival by sharing opportunities that can benefit the group or its members directly.

Unemployed people use their network of contacts to identify potential job opportunities. Professionals use their network of contacts for referrals of business (for example, the general medical practitioner refers those with broken bones to orthopedic surgeons).

Outsourcing allows us the opportunity to become a part of the provider's network of other customers, suppliers, affiliated companies, and so on. For example, for organizations that hold small market shares, that are trying to get access to key suppliers, that are struggling with regulatory requirements, or that need sources of capital, these networks can offer everything from valuable information to introductions to new distribution systems to actual sales to capital infusions. It's obvious that it is in the provider's best interest to help your business grow because it will result in their services and revenue growing as well.

Part Four
Analyzing Costs and Performance

Chapter 10

Existing and Projected Costs

Overview

In order to evaluate the decision to outsource (often referred to as the "make or buy" decision), it is necessary to understand the costs of the activities of the target function. This requires research and analysis. American biochemist Albert Szent Gyorgyi said, "Research is to see what everybody else has seen, and to think what nobody else has thought." Most people would think that a function's monthly financial report would be sufficient to analyze the costs. The project team should think differently.

A good place for the project team to start is with the function's activities and how they fit into the organization's overall processes. To which processes do the function's activities contribute? The project team might create a high-level process map of the function, showing all of its inputs and outputs. Inputs are the documents or other media that are provided to begin an activity. Outputs are the results (other documents, decisions, data base information, and so on) of performing it.

Existing costs are measured in order to understand the nature of those costs and how those costs would be affected by future events and by outsourcing. Later the project team will use this information, along with the providers' pricing proposals, to determine if outsourcing makes financial sense.

In looking at costs over the period of a potential functional outsourcing contract, it may seem logical to take a shortcut and simply use the function's total cost from the accounting records, apply some future inflation rate, and estimate the future costs. There are risks to this shortcut:

- The nature of current costs within the function may vary by activity.
- The nature of future costs within the function may vary by activity.
- The nature of current costs which are external, but related to the function, may vary by activity.
- The nature of future costs which are external, but related to the function, may vary by activity.
- Seldom does it occur that all of a function's activities get outsourced or disappear when outsourcing occurs.
- Seldom does it occur that there are not additional, supplemental costs that result from outsourcing, which may vary by activity.

Unless the project team studies the nature of the costs at the activity level, these nuances are likely to be missed. For example, the current costs of labor-intensive activities may be related to the organization's human resources practices and compensation plans, whereas the cost of technology-related activities might be related to speed and innovations in an ever-changing technology market. Future costs of labor-intensive activities may increase with the cost of living, while the cost of technology decreases with the lower costs of equipment. This might also hold true for the external (but related, current and future) activity costs for providing inputs to the function and receiving outputs from it.

Generally, 100 percent of the function's activities does not get outsourced. For example, the nature of the function's management activities may change, from managing people to managing a provider relationship, but a "managing" activity still exists. As a result of outsourcing, there may be unused capacity costs for facilities (the function disappeared, but not the facility) and unused executive management costs (the function's immediate superior, the executive vice president, is still in place, with less to manage).

Outsourcing brings additional costs, and their nature must be understood by the project team. With component parts outsourcing, for example, there may be additional costs for inspections, transportation, handling, and storing the parts, as well as additional invoice/cash disbursements costs.

Costs should not be the only issue in the make or buy decision,[1] because cost reduction is not the only reason to outsource. But comparing

---

[1]"Make or buy" means make the product or perform the service yourself, or buy the product or service from a provider.

the costs of outsourcing to continuing to perform activities internally will always be an important evaluation point and hurdle, in any outsourcing decision. One of the greatest opportunities to reduce costs comes not through outsourcing the activities, but by driving the related overhead out of the organization. Understanding that overhead and its costs will help the project team accomplish this objective.

Measuring Existing Costs

Most functions and processes are provided with monthly or quarterly financial statements on a "cost element" basis, for example, showing the following cost elements:

Element	Amount
Salaries	$4,500,000
Benefits	1,500,000
Communications (e.g., telephone, postage)	800,000
Third-party reports	400,000
Technology	300,000
Employee travel	350,000
Depreciation	300,000
Training	200,000
Supplies	150,000
Facilities and other overhead	500,000
Total	$9,000,000

In looking at this financial information by cost element, it is impossible to determine what the function actually does. This information is valuable for summary purposes in comparing results with budgeted expectations. This information is then consolidated into financial statements and presented to the organization's stakeholders (for example, the owners, lenders, and regulators) for purposes of review. Unfortunately, this information does not contain enough detail on the nature and costs of the actual activities that might be outsourced.

In this and the next chapter, we will use an underwriting function as an example of an outsourcing opportunity. The following discussion will be used to describe how the project team might consider addressing this problem of insufficient information.

Identifying Activities

The primary ten to fifteen activities of any function can be identified. Within each of these activities, there are many tasks. It is important to focus at the activity level and not move to the task level, because the overly cumbersome volume of detail will quickly drag the project team into a pit of quicksand. British author Anthony Burgess observed, "A sure sign of an amateur is too much detail to compensate for too little life." It is better to understand the activities and costs, than to have little understanding of finite details. A good rule of thumb—using Pareto's 80/20 rule—is that 20 percent of the activities will consume 80 percent of the costs. It in important scrutinize those activities.

Having said that, if the reasons to outsource are not focused on cost, the project team should also consider focusing on activities that are directly related to the "reasons to outsource." For example, let's assume that the reasons to outsource underwriting activities include improving the quality of activity performance and compressing the cycle time. The project team should also analyze the activities that cause waste, errors, and rework and the higher cycle time needed to perform the underwriting activities.

In identifying the activities, the project team should interview knowledgeable people within the function and concentrate on production factors such as:

- People
- Facilities (space and related services)
- Equipment
- Software
- Third-party contracts

What activities do the factors of production perform? To answer this, the project team should first determine the inputs they receive and the outputs they produce. Their activities are what they do to turn the inputs into outputs.

Inputs ⟶ Activities ⟶ Outputs

What the project team will discover is that there are inputs to the function that come from outside it (for example, the application comes from the sales, loan, or customer service representatives). There are outputs that go outside of the function (for example, an underwritten application goes to the policy or loan-processing functions and the entries go to a companywide database). Understanding the external inputs and outputs will help the project team know who interacts with the function—so this can be communicated to providers during their due diligence—and in documenting the provider's deliverables (outputs) in the term sheet and contract (see Exhibit 10.1).

For example, in analyzing the underwriting function (for insurance policies or home loans, for example), the following might be applicable:

- Receiving applications
- Screening applications

Exhibit 10.1   Inputs, Activities, and Outputs

Inputs	Activities	Outputs

- Data entering application information
- Investigating applicant's history (e.g., credit, health, or driving record)
- Processing applications
- Evaluating risks (e.g., nonpayment, death, accident)
- Evaluating asset collateral (e.g., real estate to be mortgaged)
- Making an underwriting decision
- Communicating the results
- Interacting with other functions
- Training underwriters
- Managing underwriters
- Administering the function (e.g., weekly reports, budgets)

If the project team is looking at this underwriting function as an out-sourcing candidate, it might ask which activities should be considered for outsourcing? This example was chosen because an underwriting function is not often outsourced. The reason is that if its decisions are poor, it can lead to future losses (such as customer bankruptcies, foreclosures, and insurance claims). But how many of the activities really affect the under-writing decision? It is fairly common today, for example, for underwriters to rely on outside technical specialists such credit agencies, doctors, and real estate appraisers in making underwriting decisions. Perhaps many of the other activities could be outsourced as well. In order to answer this question from a financial perspective, the project team will need to analyze the cost (below) and performance (following chapter) of each key activity. Activity-based costing (ABC) is useful in reaching this level of cost detail.

Activity-Based Costing

In reviewing this list of activities, the project team should identify the costs of each activity. To accomplish this, the team should request:

- The financial statements for the last twelve months (these are prob-ably prepared on a cost element basis) showing the overall costs of the function
- The assistance of a financial staff member such as a cost accountant familiar with ABC methods or an outside specialist, such as a CPA
- The assistance of knowledgeable personnel within the function

To oversimplify slightly, the ABC methodology for determining activity costs can be summarized as follows:

- Identify all of the activities.
- Group similar activities (ten to fifteen maximum, with no one representing more than 20 percent of the total cost).
- Determine the activity drivers—what best measures the consumption of the resources (the cost of the factors of production as shown in the financial statements) by the activities For example:
  - ▲ Labor driver (for example, the percentage of people's time used by an activity)
  - ▲ Nonlabor-related driver (for example, office space equals the number of square feet used by an activity; or equipment usage equals the number of machine hours used by an activity)
- Using the activity driver information, trace the resources (costs) to the activities.
- Produce the list of the costs related to each activity, called an activity cost pool.

The resulting activity cost pool would look something like the following:

Activities	Amount
Receiving applications	$ 190,000
Screening applications	540,000
Data entering application information	325,000
Investigating applicants' histories	1,040,000
Processing applications	1,110,000
Evaluating risks	1,770,000
Discussing risks in meetings	760,000
Making an underwriting decision	680,000
Communicating the results	580,000
Debating the results w/applicants	385,000
Interacting with other functions	465,000
Training	405,000
Managing the function	750,000
Total	$9,000,000

Now compare the value of the information in the activity cost pool above to the cost element financial information previously presented (see "Measuring Existing Costs" in this chapter). Which picture of the underwriting function provides better information about what is really happening within it? If the project team is thinking about outsourcing all or part of the function, which picture helps them more? Clearly, the activity cost pool presentation is far more effective.

Any manager who has this type of information can immediately spot activities that cost too much. You may know nothing about underwriting but still have reacted to certain activities, such as the cost of receiving the applications. This is precisely the type of information that providers can gather quickly, in order to identify areas for immediate elimination or streamlining.

Further, in order to understand the external, nonunderwriting activities and costs directly related to the underwriting function, the project team should also analyze activities external to underwriting that affect the inputs and the outputs. This information will be important in the "make or buy" decision about which company-wide activities and costs will be eliminated by outsourcing, and which will not, and which additional activities and costs are likely to be incurred as a result of outsourcing.

Scenarios on Projected Internal Costs

It is also important for the project team to estimate the future operating costs and asset investments for these activities under differing scenarios. For example, the future may vary with the volume changes of transactions, the cost of labor (inflation, for example), the use of newer technologies, and so on.

The three phases of projecting internal operating costs into the future involve:

1. Obtaining existing assumptions and planning scenarios about the future
2. Determining the cost drivers for each activity
3. Using the assumptions, scenarios and cost drivers to make the projection

The project team should first ascertain the assumptions that are being used in the organization's strategic planning and financial forecasting.

There may be assumptions relating to production volumes, product/ service mix, inflation rates, interest rates, investment yields, projected labor rate increases, number of locations, and many more. Are these the appropriate assumptions for projecting future costs? These assumptions may feed models that represent best-case, baseline and worst-case scenarios, and maybe several in between. To the extent that these assumptions, scenarios and models already exist and are current and relevant for the project team's purposes, they should use this information so as to not duplicate previous efforts. This will also help the reviewers who are probably familiar with the existing information (and don't want to rethink its validity).

If the assumptions, scenarios, and models do not exist or are not valid for this projection exercise, they must be created. This requires the project team's giving some thought to scenario planning. As Paul J. H. Schoemaker has explained, "Scenario planning is a disciplined method for imagining possible futures that companies have applied to a great range of issues. . . . It simplifies the avalanche of data into a limited number of possible states. Each scenario tells a story of how various elements might interact under certain conditions. When relationships between elements can be formalized, a company can develop quantified models."[2]

Next, the project team should address the cost drivers for each activity being projected. Cost drivers are the factors that cause activity costs to occur, or they influence the amount of the activity/cost. The project team might consider using activity-based management (ABM) concepts as a tool in this exercise. ABM is a sister tool to ABC, as they both are focused on activities. ABC tends to focus on improving the cost information about activities, which in turn can improve the information about the costs of products and services, customers, contracts (outsourcing, for example), and so on. ABM tends to focus on improving the costs, costs drivers, and performance measures in order to improve performance. ABM will help the project team root out non value-added and bureaucratic activities. U.S. Senator Eugene McCarthy once said, "The only thing that saves us from bureaucracy is its inefficiency."

Continuing the underwriting example, the cost driver for a number of the activity's costs, such as receiving, screening, data entering, and processing, would appear to be the "number of applications." Intuitively, we understand that the more applications that come in, the more effort and costs will

[2]Paul J. H. Schoemaker, "Scenario Planning: A Tool for Strategic Thinking," *Sloan Management Review,* Winter 1995.

be incurred by most of the underwriting activities.[3] (On the other hand, the number of applications should have little impact on training under-writers.) There are other cost drivers as well. For example, the completeness and accuracy of the applications will strongly influence the amount of time spent screening, investigating, and processing the activities, and hence their costs. The design of the application is another possible cost driver that could affect the completeness and accuracy of the finished applications.

Using the existing assumptions, scenarios, and cost drivers, the project team can make the projection. For example, focusing on the "evaluating risks" activity, the project team learned that:

- Current resources can handle volume changes of 2.5 percent, plus or minus, without cost changes.
- Thereafter each increase in volume of up to 10 percent will increase costs by 8 percent for new employees and equipment—this then creates a new dead band plateau.
- The volume assumption is that volume will increase 2.5 percent next year and 10 percent in each of the following years, over the prior year.
- Salary and benefits will increase at 4 percent per year over the prior year.
- Improving the completeness and accuracy of applications will improve current costs by 10 percent, and there are sales rep training programs in place to accomplish this, phasing in over the next three years.

Accordingly, the project team calculates that there will be the follow-ing net increases in processing costs:

- *Year 1:* 67 percent over current costs (no volume related increase next year, 4 percent salary and benefits increase, and a 3.3 percent decrease related to applications improvement) $1,770,000 \times 1.0067 = \$1,781,859$

- *Year 2:* 8.7 percent over year 1 costs (10 percent volume related increase = 8 percent cost increase, 4 percent salary and benefits increase, and a 3.3 percent decrease related to applications improvement) $\$1,781,859 \times 1.087 = \$1,936,881$

---

[3]However, costs may not go up or down *directly* with volume, because some of the costs are fixed, not variable. There may be volume ranges (dead bands) within which costs remain rel-atively unchanged. If so, this is important information to know in determining if the providers' proposals for pricing volume changes is fair.

■ *Year 3:* 8.6 percent over year two costs (10 percent[4] volume related increase = 8 percent cost increase, 4 percent salary and benefits increase, and a 3.4 percent decrease related to applications improvement) $1,936,881 × 1.086 = $2,103,452

In this exercise, it is also helpful to determine how isolated changes in specific business conditions will affect overall costs. For example, how will these activity costs fluctuate with changes in volume only? Are certain costs relatively fixed (such as managing and training), while others are variable with volume? What is the marginal increase in costs at incremental volume increases (5 percent, 10 percent, 15 percent, and so on). These are typical questions that must be answered when negotiating the term sheet, because providers will expect to be paid extra as volume increases.

Finally, the project team should project the capital investments (for example, purchasing assets) that will be necessary to continue to support the underwriting function internally. Will new equipment or technology be needed? These projections should be made for each year of the anticipated outsourcing contract. If significant technology investments are involved, experience indicates there may be a decreasing cost over the anticipated contract period. This has been particularly true in the long information systems and technology outsourcing contracts. If so, the project team should consider this in rethinking its operating cost projections.

Cost-Level Comparisons and Standards

This current and projected cost information then allows the project team to compare the internal unit's current and future projected operating costs and asset investments to:

■ The organization's desired level of costs and investments
■ Other firms' similar activities and costs and investments (benchmarking)
■ The provider's pricing in the proposal

[4]The 10 percent improvement will be assumed to occur as the new training is phased in over the three years.

How does this new activity-based cost information compare with what the organization wants to spend on underwriting, or on specific activities within it? How much is the organization willing to invest in assets to support underwriting? The project champion may have a feel for senior management's position on this. In the pricing of the organization's services, the marketing function may have specific assumptions about the antici- pated costs of underwriting. In the budget there are standards set for cur- rent year performance. Answering these questions now may save time later, if decision makers tend to discuss the details during presentations or ask for further investigations, thus delaying decisions. It can be quite effective to anticipate questions and answer them before they are asked.

How does this new activity-based cost information compare to other firms, such as existing competitors or world-class organizations (in other industries), with similar activities? How much do other organiza- tions invest in assets to support the function? This type of activity-based cost information allows the project team to benchmark the internal unit's activities and costs against other organizations' similar activities and costs. Benchmarking has been defined as "a continuous, systematic process for evaluating the products, services, and work processes of organizations that are recognized as representing best practices for the purpose of organiza- tional improvement."[5] If the team can identify similar organizations with similar units—who are known to have superior cost structures—it would be quite valuable to benchmark these other organizations in order to gain a better understanding of how the activities and costs might be improved.

In addition to benchmarking a unit's costs in other organizations, the project team might also take the opportunity to benchmark their out- sourcing process and experience, if these exist. This could provide valuable insights on what to look for in providers, how to manage the relationships, potential pitfalls to watch out for in outsourcing, and other practical tips. In benchmarking, each organization is a partner in sharing information[6] and is looking for benefits. The project team should be prepared to

---

[5]Michael J. Spendolini, *The Benchmarking Book* (New York: AMACOM, 1992), page 9.

[6]Those who have not been educated in benchmarking may express concern about propri- etary information leaving the organization or antitrust issues (e.g., price fixing or market share manipulation). The project team should be prepared to address this, and educate those individuals in the concept of benchmarking. There are rules of benchmarking that cannot be crossed.

describe the internal unit's costs and performance, its outsourcing process and experience, and provide insights as well.

This new activity-based cost information will also allow the project team to better evaluate the pricing details in the providers' proposals and more effectively evaluate the financial aspects of the "make or buy" decision. The projections for asset investments will also help the project team question the providers' anticipated level of investments. If the project team expects to negotiate true cost savings, they must have a clear understanding of the nature and amount of the unit's current and projected activities' costs and asset investments. This is covered further in Chapter 15's discussion of comparing and evaluating proposals.

If the providers' suggested solutions are expected to be very different from the existing activities, the project team will probably need to take an additional step—to engage the services of an outside consultant with technical expertise related to the anticipated solutions. Outside consultants can help in projecting the costs, market pricing, and necessary asset investments for complex activities, functions, or processes not previously used by the organization. For example, if the organization were expecting to move from mainframe legacy systems to client server systems, then the outside consultant would estimate the necessary asset investments and the costs of migrating the systems as if it were to be done internally. Then the consultant would estimate the market pricing for such a migration as if it were to be outsourced. Although the market will determine the price through the RFP process (as providers compete), because the project team has no previous experience in this area, the consultant's estimates will help provide a benchmark and background material on which the team can rely in their discussions with providers.

Another Reason to Outsource:
Improve Management and Control

Sometimes functions or processes are operating poorly, and our assessment is that there is a management problem. In addition, that weakness hurts our other functions or processes. For example, if the shipping department is performing poorly, this can affect the:

- Invoicing of customers (accounts receivable department)
- Tracking of shipments (outbound logistics process)
- Inventory management (inventory control department)
- Internal accounting controls (accounting department and internal audit department)
- Number of customer complaints (customer service department)

We could send in a swat team to clean up the area, change procedures, solidify controls, and so on, in order to stop the bleeding. We could bring in stronger management to launch a new improvement program. We could reengineer the function and processes. We could add technology. But think of the costs and investments. What are the probabilities of success, and when?

We could do a lot of different things that might make sense if this was a core area or even a near core area. But if it's not one of these, maybe we should consider outsourcing. We probably have to stop the bleeding now, but the provider has the expertise and systems to make the fastest, most effective improvements, with a high probability of success.

Outsourcing allows us another option to bringing in new management and incurring the costs associated with turning around poorly managed areas.

Chapter 11

Performance Standards

Overview

The project team should not only measure existing and projected *costs,* as discussed in the previous chapter, it should also measure existing and projected *performance.* When a baseball hitter has a .300 batting average, or a singer has a gold record, or a child has no "tardy arrivals" on the school attendance record, or a track star runs a mile in under four minutes, we immediately understand the high level of performance. These are well-understood performance measures of productivity, sales output, timeliness, and cycle time, respectively.

Organizations should have performance measures for their significant activities that support their strategies. In the words of the renowned British scientist Lord Kelvin, "when you can measure what you're speaking about, and express it in numbers, you know something about it; but when you cannot measure it, when you cannot express it in numbers, your knowledge is of a meager and unsatisfactory kind. It may be the beginning of knowledge, but you have scarcely, in your thoughts, advanced to the stage of science."

Knowing the performance measures for the activities being considered for outsourcing helps the project team make judgments. If performance measures do not exist for these activities, then they should be created and determined. The project team should understand the gap between the actual performance and the desired performance, the competitors' performance, and the outsource providers' promised performance.

PROVIDER:	Ryder Transportation Services (a division of Ryder System, Inc.)
CUSTOMER:	Deere & Company
SCOPE:	Logistics support
LOCATION:	Three tractor manufacturing facilities in Waterloo, Iowa
REASONS TO OUTSOURCE:	Deere's reasons to outsource included focusing on their core competencies, increasing production by freeing up floor space on the line at the central manufacturing facilities, implementing a more flexible manufacturing system they could modify to meet seasonal and economic cycle demands, reducing inventory stocks, and maintaining continuous improvement.

CONTRACT:

Duration:	1995–1999
Amount:	$10,000,000
Type:	Fixed price

Deere, headquartered in Moline, Illinois, is a worldwide manufacturer of farm, industrial, and lawn care equipment. The company has approximately 36,000 employees worldwide.

Ryder, headquartered in Miami, Florida, is best known as a full-service lessor of commercial trucks, trailers, and tractors; however, it also transports 500,000 students by school bus, and it operates more than 100 public transportation systems. Ryder's integrated logistics services provide transportation, information systems, and logistics tracking services for a wide array of clients such as Xerox, Ford, Hewlett

Packard, Bell South, General Motors, Northern Telecom, and Chrysler. Ryder has 44,000 employees worldwide.

In order to increase production at its Waterloo, Iowa, plants in order to meet the demand for its tractors, Deere needed to change how components were stored and delivered to the line for assembly. Ryder and Deere signed an outsourcing agreement in which Ryder built a 300,000-square-foot logistics center in Waterloo. Working closely with Deere's management team, Ryder introduced its logistics expertise, including just-in-time manufacturing, "demand flow technology," and an electronic data interchange to link the plants with the logistics center. Through its management and information systems, Ryder manages all aspects of the flow of component parts within its logistics center, from receiving, checking, storing, and container management to selection. These systems are also integrated with the inbound and outbound transportation network. Ryder's employees also provide a value-added service by combining component parts into packages for delivery to the line.

As a result of this outsourcing initiative, valuable space in the plants was converted from inventory storage and made available for tractor assembly. In the new logistics center, Ryder receives, bar codes, scans, and stores more than 5,000 SKUs, and then, most importantly, delivers the correct component parts to the assembly line in time for assembly. Deere can now manufacture more tractors at the Waterloo plants. Ryder also assembles spare-parts kits and distributes them worldwide for Deere.

Measuring Current Performance Levels

Although performance measures will vary by type of organization, there are several generic measures[1] that might be customized to fit the organization's application:

Productivity:	Measuring inputs ÷ outputs
Quality:	Measuring waste, errors, and rework
Timeliness:	Measuring the meeting of deadlines
Cycle time:	Measuring elapsed time from start to stop in minutes, hours, days, etc.
Utilization:	Measuring time invested in a specific activity ÷ total time available (for example, 2,080 hours is a typical work year, based on 40 hours × 52 weeks)
Creativity:	Measuring artistic achievement (such as design) or new ideas, discoveries, products, etc.
Outputs:	Measuring the results of activities
Financial:	Measuring certain financial objectives (such as budgets, net income, earnings per share, and economic value added)

The performance to be measured should be directly related to the "reasons to outsource." For example, continuing the underwriting example from the previous chapter, let's assume that the reasons to outsource underwriting activities include improving the quality of activity performance and compressing the cycle time. The project team should measure waste, errors and rework, and the elapsed time it takes to perform the underwriting activities. In any situation, there will be a number of alternative measures, and the project team should try to select the ones that are the best indicators of performance.

Because some activities have a greater impact on these measures, the investigation should start with them. The following questions can be used the help find the reasons for poor performance:

- What factors cause the waste, errors, rework, and long cycle times? (With each successive answer, ask "why" five times to get at the root causes.)

[1]Adapted from William F. Christopher and Carl G. Thor, eds., *Handbook for Productivity Measurement and Improvement* (Portland, Ore: Productivity Press, 1993), Chapter 2-9, "The Family of Measures for Improving Organizational Performance."

- What changes would affect these factors?
- Would these changes positively or negatively affect the factors?
- By approximately how much?
- Are there better ways to measure performance?

Once again, the activity-based management tool previously described can be useful here. There is no suggestion that this investigation should lead to the perfect solution or to the actual implementation of any solution, because that is beyond the project team's scope. In fact, the provider will be more qualified to make these analyses and provide solutions. However, this information will provide valuable insights for further discussion with providers (they will be exploring these same questions during their due diligence) and for comparison purposes when reviewing provider proposals.

Estimated Cost of Poor Performance

After making these measurements, the project team should estimate what the effect of poor quality and cycle time performance is on the overall organization's costs and revenue. In this example, the project team might explore the answers to these questions:

- What are the costs of poor underwriting decisions resulting from errors, for example, ultimate losses on insurance policies or loans that would not otherwise occur?
- What are the cost impacts of the slow cycle times on the underwriting function and other functions as well?
- How is revenue hurt by customers growing tired of waiting for an underwriting decision and taking their business to competitors?
- What are the costs of wasted management time spent trying to improve the poor performance and stop the conflicts it causes?

In effect, the project team is estimating the financial impact of the difference between poor performance and above-average performance. It would be unfair to expect that an internal function, which should not have superior resources, would be able to achieve world-class performance. Consequently, it would be unfair to make the comparison to such high performance. These financial impact estimates will be used in the make or buy decision (see Chapter 12).

Scenarios on Projecting Internal Performance

Once existing performance is understood, projections of future performance can be made. The following questions should be addressed:

- What factors will drive future performance?
- How much control do we have over those factors?
- Will performance likely improve or deteriorate?
- What further investment (equipment, transformation project such as reengineering, stronger personnel, and so forth) will be required for improvement, and how much?

The forecasting scenarios used in the previous chapter should be used consistently through this chapter as well. For example, in the "growth scenario," if a 25 percent increase in underwriting applications could be expected in the next three years, how will this affect the factors that cause waste, errors, rework and long cycle times?

Then, using the information about the future from above, what impact will these factors have on performance? Don't focus on past and current performance, but on how future scenarios should change them. U.S. President John F. Kennedy said, "Change is the law of life. And those who only look to the past or present are certain to miss the future." Perhaps without any changes other than growth, quality and cycle time would deteriorate by 20 percent. With internally improved processes (such as reengineering, stronger management, and inspections), the team might conclude that instead of 20 percent deterioration, perhaps there would be a 10 percent improvement, and bringing in the advanced technology should add another 5 percent improvement. While these are rough estimates, it gives the team a starting point for further discussions with providers.

Performance-Level Comparisons and Standards

This current and projected performance information then allows the project team to compare the performance of the internal unit to:

- The organization's desired level, or standard of performance
- The other firm's similar activities and performance (benchmarking)
- The provider's promised level of performance in the proposal

How does this new information compare with the level at which the organization wants underwriting to perform or on its specific activities? The project champion may have a feel for senior management's wishes about this. In the pricing of the organization's services, the marketing function may have specific assumptions about the anticipated performance of underwriting. In the business plan there may be certain underlying assumptions that were set for current year performance. A 15 percent improvement may not be satisfactory, given the necessary capital investments and the risk that it might not actually occur. The organization may need a 20 percent performance improvement in order to avoid future losses from poor underwriting.

How does this new performance information compare with that from other firms, such as competitors or world-class organizations in other industries that have similar activities? This information allows the project team to benchmark the internal unit's performance. If the team can identify similar organizations with similar activities, which are known to have superior performance, it would be valuable to benchmark these other organizations to gain a better understanding of how activities and performance can be improved. The team may learn that underwriting is 15 percent behind competitors and sinking slowly, and is 30 percent behind world-class organizations (which shows the potential for improvement).

Perhaps most important, this new performance information will allow the organization to better evaluate the performance details in the providers' proposal. It will also make it easier to evaluate the providers qualifications (see Chapter 15).

Specific Risk Analysis

Specific risks can be defined as the exposure to adversity (loss) resulting from specific events. The project team should evaluate the risks associated with either outsourcing or not outsourcing the area. Because the specific risks are often the ones that threaten a project, this is precisely the area to which the project team should devote substantial time.

Once identified, risks can generally be managed in several different ways:

- The risk may be avoided.
- The risk may be retained.
- The risk may be reduced.

- The risk and any related loss may be transferred.
- The loss from the specific event may be reduced.

For example, a risk of outsourcing (say the provider does not perform to expectations) may be avoided simply by not outsourcing. Then, however, the risk of continued poor internal performance must be confronted. The risk of poor provider performance may be retained (accepted) by signing a contract with any provider that shows up. The risk of poor provider performance may be reduced by following the methods in this book so that there is a higher probability of finding a top provider or that the monitoring controls will make it easier to predict risk and make it more manageable. The risk of poor provider performance may be transferred through an insurance contract (performance bonding, for example). The loss from poor provider performance may be reduced by including liquidated damages in the contract, in case poor performance actually occurs.

The specific risk analysis does not just address outsourcing risks only, because this would be a biased analysis—against outsourcing. The analysis also includes the risks of not outsourcing as well. It is done so that an appropriate comparison of the risks can be made. The project team should assess what the risks could be if:

- The function makes no changes and continues to perform below the desired levels of performance.
- An outsource provider is brought in, irrespective of the results (business risks).
- An outsource provider is brought in:
  - ▲ And it successfully improves performance, but not to desired levels of performance.
  - ▲ And it is unsuccessful in improving performance.
  - ▲ And the performance deteriorates.

What are the risks if the existing underwriting function continues to perform below the desired level? Perhaps the losses that come from accepting unsuitable insureds (insurance policy, for example) or credit unworthy borrowers (loans, for example) can be measured. Is there a historical pattern of excessive losses or extra costs that can be correlated with past underwriting practices? A regression model or actuarial studies would be helpful in identifying the variables that are related to poor underwriting performance.

What are the business risks of the area being considered for outsourcing? The project team should explore whether there are risks relating to non-compliance, confidentiality, accuracy, safety, controls, and so on. Are there financial, labor, technological, or environmental risks inherent in the function?

The project team should talk to senior management, the project champion, and other knowledgeable employees about organization-wide business risks. It may be that if costs are not dramatically reduced the organization cannot survive, or if innovative processes are not introduced, its products will become obsolete. Perhaps outsourcing a relatively important, but non-core, function, such as underwriting, would damage the organization's reputation in the market, making it difficult to hire higher-level executives.

Then the project team should think about the impact of outsourcing on these business risks. Does outsourcing increase, decrease, or change these risks? Think about such things as the personalities, cultural dynamics, organizational structures, and management styles involved. How would these factors affect the provider's probability of success? Turning this around, how would outsourcing affect these same factors?

According to press reports, CVS Pharmacies, the large drugstore chain, outsourced its prescription follow-up in selected markets to a third party who would send letters to customers who had not had their prescriptions refilled at the pharmacy. While CVS viewed this as a valuable service that helped customers remember to keep taking their medications, a number of customers were outraged that their sensitive medical information was now outside the ethical boundaries of pharmacist-patient confidentiality. This led to a deterioration in customer satisfaction. Was this a risk that was originally identified?

What are the risks if the new provider improves performance, but not to the desired levels? Or if it makes no performance improvement or even lowers performance? The project team should analyze these potential pitfalls from the organization's perspective, as well as from the perspective of its stakeholders—customers, owners, employees, suppliers, lenders, regulators, and so on. How will this event, if it occurs, affect these groups? If the provider doesn't improve the underwriting function's cycle time, the organization may not be able to compete effectively. How will this affect new business? If the provider causes deteriorating cycle times, the regulators may step in to clean up what they perceive as unfair and unacceptable market conduct.

Once the risks are identified, the project team should evaluate the possible ways of managing them. Outsourcing risks cannot be completely avoided unless outsourcing is avoided. Otherwise, the project team should explore the causes of these risks to determine what controls might be put into place to address these risks. These controls may involve everything from adjustments in the outsourcing initiative plan, provider criteria, RFP language, and so on, to engaging additional outsourcing advisers, adjusting employee communications, and meeting with regulators. Generally, the benefits of outsourcing far outweigh the risks. As the American test pilot Chuck Yeager once put it, "You don't concentrate on the risks. You concentrate on the results. No risk is too great to prevent the necessary job from getting done."

Setting Outsourcing Priorities

The new performance information also aids in deciding how the outsourcing initiative should continue. In the underwriting example, because its current and future expected performance is average or worse, the project team will likely recommend getting proposals from providers to outsource some or all of the unit's activities.

On the other hand, changing the example slightly, if after measuring the underwriting unit's performance, the team concludes that it is above average to exceptional, there are several options that might also be considered besides outsourcing. The project team might recommend spinning off all or part of this unit so that its value might be realized. This could be accomplished by:

- Selling the unit to a third party.
- Setting up a joint venture with a partner (perhaps an outsource provider) to commercially exploit the unit's special skills.
- Providing the unit with enough time to set itself up as an independent business and acquire the talent for the newly required roles (for example, marketing, sales, and accounting). With this lead time and an initial contract for the unit to provide services to the organization, the unit could jump-start its business.

But if the unit performs so well, why not just continue to use its services internally? Because it has been determined that the organization's core competencies are not to be found in this unit. These activities are very important, but not core. Accordingly, restrictions should now be placed on the resources allocated to this unit, which will probably result in the deterioration in performance over time, to average at best.

Exhibit 11.1 Plotting Internal Units to Determine Sourcing

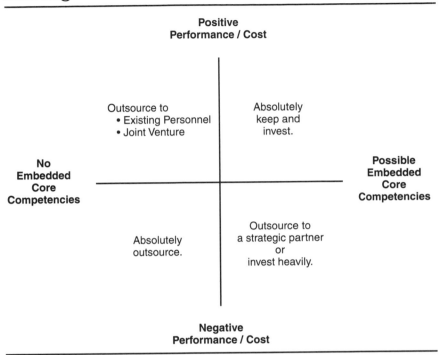

Positive
Performance / Cost

Outsource to
• Existing Personnel
• Joint Venture

Absolutely
keep and
invest.

No
Embedded
Core
Competencies

Possible
Embedded
Core
Competencies

Absolutely
outsource.

Outsource to
a strategic partner
or
invest heavily.

Negative
Performance / Cost

Contribution Value

Once the current and future costs (see the previous chapter) and the performance have been measured, analyzed, and projected, the project team can begin to look at the relative value that a unit contributes to the organization. If the reasons to outsource include cost and performance improvement, the team can determine how the internal unit stacks up against management's desires and against other organizations. For example, a low-performing, high-cost unit might be outsourced before a high-performing, low-cost unit is.

Exhibit 11.1 provides a framework for the project team to think about when it considers where the internal unit stands in relation to the normal decision for outsourcing:

This may be an appropriate time for the project team to meet with senior management to review their progress and findings. They can discuss their analysis of the internal unit as compared to:

- The organization's desired level for costs and performance
- Other firms' similar activities, costs, and performance (benchmarking)

In preparing for this meeting, the project team should determine, based on this information, if it makes sense to continue to pursue outsourcing. Does the information lead the project team to believe that providers can bring, at a reasonable cost, the benefits of outsourcing? This is not the final decision, only one on proceeding to the identification of potential providers and preparing the request for proposals. Then the project team should make a recommendation on whether to proceed.

If the outsourcing initiative is to move forward, the human resources function needs to assess further the impact of outsourcing on the employees and organization. This assessment goes well beyond the calculation of potential severance packages to include personnel security, employee morale, and similar issues. It is very important that the organization's interests and the 99.9 percent of the employees who are mature, honest, and mentally sound be protected from those few employees who do not meet these criteria. With each passing phase in the outsourcing initiative, there is additional pressure on those employees who feel they may lose their jobs. For example, human resources should review building security to determine if unhappy employees could sabotage assets or, worse, bring violence into the workplace.

Another Reason to Outsource:
Improve Credibility and Image by Associating With Superior Providers

Why do organizations sign famous athletes, actors, and other celebrities to endorse or speak for their products, services, or causes? Because these people lend their name, which stands for success, credibility, and image, and this gives the organizations' products, services, and causes recognition.

Think about some of the premier organizations in the world serving as outsource providers. Microsoft and Intel deliver the operating systems and micro-processors, respectively, to most of the world personal computer manufacturers, and Sony operates as an outsource provider in manufacturing miniature electronics (including the development of Apple's notepad computer). Arthur Andersen delivers accounting services (beyond its traditional audit, tax, and consulting services) to companies of all sizes, and Marriott delivers food service operations in many organizations' headquarters.

American Airlines (through a subsidiary, Sabre Group) delivers reservations systems to travel agents, hotels, and other airlines. Robin Kane owns Classic Travel, a travel agency with several locations in the Baltimore area. One of the top concerns for travelers when making reservations is that the reservations be accurate. When travelers show up at the airport check-in counter or hotel, they don't want any problems. Robin and her staff assure concerned customers at the point of reservation that Classic Travel uses American Airlines' Sabre reservation system and as a result, reservation accuracy should not worry them. The name recognition of American Airlines and its Sabre reservation system, considered one of the industry's finest, bring customer peace of mind and enhance Classic's credibility.

Outsourcing allows us to associate with superior providers that have name recognition, and thus improve the credibility and image of our products and services.

Chapter 12

Other Financial Issues

Asset Identification and Capital Budgeting

The project team identifies which assets, such as facilities, equipment and technologies, are related to each activity. If an activity is then outsourced, consideration can be given to the disposition of each asset (it will or won't go to the provider).

Several questions need to be asked. What is the nature of these assets? Are they shared resources or are they directly tied to specific activities? If an asset is a shared resource and will not go to the provider, will it be used enough by replacement activities to operate at least at existing capacity, or will the asset operate at under existing capacity? Should the assets be sold or leased to the provider? What are the fair market values of these assets?

Of particular importance to the project team is their understanding of:

- The impact of these assets on the provider's costs
- How the need for these assets will change over the contract period
- What the nature and timing of their replacement will be

For example, if the facilities, equipment, and technologies are significant to the provider's being able to perform the activities and deliver the outputs, then they will probably be an important element of the cost (which the project team should understand). Will the need for these assets change during the contract period? If these assets are the objects of rapid innovation in the marketplace, this will affect the estimate of their useful lives, the timing of their replacement, and the operating costs that are incurred as they are replaced.

If the cost of new equipment and technologies are expected to decrease, as has occurred in computer-related systems, this would affect not only the estimated future costs (see Chapter 10), but also the length of contract being sought. There is no reason to lock into a long-term contract using today's cost/pricing assumptions when the anticipated degree of innovation and its effect on replacement costs are unclear. Otherwise the provider may receive an unfair benefit as its costs go down over the contract period.

If the depreciation costs for the accounting records or tax returns are based upon accelerated depreciation methods (double declining balance method, for example), there may be a difference between the fair market value and the undepreciated value, resulting in a gain (probably) or a loss. While this is irrelevant to the project team, they may want to point this out in their final report—if outsourcing is recommended—so that the appropriate financial planning can be updated.

Based upon this information, the project team can prepare a capital budget[1] (and estimate the related annual depreciation) for each year in the anticipated contract period, showing the anticipated cash outflows for new facilities, equipment, and technologies related to the "make" activities.

Asset Values

It is important for the project team to understand the market value of any assets that will be transferred to the provider. This will ensure that the organization receives fair compensation for these assets. There are a number of factors that determine the value of an asset, including the following:

- Market demand
- Replacement cost
- Original cost
- Remaining useful life
- Condition
- Features

---

[1]The purpose of this exercise is to estimate the future net capital cash outflows (acquisitions of facilities, equipment and technologies, net of disposals) relating to the "make" activities. If the future net capital cash outflows are either insignificant or are expected to approximate the historical pattern, this exercise is unnecessary. Accordingly, historical depreciation expense can serve as a surrogate (or substitute) for future net capital cash outflows. If projected capital outflows are used, the present value of those generally should not be less than the present value of the depreciation, or it may bias the exercise—why would a unit be investing less than in the past?

- Maintenance requirements and costs
- Output

If the assets to be transferred are of significant monetary value, and represent a significant benefit to the outsourcing deal, the team may want to commission an independent appraisal. If the assets are commodities, or do not represent a significant benefit to the deal, then the team may choose to let the open market RFP environment help set a range of fair asset values. Generally, providers will pay fair value. If significantly higher value is offered, be assured that the pricing is adjusted elsewhere to make up for this higher value.

Make or Buy Financial Decision

The traditional "make or buy" is simply the present value of the net cash outflows of making the products/services as compared to the present value of the net cash outflows of buying the product/services. Further, this decision has traditionally been driven primarily by the costs of the internal unit as compared to the cost in providers' proposals. But the suggested "make or buy" decision needs to be more robust. It should take into account the importance of analyzing the provider's contributions beyond simple cost implications. This is done by quantifying the provider's favorable effect on the organization's revenue and financing. The decision should also consider that the internal unit's poor performance causes negative impacts on the organization's overall costs and revenue.

The financial elements can be complex, and if performed poorly, can lead to the wrong decision. The financial elements of the make or buy decision are as follows:

Make

What will be the cost to continue to make the products or perform the services?

Activity costs (see previous chapter), inclusive of labor and overhead,[2] for a specified projected volume

---

[2]Normally depreciation expense is included in overhead. If the future net capital cash outflows (acquisitions of facilities, equipment and technologies, net of disposals) for the "make" activities are either not significant or are expected to approximate the historical pattern, historical depreciation expense can serve as a surrogate (substitute) for future capital cash out-

+ Raw materials, inclusive of direct shipping, storage, handling, and overhead, for a specified projected volume

= Total Costs.

Adjustments

Cost of invested capital

+ Estimated impact to overall costs and revenue of poor performance

+ Other

= Total Make, to Be Present Valued for Comparison to the "Buy" Option.

Buy

What is the cost to buy the products or the services?

The providers' proposals for a specified projected volume (same as above)

+ Anticipated future pricing adjustments in the providers' proposals, at the same specified projected volume (for example, cost of living adjustments)

= Total Provider Price.

Adjustments

Costs that don't disappear if outsourcing occurs

+ Additional one-time costs that occur with outsourcing

+ Additional ongoing costs that occur with outsourcing

± Other financial implications of outsourcing

= Total Buy, to Be Present Valued for Comparison to the "Make" Option.

This calculation should be made for each year in the anticipated contract period; thus the aforementioned elements (described further below)

---

flows. Therefore, depreciation should be included on this line. If future net cash outflows are expected to be significant or different from the historical pattern, depreciation should not be included on this line and the projected net capital cash outflows should be included as an "other" "make" adjustment in the make costs.

should be estimated for each period. Up to this time, the team has been working primarily on the cost elements of the "make" calculation. It is more efficient to estimate the remaining financial elements of the "buy" calculation now. At this point, the only element that is unavailable is the providers' proposal pricing. When the providers' proposal pricing comes, the "buy" information will then be finally completed (see Chapter 15).

Cost of Invested Capital

The assets involved in the "make" decision include any facilities, equipment, and technologies that are used by the "make" activities. While these assets are included in the make costs as depreciation (for example, if not identified separately, depreciation may be included in overhead), the cost of the funds used to acquire these assets (for example, the cost of capital) is not generally pushed down to the process or functional level. In effect, this amount is the imputed annual financing costs for these assets (and any future projected asset acquisitions in the anticipated contract period).

Nowadays, managers are typically not charged for the cost of the funds used to acquire the assets they employ. Because these costs are not allocated to the manager's budget, most don't think about it. Let's use a loading dock example, in which its manager is responsible for unloading trucks and temporarily storing the items unloaded. The assets available to that manager are the facility (loading dock and storage area), shelving, and five forklifts:

Assets	Original Cost	Useful Life	Remaining Life	Net Book Value
Facility	$2,000,000	20 years	10 years	$1,000,000
Shelving	500,000	10 years	5 years	250,000
Forklift 1	30,000	5 years	1 year	6,000
Forklift 2	35,000	5 years	2 years	14,000
Forklift 3	40,000	5 years	3 years	24,000
Forklift 4	45,000	5 years	4 years	36,000
Forklift 5	50,000	5 years	5 years	50,000
Total				$1,380,000

The imputed financing costs can be calculated for each asset over the anticipated contract period until it becomes fully depreciated. If a five-year contract is anticipated, then the acquisition at the end of each year of one additional forklift should probably be projected.

The CFO or treasurer will know the cost of capital rate to apply to the net value (generally the average balance) of the capital assets (or portion thereof) used. Assuming a 12 percent cost of capital, the resulting year 1 total imputed financing costs can be calculated by taking the average net asset balance over year 1 of $1,312,500[3] × 12 percent = $157,500. This should be calculated for each year of the anticipated contract period and added to the make costs.

If managers had this information and understood its effect on the bottom line, their behavior might change. If managers' compensation was based on how they managed their total costs, including the cost of capital, their behavior might change. Robert Townsend, American business writer and former president of Avis, once said, "Make every decision as if you owned the whole company." Could the forklifts really last an extra year or two if properly maintained? If volumes increased, does that necessarily mean another forklift must be purchased? If volumes decreased, could some forklifts be sold? If volumes decrease, could part of the facility be subleased? These questions are too seldom asked. The concept of economic value added, as a performance measure, is beginning to unmask this type of hidden cost that must be better managed.

Estimated Impact of Poor Performance

In looking at the organization as a whole, the project team should estimate the impact of the function's poor performance on overall costs and revenues. For example, what are the costs associated with poor quality, slow cycle times, missed deadlines, wasted management time, and so on. This was estimated in the preceding chapter.

Costs That Don't Disappear With Outsourcing

On the surface, it might appear that all of the costs to "make" a product or provide a service would disappear with outsourcing, but they typically do not. In effect, the project team should determine the costs that will and will not go

---

[3]Beginning of the year net value = $1,380,000 − year 1 depreciation of $190,000 + year-end forklift acquisition of $55,000 (projection) end-of-year net value = $1,245,000; thus the average balance for the year is $1,312,500 ($1,380,000 + $1,245,000) divided by 2.

away by outsourcing. Accordingly, on the "buy" side of the decision, the price quote should be adjusted for any make costs that will not go away with the outsourced activities so that there can be an apples-to-apples comparison with the "make" costs. An estimate of these costs should be made using reasonable assumptions about the time when this cost will disappear in the future.

Costs related to the make activities that often do not go away with outsourcing include the following examples:

- Unused portion of facility capacity
- Unused portion of equipment (production, logistics, computer, and so on) capacity
- Unused portion of managers' capacity
- Unused portion of materials handlers
- Other overhead being absorbed by the product or service
- Cost of invested capital related to the unused capacity of capital assets that will not go away
- Other

By understanding the nature of the costs (see Chapter 10), the project team should be able to estimate which costs do not disappear with outsourcing. Direct costs typically disappear and overhead doesn't. Will another activity fill the portion of the facility currently used by the outgoing function's activities or will it sit idle? If a resource (for example, the manager) won't disappear, does the resource assume new value-adding responsibilities? Of course the project team should challenge management to make these costs disappear by reallocating or terminating these resources.

For example, a manufacturer wants to explore outsourcing component parts #1001, #1002, and #1003, because they are commodity products. The parts represent 30 percent of Plant 2's capacity and current output. The team might discover that Plant 2 only has new production to replace 80 percent of this 30 percent capacity in the foreseeable future, so 6 percent (20 percent of the 30 percent) of the related plant's costs, equipment costs, plant foreman costs, materials handlers costs, and cost of invested capital, and so on should be added back. The project team should challenge management to reallocate these resources for the benefit of other product production, sublease the unused space, sell the unused equipment, or terminate the personnel.

Upon further investigation of the manufacturer's costing system, the team might also learn that these component parts are being unfairly burdened with certain unrelated overhead from old Plant 1, which has been sitting idle for six months. These overhead costs that won't disappear should not be added back, as old Plant 1 is unrelated to the make activities.

Additional Costs With Outsourcing

On the "buy" side of the decision, the provider's quoted price in the proposal should be adjusted for those additional costs that will be incurred as a result of outsourcing. These are costs that are often hidden and can add up to significant amounts. The team should estimate these additional costs now.

Continuing the manufacturing example, the team might identify the following examples of additional costs to be added back:

One-Time Additional Costs: Examples

- Severance and other benefits (for example, for certain employees the provider will not hire)
- Transfer costs of the factors of production (for example, moving equipment and transferring maintenance contracts and technology licenses)
- Training costs (for example, for the provider's staff regarding existing parts specifications and equipment operation)
- Other

Ongoing Additional Costs: Examples

- Training provider's staff (for example, for future changes in parts specifications)
- Inbound shipping (for example, from the provider's plant)
- Higher inventory carrying costs (for example, to assure stocks are available)
- Additional material handling and storage (for example, from the loading dock, to inventory, to the line, as opposed to the previous continuous processing)
- Additional inspection and rework (for example, upon delivery, for quality)
- Additional paperwork (for example, handling provider invoices and cutting checks)
- Travel and long distance telephone calls (for example, to/from the provider's operation for meetings)

- Additional costs of working capital for extended operating cycle times (for example, if outsourcing increases cycle times)
- Managing the provider relationship (for example, cost of the relationship manager and the relationship team)
- Other

These costs would not be incurred without an outsourcing initiative. The human resources function should be asked to calculate the severance benefits for the outsourced area. The project team can estimate the remaining costs by discussions with other personnel.

Other Financial Implications

There are many reasons to outsource, some of which can have profound impacts on revenue, performance (other costs), and financing. The project team should explore the reasons to outsource and the implications these might have, quantifying where possible the financial impact.

Continuing the manufacturing example, the project team recognizes that there are several potential benefits to be estimated:

- The providers are all more technologically advanced and are willing to share that knowledge without charge (other costs can be lowered).
- The providers are willing to buy the existing production equipment for the component parts at fair value, providing cash not otherwise obtainable, to purchase new advanced robotic equipment for the replacement production in the plant (lowering overall costs).
- If an outsourcing deal can be struck, one provider has expressed interest in buying old Plant 1, providing additional cash for modernizing equipment (lower costs) and product development (increased revenue), net of the cost of the sale.
- The additional equipment will increase property taxes.

These are all potential benefits and costs that will affect the make or buy calculation. This same cost-adjustment process should be done for the future scenarios in each year of the anticipated contract. The final calculation is made to determine the net present value of the "make" cash inflow and outflow streams, represented by the "Total Make, to be Present Valued for Comparison to the Buy Option" line. The present value of the "buy" cash inflows and outflows will be calculated when the providers' proposals are received (see the discussion of comparing and evaluating proposals in Chapter 16).

Pricing Models

There are many pricing models that can and should be considered, depending on the circumstances. If the organization has a preferred model, it should be stated in the request for proposal (RFP). If a particular model is unacceptable, that should be stated as well. Care must be taken to match the models with the provider relationship that is being sought, the reasons to outsource, and the existing environment.

The following examples can be used for the entire outsourcing initiative, or it can be broken down into segments and different pricing models applied to each segment:

- Fixed price (in total or per unit, transaction, keystroke, etc.)
- Cost plus
- Management fee
- Hourly fee
- Pay for performance
- Gain sharing
- Value-based
- Other (see financial engineering)

From the organization's point of view, fixed price terms are often used when:

- The services to be performed are well understood in the market and their scope and volume are reasonably predictable.
- There are a number of qualified providers from which to choose.
- The organization wants to shift much of the financial risk to the provider.

For example, payroll processing, janitorial services, and accounting services probably fall into this category. Production of commodity component parts would also fit the fixed pricing model. These tend to be fairly competitive markets with tight margins in this environment. If the organization asks for a fixed price, one of two things will likely happen unless it is a commodity service:

- You get a very high price—which covers every contingency.
- You get a very low price—which covers only the minimum specifications—and change orders will be prevalent (and costly).

Accordingly, getting competitive bids is important in forcing providers to detail which option they selected, and to sharpen their pencils in making the price the lowest they can make it.

From the provider's point of view, fixed pricing is preferred when they can quickly improve the costs or performance and can quickly capture these benefits to improve their bottom line. For example, in activities with heavy reliance on fast-changing technology, such as IT outsourcing, providers signing long-term fixed-priced contracts have reaped healthy profits as the decreasing costs of newer technology lowered their costs over the contract period.

From the organization's point of view, cost plus pricing terms are often used when they want to retain the decision rights over the level of resources to be applied. Examples of this would include organizations that need outside expertise but do not want to commit to contracts sufficiently long to attract providers—or there is the imminent possibility of dramatic advances in technology or equipment. From the provider's point of view, cost plus pricing is preferred when there are significant uncertainties that create undue risk or unclear rewards for the providers. Examples of this would include services to an organization that is in a turbulent period (with an uncertain future), or the provider does not want to (or cannot) assume the financial risk of a fixed price contract.

From the organization's point of view, the management fee and hourly rate pricing models are used when it wants virtually all of the decision rights, risks, and rewards. An example would be a case in which an organization is unhappy with its management in a certain area and thus needs specialized expertise over the short term and can buy the time and talent to reach a more permanent decision on staffing versus outsourcing. From the provider's point of view, these models work well when significant uncertainties exist or they have excess capacity. An example would be a case in which the provider has recently lost a major contract and has excess capacity. Of course, this also gives them a foot in the door to learn about the operation and prove their expertise and value. Fees tend to be higher because of the shorter duration and more uncertain workload.

Pay for performance models set a lower baseline price with a significant bonus if the provider meets the challenging performance objectives. A variation of this is gain sharing, in which the provider gets a more normal baseline price, with a bonus incentive to improve the operations, that is paid out of the savings generated. Another variation on this is value-based pricing, in which the provider's price is tied to a particular financial measure (for example, increasing revenue or market share), such that the typically larger provider has every incentive to use its vast resources (network, capital, and so on) to help the organization improve. From the organization's point of view, these models work well when there are significant uncertainties, but the provider has the expertise to meet the challenge —if properly focused. From the provider's point of view, these models encourage it to apply its resources for the organization's benefit and to achieve a greater profit than might otherwise be available—and the risks are manageable.

Agreements are typically built on a fixed price or cost plus model. In each of these models, a price for agreed upon volume or services scope as well as additional fees for excess volume or services scope are negotiated. The RFP should ask the provider to indicate in the proposal how future changes in volume or services scope will be handled. While it is almost certain that changes will occur, and it is impossible to provide for every eventuality, a price adjustment mechanism should be set forth in the contract.

The desired pricing model set forth in the request for proposal sends a message to the providers, and should be thought through carefully. If you focus on a short-term, low-price contract, you encourage your providers to operate opportunistically and favor their other customers who treat them with respect. The relationship should benefit both parties. To get the service you need, your provider must have a profitable contract. As American publisher and founder of *Forbes* Magazine B. C. Forbes explained, "Any business arrangement that is not profitable to the other fellow will in the end prove unprofitable to you. The bargain that yields mutual satisfaction is the only one that is apt to be repeated."

Financial Engineering

Other pricing models have been developed by providers to meet organizations' needs. They want make deals and can provide powerful incentives to convince their customers to say yes.

For example, if an organization needs quick cost reduction or higher up-front cash flow from the sale and transfer of assets, providers can adjust the pricing to meet these needs. In effect, the provider is front-loading the contract benefits to the organization, and will charge a higher fee over the contract period for this additional risk and financing.

Another Reason to Outsource:
Expand Sales and Production Capacity During Periods When Such Expansion Could Not Be Financed

The market is booming! The CEO asks, "Why can't we turn out the products and services faster to benefit from this market?" The response, "We don't have the funds to expand!" Irrespective of the economic times, organizations will have neither equal access to capital, nor equal cost of obtaining it.

When the market is booming and expansion is critical to maintaining market share, those organizations that cannot obtain the capital to expand will be left in the dust. Perhaps your organization has suffered several down years and either cannot obtain new capital or only at a higher cost than competitors. Now the new product line introductions necessary to turn around the business may not be financially feasible. The research and development is complete, and the marketing tests indicate the products will be well received. The products can be priced very profitably. But without capital, they cannot be made.

Outsourcing allows us to transfer the responsibility for production of certain items, components, or services to the provider. If the provider has superior access to capital and/or to a lower cost of capital, and is willing to share that access, you can expand your sales and capacity by this transfer of production responsibility. The provider wins by sharing capital at reasonable rates and increasing volume at profitable pricing. The organization wins by increasing sales and market share.

Part Five

Selecting Providers

Chapter 13

Service Providers

Identifying Potential Providers

Once a decision has been made on which areas to consider for outsourcing, the project team should begin researching providers. This is where the team member having the strongest research skills—or support from the organization's librarian—will be most useful. But what if the team doesn't have such a person? The recent college graduates on staff are probably familiar with current research techniques, or perhaps the outsourcing adviser can do the job.

This might seem to be a simple research task, but the information is often not readily available—or that which is available is incomplete. For example, the organization might be able to come up with the names of the largest five providers in a particular function right off the top of its head. But is size so important? It may be, if factors of production having significant value will be transferred, making the provider's strong capitalization and financial stability very important. But if that is not the case, and service and responsiveness are most important, a small, high quality provider located nearby may be the perfect choice. Without research, the perfect choice may not have even been considered.

The first objective is for the project team to identify the greatest number of providers who might have the right qualifications and might be interested in providing the services. This involves networking with contacts in the industry and doing the research. Networking consists of calling knowledgeable people in the industry, briefly explaining the outsourcing initiative, and asking a series of questions:

- Do you know of any organizations in our industry that have conducted a similar outsourcing initiative (this is done to expand the contact list)?
- Do you know of any providers who deliver this type of service?
- Are there other people that I should talk to, to learn more about providers who deliver this service?
- Are there other resources you know of that might be helpful in identifying providers who might deliver these services?

When the calls on the knowledgeable contacts list have been completed—including those added as a result of the calls—continue the networking by calling the providers as well. After explaining the initiative, ask the same questions, and add a fifth. "Would you be interested in receiving a proposal?" With luck, they will give additional names for follow-up.

In addition to resources identified through networking, consider these:

- Industry association directories
- Internet web pages
- Speaker and participant listings from outsourcing seminars
- Outsourcing directories
- The author of this book (by e-mail, grvrassoc@aol.com)

The second objective is to pare this list down, based upon preliminary discussions with providers, to a manageable size for mailing out RFPs. It is counterproductive to both the organization and the providers to send the RFP to providers who are probably unqualified, who would probably not be interested in providing this service, or could probably not price their services competitively. If the team is thinking about sending out more than ten to fifteen RFPs, sufficient screening has probably not been done.

Someone will have to talk to each provider, satisfy the providers' due diligence requirements, review and evaluate proposals, and reach decisions. The providers will have invested significant resources to submit proposals, and they deserve serious consideration. It is far better to do the screening up front than to do more work on the back end.

In some outsourcing markets, for complex transactions for large global organizations there may only be a few providers who could handle the scope. For example, for Fortune 500 companies wanting to outsource their information systems and technology operations globally, there are only a handful of providers who have the size, breadth of scope. and financial resources. Providers such as EDS, IBM/ISSC, CSC, Andersen Consulting, Perot Systems, and maybe several others end up battling for these opportunities.

Matching the providers and the organization's needs is just as important. The "big boys" of IS and IT outsourcing may not be the best choice to deliver services for small and mid-sized organizations not located near one of their service centers. The organization would be a small fish in a large pond (or more likely, giant ocean) and probably wouldn't get the hands-on service it needs. This type of organization would be much better off identifying local (including regional) service providers who are closer and smaller. In addition to size, scope, and financial resources fit, there are many other criteria to consider, which are covered in this chapter.

The final objective is to get five to seven proposals from the most qualified, interested, and cost-competitive providers, and to evaluate those proposals efficiently.

Provider Qualifications

A list of examples of qualifications follows, summarized by hard and soft qualifications (in no particular order). The hard qualifications are those that are primarily historically based and can be reasonably verified by due diligence. The soft qualifications are those that are more attitudinal, may or may not be verifiable, and could change based on the circumstances:

Hard Qualifications	Provider	Process	Personnel
Demonstrated ability to deliver today	x	x	x
Experience to deliver	x		x
Provider strengths	x	x	
Superior performance	x	x	x
Deserved positive reputation	x	x	x
Proven customer satisfaction	x		x
Strong capitalization/financial stability	x		
Proven management capabilities	x		x
Shared approach to problem solving	x		x
Commitment to continuous improvement	x		x
Strong transition experience	x		x
Commitment of specific resources	x		x

Soft Qualifications	Provider	Process	Personnel
Trust/Security/Confidentiality			x
Positive attitude			x
Good chemistry			x
Good cultural fit	x		x
Flexibility to change	x	x	x
Cost conscious	x		x
Willingness to share cutting-edge knowledge		x	x
Clear vision of their market	x		

The project team should consider whether this list is complete and add to it where appropriate. For example, if the provider would be involved in transportation or medical services, then "safety" or "sterile environment" would be important. Further, not all of these qualifications apply to each situation, and the project team should determine which should apply and which should be eliminated. Reflect on the reasons to outsource in reaching a conclusion about the necessary qualifications criteria.

Let's address the example qualifications:

■ *Demonstrated ability to deliver today.* The provider should be able to demonstrate with its people and processes, including site visits if necessary, that they have the ability to deliver the desired result at this time. Does the provider have customers to whom this service is being delivered today? Of course they do. How similar are those customers and their needs to the organization and its needs? How much of the provider's revenue would the organization's business represent (for example, a concentration concern)? Does the provider have the size and scope to handle the service? A small provider probably cannot handle a Fortune 500 company's international scope.

■ *The experience to deliver.* Solid experience in performing the service should generally be important. Is there a track record of experience, as a firm, and/or individually in delivering these services? Is experience in the organization's industry important, and if so, does the provider have it? Does the provider hire individuals that have specific education, certifications and experience levels? How are these people trained, developed and promoted? On the other hand, if price is most critical, accepting less experienced providers or start-up operations (with experienced personnel) may be satisfactory (and necessary).

■ *Provider strengths.* The provider should have strengths in those areas that relate to the reasons to outsource. For example, if flexibility is critical because technology advances are uncertain, the provider should have superior flexibility. Expectations are that the provider's core competencies will complement the organization's core competencies.

On the other hand, if the provider's core competencies and product/service must be integrated into the organization's final product/service (for example, manufacturing of outsourced high quality component parts), then identical core competencies would be important.

■ *Superior performance.* Improved performance and lower costs are often cited outsourcing reasons. While there may be trade-offs here and there, the provider should have superior performance (to the internal unit). If shorter cycle times are an important reason to outsource, the provider's cycle time should be shorter than the internal unit's cycle time. For the performance areas related to the reasons to outsource, is the provider's performance better than the internal unit's performance?

■ *Deserved good reputation.* If employee resistance is likely, perhaps because the internal unit is well regarded (just not core), the provider will need a good reputation to be accepted. Or if the organization is hoping to network through the provider to increase sales, or improve its credibility and image through association with the provider, identifying a provider with a top-flight (not just in the outsourcing area) reputation would be important.

■ *Proven customer satisfaction.* If the organization has not been satisfied in the past with other providers' performance (of any type), then this could become an issue with internal customers. For example, is the provider responsive to the customer's needs and requests? Does the provider measure customer satisfaction through surveys? The provider may claim superior customer satisfaction, but what do the customers say? Is the provider responsive in a timely fashion when confronted with issues?

■ *Strong capitalization/financial stability.* If the provider must purchase significant factors of production (for example, assets such as equipment and technology), now or in the future, then their ability to meet their commitment is dependent on their capitalization and financial stability. This would be much less important in an outsourced service in which labor is the primary factor of production.

■ *Proven management capabilities.* Several of the decision rights that are often transferred to the provider relate to the management of resources and processes. Management expertise requires the ability to oversee people and equipment and set up effective processes and controls. If human labor is significant or advanced processes and controls are necessary, then this would be important.

■ *Shared approach to problem solving.* In the best of outsourcing situations, problems will arise. How does the provider address such problems? Beware the provider who has all the answers. Most outsourcing problems require that both parties address them, and share in finding a resolution. Are the provider's people defensive when confronted with problems or do they try to work through them to a solution?

■ *Commitment to continuous improvement.* The provider may have outstanding performance or cutting edge technologies now, but what will happen over the length of the outsourcing agreement, which is typically several years at least? Will the provider continue to improve? How does the provider attract, train, and compensate their personnel? How does the provider manage knowledge? How does the provider evaluate new technologies? The organization's competitive advantage may be tied, in part, to the provider's continuous improvement.

■ *Strong transition experience.* This will be important in the first few outsourcing initiatives an organization undertakes. A foul-up in the transition can doom the initiative, and/or make it sufficiently painful that the organization will avoid future outsourcing. This will always be important in significantly large transfers of factors of production (for example, large functions and processes). Most organizations cannot afford to (and should not) miss a beat during the transition.

■ *Commitment of specific resources.* The provider should be able to identify its key account team members, and commit to their involvement. What is the provider's track record of turnover (voluntary or involuntary)? How do they treat their people? Are they satisfied and challenged? How are they organized? How do they assure quality? How is job performance evaluated, and what are the results? What is their bench strength and emergency backup plan? Understanding who these people are, how they operate, and how you feel about them, is an important part of the soft qualifications that follow.

■ *Trust, security, and confidentiality.* Access to everything from assets to proprietary information may occur through outsourcing. What are the risks? There will be a claim made by those attempting to defeat outsourcing that outsourcing providers cannot be trusted. This also applies to trust in simple things, such as keeping promises. What are the provider's policies on trust issues? How does the provider screen and hire employees? How does the provider handle breaches of trust? How does the provider secure your information? What kind of contingency plan and disaster recovery plan for operations does the provider have? Only providers having high integrity and quality security should be considered. This applies in virtually every case.

■ *Positive attitude.* Working alongside a provider's personnel is no different from working with a peer employee. Who wants to work with a difficult person? Outsourcing can be challenging at times, and it's far better to start each day with a can-do, positive approach and know that the provider's personnel think that way too.

■ *Good personal chemistry among key staff people.* Based on the interviews and presentations, how do you feel about the provider's key people? Are they the types of people the organization would hire if filling an internal position? Employees tend to work better with people they like.

■ *Good cultural fit.* Look at the organization's and provider's cultures. What are their basic beliefs and values? Is their service high touch or high tech? How do they fit? The organization might be solid with conservative growth, while the provider is loose and on a fast track—not a particularly good fit. Different cultures tend to see, approach, and solve problems very differently.

■ *Flexibility.* Flexibility should be tested from day one; inflexibility may be a deal killer. The one thing that can be assured is that the assumptions that went into the original agreement will change. Volume will be more than expected, new technology will require scope changes, a location will be closed, a key employee will leave. Does the provider have multiple resources, skills, and options available? Is their process flexible or inflexible? How do the provider's people think about change?

■ *Cost-consciousness.* Sometimes provider costs and pricing are critical to the make or buy decision. Sometimes you may be willing to pay a premium for differentiated service. But either way, you don't want to pay more for the service than is necessary. How does the provider measure and monitor costs? What is the provider doing to avoid waste, errors, and rework, to improve productivity, and so on? How does the provider achieve its lower costs (for example, economies of scale)? Providers should be conscious of their costs and how they affect the organization.

■ *Willingness to share cutting edge knowledge.* Providers who specialize in a niche service generally do it better. How open are the provider's personnel to inquiries? How willing are they to share that knowledge? If you better understand what they are doing, and how they are delivering the service, you can better integrate them into your company (not cut them out). Many providers will share information, but few share knowledge. You want to choose one that can share knowledge in such a way that together, you can turn it into a competitive advantage.

■ *Clear vision of their market.* You don't want to associate with a provider who doesn't know the market, where it will be in several years, and where they will be within in it. What is their commitment to outsourcing? Do they have a clear vision of their market? Their answer may tell you a great deal about their sophistication in the marketplace and what you might expect in terms of service in the agreement's out-years.

Notice also that "price" was not included in the qualifications (see Chapters 12 and 15). Experience shows that in evaluating proposals, it is better to separate price from the other criteria. If the evaluators know the price, it may unduly influence the evaluation.

A qualification that should be focused on, and is thus discussed separately, is the provider's willingness to hire a significant number of the employees from the unit being outsourced. In a number of outsourcing transactions, this is not a problem because this is the only way the provider could deliver the services. The employees' skills may be scarce in the marketplace, the organization's location may not be particularly attractive to the market as a whole, and so on

On the other hand, there are many situations in which the provider hopes to use their existing resources' excess capacity to deliver the services without taking any of the employees (or other factors of production). This intention should be questioned at length. Unless these employees will be absorbed by other operations within the organization or the local market is such that they will have no trouble immediately finding other employment at equal levels, the project team should strongly consider providers who are willing to hire these employees.

The two primary objectives of listing these qualifications criteria are (1) to think through the necessary qualifications so they can be communicated in the request for proposal (see the discussion on developing the RFP in Chapter 14) and (2) to try to make the provider evaluation and selection phase as objective as possible (see Chapters 15 and 16).

Evaluation Criteria

Not all of the qualifications just discussed (or the new ones that the project team identifies) are of equal importance. Accordingly, the team should assign the appropriate weightings for each separately. This is done now to eliminate any bias that might result from a reviewer reading a particular proposal and setting the criteria and weightings to give that proposal an unfair advantage.

In setting the criteria weightings, think again about the reasons to outsource. Start by listing the reasons and judging their importance to the outsourcing decision. Then apply that information in order to weight the qualifications (see Exhibit 13.1).

There are other ways of thinking about this as well. If the team believes that qualifications and price should receive equal weight in making an evaluation, think about the standard "value" formula, in which value = performance (for example, qualifications in the proposal) divided by price. If obtaining the highest overall value is important, this formula should work well.

On the other hand, in the unusual circumstance where obtaining the lowest price is critical to survival, the price may be virtually 100 percent of the evaluation criteria. In this case, the qualifications review exercise is primarily limited to getting assurance that the provider can produce at the absolute minimum acceptable standards.

A final question relates to whether any one provider is likely to have all of the qualifications as they are weighted. In outsourcing large, complex functions or processes, multiple providers may make sense. In this way, the organization can get the benefit of each provider's core competencies. Another way of achieving the same result is to encourage single providers to use subcontractors and to set the performance levels high enough to encourage them to do it. In the case of multiple providers, the initiative's later phases (RFP, evaluations, and so on) should be separated according to the different types of services, but the providers should be expected to coordinate their services so that they are not only operating seamlessly with the organization, but also with one another.

Decision Time

Up to this point in the initiative, the team has been engaged in an information gathering and analysis exercise. The project team has:

- Organized itself and the project.
- Sought the assistance of advisers.
- Explored the organization's strategy, structure, core competencies, and reasons to outsource, and aligning them.

Exhibit 13.1   Identifying and Weighting the Qualifications

Reasons to Outsource

Provider Qualifications	Total Weighting						
Total	100%						

Identify the related qualifications for each reason to outsource. Then assign weights to each appropriate box (matching reason and qualification), so that the total numbers in all of the boxes add across and down to 100 percent (shaded areas).

- Reviewed the unit's costs and performance, both existing and anticipated.
- Identified the providers' qualifications and criteria for choosing the provider.

Now is the time for the project team to be decisive. There are two questions that should be asked:

1. What will be described in the request for proposals (RFP)?
2. Is there any reason to shortcut the full RFP and provider selection process?

First, the reasons to outsource, anticipated scope of services, provider qualifications, and so on should be reduced to writing in a "request for proposal." Any confusion or disagreement on the project team should be resolved. This can be a time of frustration and confrontation.

For example, there may be disagreement on which activities should be outsourced. Some team members may support total outsourcing for the internal units under consideration, while others may support selective outsourcing of certain activities within the internal units. Some team members may prefer a more strategic partnering with the provider, while others prefer a more routine supplier relationship with the provider. Some team members think provider qualifications are more important while others think provider costs are the key issue. Some team members like the fixed-price model to transfer much of the risk to the provider, while others like the pay-for-performance model in which benefits are shared. Some team members are excited about outsourcing, while others feel the pressure and are tired of thinking about it. Here, the project leader (and advisers), under the project champion's guidance, should be able to bring the group to consensus and gain management's support for the result.

Second, the project team needs to confirm that the initiative should move forward with the suggested methodology. In certain situations, there may be shortcuts that might work:

- Sole sourcing with a provider with which the organization has a relationship
- Allowing the internal unit to make a proposal, leading to a future spin-off
- Engaging the outside adviser to carry more of the load

Most people do business with people they like and with whom they have a relationship. There may be fear of people you don't like or don't know. As Henry Quadracci, president of Quad/Graphics, put it, "One of our iron-clad rules is 'Never do business with anybody you don't like.' If you don't like somebody, there's a reason. Chances are it's because you don't trust him, and you're probably right. I don't care who it is or what guarantees you get—cash in advance or whatever. If you do business with somebody you don't like, sooner or later you'll get screwed." Unfortunately, in outsourcing situations the organization often doesn't have a relationship with qualified providers of certain services because those services were previously performed internally. The organization is starting from scratch.

If one of the organization's valued service providers is qualified to perform the requested services and is interested in doing so, then sole sourcing may be an alternative. The obvious advantage of this shortcut is to reduce the time and effort and get to a decision when a well-known provider would have an inherent advantage in the competition anyway. The obvious disadvantages include: (1) there is no open market competition and the related benefits, such as competitive pricing, are lost; (2) the chance for getting innovative ideas from many sources is lost; and (3) there may be failure to discover providers whose performance would be superior. If this shortcut makes sense, the RFP could only be sent to the well-known provider. If this approach is used, keep the contract short and give the provider a chance to prove their performance in this new area before making a longer commitment.

Another variation on sole sourcing is to allow the internal unit to make a proposal for delivering the services. This typically occurs only when the internal unit has achieved both low costs and superior performance. If this is the case, the project team could negotiate with the internal unit on the basis that if a contract could be drawn up, the unit would be spun off as a separate entity. The advantages and disadvantages are similar to sole sourcing, except the internal unit is unproven as a separate business. Accordingly, it would make sense to allow the unit some time, while still in the organization's employ, to develop the necessary business skills and to acquire new positions, such as marketing, sales, and accounting, that were not needed in the internal unit. An obvious added advantage is that this can be a tremendous morale booster, not just for the internal unit's employees, but for all employees. If they can produce low costs and superior performance, any employees not in a core competency area have a chance to spin off into a separate business. Think how the organization could benefit if each internal unit could achieve such results.

If the project team members have needed more time than had been hoped, getting the outside adviser (who would report to the project leader) to perform more of the duties (for example, outsourcing!) may be an alternative. The outside adviser could prepare the RFP, coordinate the competition, handle the communications with providers, do the preliminary evaluations of the proposals, expedite the discussions to cut the candidates to the short list, coordinate the formal presentations, and then facilitate the project team members' evaluations to select the final candidate. Less team member effort is required, and greater experience is brought to bear. The obvious disadvantages include higher adviser fees and less involvement by the project team members which might weaken their decision-making ability later.

Another Reason to Outsource:
Turn Fixed Costs Into Variable Costs

For most companies, employee related costs and the associated overhead are relatively fixed. Product or service demand can vary, but these costs generally remain the same. This can be costly when demand slackens. Should we hire or downsize at every demand change? Of course not.

Outsourcing allows us to turn fixed costs into variable costs. Providers can handle varying demand more efficiently because of their economies of scale. Assume that the provider's capacity is 100 million units (transaction counts, items processed, lines of code written, and so on) and your operation's capacity is 5 million units. A 1 million (20 percent) unit swing in your demand can be devastating to your organization, but is a mere blip (1 percent) on the provider's capacity screen. Accordingly, providers can price for variable demand, assuming some slight increase in risk, compared to a fixed volume contract—at substantially less risk to you.

Chapter 14

Developing the Request for Proposal

Overview

Providers are limited in their ability to respond to requests for proposals (RFPs), and their responses, often in the form of written proposals, require significant investment. Proposals for long-term, capital-intensive contracts, such as information technology, can cost a provider $1 million or more. This heavy investment, coupled with stiff competition and tight profit margins, create a real business risk and force providers to carefully assess which RFPs to respond to. There must be a reasonable probability of success, or a provider will ignore the RFP.

Remember that the RFP is typically the first communication with providers, in establishing the relationship. Accordingly, it should establish a process that is fair, disciplined, and smooth. What do providers want to see in a proposal process? The following list summarizes what providers want to see in a proposal process:

- A clearly written RFP
- Sufficient information (to shorten their time investment)
- Reasonable time to respond to the RFP
- Access to the organization's decision makers

As we will explore further, a healthy competitive environment is essential to a successful RFP process. As a result, the RFP must be clear and comprehensive, in order to allow providers to assess quickly and accurately

PROVIDER   Computer Sciences Corporation
                     (CSC) and Andersen Consulting

CUSTOMER: E. I. du Pont de Nemours
                     (DuPont)

SCOPE: Information technology

LOCATION: Global

REASONS   In 1997, DuPont created a
TO OUTSOURCE: breakthrough information tech-
                     nology alliance. The reasons for
                     this "creative sourcing alliance"
                     were to:

- Strategically support growth and shareholder value rather than mere cost reduction.
- Achieve significant changes globally in services, technologies, and speed.
- Provide the flexibility and speed to focus on growth and diversification.
- Access leading-edge technologies and know-how.
- Ensure a competitive and affordable information technology base.
- Improve operational reliability and provide infrastructure renewal.

CONTRACT:
    Duration: 1997–2007
    Pricing: Fully variable and consump-
                       tion-based; joint-benefits
                       based upon best-practice
                       leverage.

To drive worldwide, profitable growth, DuPont's business model is changing significantly as its businesses grow globally, pursue acquisitions, and utilize joint ventures, alliances, and other third-party arrangements. In addition, the businesses have undertaken initiatives to streamline supply chains, improve operating efficiencies, and facilitate customer interfaces. This has created demand for timely, integrated business solutions to support its transformation to an enterprise focused on life-sciences, differentiated, and foundation businesses.

DuPont is headquartered in Wilmington, Delaware, and has approximately 98,000 employees worldwide. As a result of this alliance, approximately 3,000 DuPont employees were reassigned, approximately 2,600 DuPont employees became CSC employees, and approximately 400 moved to Andersen Consulting.

CSC has 45,000 employees worldwide and is headquartered in El Segundo, California. CSC is a world leader in the strategic use of information to achieve business results. CSC provides management consulting, business reengineering, and information systems consulting, integration, and outsourcing. It has annual revenues of $6.9 billion and 45,000 employees in more than 700 offices worldwide. CSC has been one of the pioneers of successful information technology outsourcing. General Dynamics has just renewed its ten-year contract with CSC for another ten years. CSC is the lead partner in the Pinnacle Alliance for J. P. Morgan and has many global outsourcing customers, including AMP of Australia and British Aerospace.

CSC manages DuPont's global information systems and technology infrastructure, including mainframe, midrange, and distributed computing, telecommunications, and cross-functional services. CSC handles more than half of all current applications work. The key applications, including SAP R2 & R3, are those specific to each of the company's strategic business units where CSC has global responsibility. It also includes about 50 percent of DuPont's global multiple business units' applications, such as payroll, finance, and human resources.

Andersen Consulting is a $6.6 billion global management and technology consulting firm whose mission is to help its clients change to be more successful. The firm works with clients from a wide range of industries to align their people, processes, and technologies with their strategy to achieve best business performance. Andersen Consulting has nearly 45,000 people in forty-seven countries.

Andersen Consulting will provide chemical business solutions designed to enhance DuPont's manufacturing, marketing, distribution, and customer service. This includes materials and resource planning, order processing, manufacturing and engineering systems, and safety, health, and environmental analyses and reporting.

As a result of this outsourcing initiative, these providers have:

- Reduced costs.
- Changed the cost structure from fixed to variable.
- Increased the flexibility and speed of solutions delivery.
- Added strategic value through increased business process change results.
- Enabled the reengineering of the corporation to a more agile entity.

their chances of success. The objective should be to attract the most responses from the most qualified providers.

The RFP should summarize the findings made so far by the project team. Specifically, it should include the reasons for outsourcing and list the key information that the organization will expect each provider to include in their proposal:

- *Reasons to outsource.* Be clear on which reasons best apply to the situation (see list in Appendix 1).
- *Scope.* Be clear on what services the provider is being asked to deliver.
- *Provider qualifications.* Be clear on which qualifications are important.
- *Performance standards/measures.* Be clear on the level of anticipated performance and how this performance will be measured.
- *Pricing.* Be clear on the desired model (for example, fixed price, cost plus), if one is preferred, and how the estimated price for such services should be presented.[1]
- *What decision makers are accessible.* Be clear on who they can talk to and when access can occur.
- *Questions.* Be clear on how any questions resulting from their review of the RFP will be answered.

Further, each provider should be asked to (1) focus their proposals on these issues, (2) confirm specifically that the requested provisions can be delivered, and (3) specify what they will not deliver. The organization thus sets the framework for the proposals, forcing some level of discipline, and allows for better comparability during the proposal evaluation phase. From the providers' perspective, this is helpful because limiting the scope of the proposal to the essential elements reduces their preparation time. Finally, give the provider the freedom to propose reasonable alternatives that would improve the desired result. After all, the provider is the expert.

Reasons to Outsource

Explaining the reasons (see examples of reasons to outsource in Appendix 1) that outsourcing is being considered is often overlooked. But by explaining this, the organization sends a clear signal on where the provider

---

[1]It is difficult in most proposals for large complex transactions for the provider to provide a firm price without substantial investigation. They know, as you know, that this is unlikely in the short time frames for responding to the proposals. Unless you are looking for an absolute firm price in the proposal (in which case this should be stated), getting a reasonable estimate should be enough to screen the proposals to the few providers who deserve to be included in the short list competition.

should focus the innovative aspects of their proposal. Providers will highlight their special on-point expertise and offer ideas for improving the outsourced unit.

Without this "reasons to outsource" statement, providers' proposals tend to make general claims of excellence. This "reasons to outsource" statement forces them to focus their proposals on opportunities for differentiating themselves in the most important areas. Accordingly, if responded to properly, it is unnecessary for the proposal evaluators to find the proverbial needle (special on-point expertise) in the haystack (the general claims of excellence). Conversely, it is difficult for providers to make insupportable claims of excellence knowing that such claims will be tested during the due diligence process.

Outsourcing Scope: Service Specifications

The most important requirement (in the RFP, term sheets, and contract) will be to set forth concisely, yet comprehensively, the scope of the outsourcing relationship. The significance of scope is that:

- Services *within* the scope of the contract are within the contract's pricing terms
- Services *outside* the scope of the contract will be priced as new or additional services (which can be expensive)

The objective is to avoid paying twice for a service—once because you thought it was in the base charge and a second time when you have to pay extra to actually get it performed.

In defining scope, the RFP should be reasonably comprehensive yet not overly detailed. The team should avoid narrowly defining specific tasks (such as "entering payroll changes to the XYZ software data base"). This can unnecessarily limit a provider's thinking (and if not revised in the negotiations and contract can later give the provider ammunition to "create a change order" and possible additional charge as the business changes). It is more effective to describe the functions and activities being performed (such as "processing payroll changes"). The provider should process the payroll changes regardless of how it's done or what technology is used.

In identifying services within scope, return to Chapter 10, which described how the team reviewed the activities of the area being considered for outsourcing. While that chapter focused on costing the activities, the exercise of identifying activities was central to the discussion.

There are several ways to frame the scope:

- Specific activities
- Broader services and functions performed by the affected personnel in the twelve months prior to transition
- Broader services and functions included in the budget categories assumed by the provider
- Inherent services and functions necessary to perform the specified services

If specific activities—as opposed to substantially all of a function or a process—will be outsourced, the activities need to be specified. On the other hand, if substantially all of a function or a process will be outsourced, then a broader definition of scope can be used. The RFP should also set forth any support-type services, such as technical consulting, administrative services, and contract monitoring/budgeting that has been previously performed by the function being outsourced, and which the provider is expected to deliver in the future.

Which factors of production go or remain should also be outlined in the RFP. For example, if the organization is expecting to transfer equipment to the provider as part of the transaction, this should be included in the RFP.

Potential Pitfalls

When misunderstandings result from an unclear RFP scope description, it usually works to the detriment of the organization. For example:

- A provider may erroneously conclude that the RFP is not worth pursuing, thus reducing the competition.
- A provider who misinterprets the scope may incorrectly overestimate the costs (and therefore the pricing), thus reducing the competition.
- Providers may interpret the scope differently, thus making their proposals not comparable, resulting in significant time/resource waste and delay later in the process.

- Providers may unnecessarily hedge their proposals, making them subject to due diligence for example, thus delaying the process or reducing the competition prematurely, if the caveats are unacceptable.

Worse still, if the competition winner turns out to have misunderstood the scope, and as a result, underestimated the costs (and therefore the pricing), then:

- The budding relationship will be derailed, at least temporarily, while the controversy is resolved.
- One of the two parties will likely feel they were taken unfair advantage of.
- The provider will have greater opportunity to adjust the scope and increase the price over the contract period.

This is the time to have several key employees in the internal unit review the service specifications to make sure they fairly represent their activities.

Provider Qualifications

As explained in Chapter 13, at this point the project team has identified the desired provider qualifications. Clearly stating the desired provider qualifications in the RFP is important because it lets the providers know what qualifications they must demonstrate in their proposal (for example, which of their existing customers/contracts to refer to and which firm specialists should be assigned to the project).

In their proposal, providers should be asked to specify why they meet the desired qualifications. They should also be asked to give supporting documentation for their claims. This would include lists of customers and proposed account team members (and perhaps their resumes or brief bios). You want to make it clear to the vendors that you are prepared to perform a thorough due diligence. Qualified providers appreciate this because they know that this will help you screen out the wannabes from the real McCoys.

Performance Measures

As explained in Chapter 11, the project team has also identified the performance improvement objectives. The performance objectives and issues should be described in the RFP, as well as the underlying problems, that the providers may have to deal with. Candor is both necessary and deserved. The providers should understand the challenges they will be facing and what the organization is looking for in terms of improvement. If quality is critical, say so. As the British writer Somerset Maugham once put it, "It is a funny thing about life; if you refuse to accept anything but the best, very often you get it." If speed or timeliness or productivity is critical, say so. If you demand certain performance in the RFP, you are more likely to get it in the proposal, in the contract, and in actuality.

Based upon the reasons for outsourcing as explained in the RFP, the provider should be requested to identify proposed performance standards and how performance should be periodically measured and reported. In particular, providers should be asked to list references showing where they have had similar experiences and were able to improve performance.

Pricing

The economics of outsourcing are complex and varied. The organization is at a distinct disadvantage, given the providers' experience and sophistication in developing advanced pricing models. Accordingly, the RFP should be designed and worded to illuminate, as much as possible, the underlying economics of the transaction. Doing so:

- Helps level the playing field.
- Helps the market's competitive environment force discipline on the competitors by signaling to the providers that this information is important and will be analyzed.
- Helps the reviewers be more effective in evaluating and comparing the proposals.

Agreements are typically based on either a fixed-price or cost-plus model. In both of these models, the provider sets a price for agreed-upon volume or services scope and charges additional fees for excess volume or services scope. The RFP should ask the provider to explain how future changes in volume or services scope will be handled. While it is almost certain that changes will occur and it is impossible to provide for every eventuality, a framework for the price adjustment mechanism should be well understood. If the organization has a preference, it should be stated in the RFP. Likewise, if a particular model is unacceptable, it should be stated as well.

In requesting pricing from providers, make sure it is broken down by each year in the contract and that the first year is further broken down into normal charges and start-up charges. If the provider will purchase any of the factors of production, ask that the estimates be broken down at least by type of equipment, so the providers' proposals can be compared.

Other Special Terms and Conditions

If the organization desires terms and conditions not usually found in outsourcing agreements, these should be so explained in the RFP. If the decision rights to be transferred are unique, this should also be noted. If the transition of the factors of production to the provider will be particularly challenging this should be mentioned. If the provider will have access to highly confidential and/or sensitive information, assets, technologies, and so on, requiring a unique confidentiality agreement, this should be pointed out, too.

Special transition considerations also need to be brought up. For example, the organization's management may want their loyal and dedicated outsourced employees to have a good chance to land on their feet by being hired by the provider. If so, the project team will want to send a strong message in the RFP about the need to hire a significant number of the internal unit's employees as the transition occurs. There might be several questions in the RFP addressing this. How do the providers feel about this? How do the providers determine who will be offered employment? What is the providers' track record for hiring employees as part of the contract? Providers should be encouraged to interview and make offers to the qualified employees as part of the deal.

If there is a need for special payment terms, that do not follow economic reality, then this should be noted. For example, if lower costs are the primary reason for outsourcing and the savings must be realized early in the contract term, this would be important information for the providers. In most outsourcing situations, most savings are realized later in the contract. Without an understanding of the organization's special needs, the providers might promise a lower cost that is spread consistently throughout the contract. Obviously, there are higher prices associated with terms and conditions if this increases the providers' risks or costs.

The project team may want to explore whether the provider is committed to outsourcing as a philosophy by asking the provider about areas it has outsourced from its own organization. After all, if the provider can benefit from outsourcing (for example, operate at higher performance levels, or at lower costs, or for the many other reasons to outsource), then the benefits should accrue in part to their customers over time. The organization should encourage providers to strengthen their value chain and examine ways of becoming more efficient, including outsourcing.

If the outsourcing initiative is large and complex, the organization may want to look at the provider's use of subcontractors. In logistics outsourcing, for example, there is the obvious need to ask about the providers' transportation and coordination expertise and assets, but there are also qualifications for handling information systems and technology issues, telecommunications issues, and so on. A subcontractor to the provider might better handle these areas.

The RFP might explain how the organization feels about subcontracting. Should the provider identify subcontractors in the proposal or wait until later? If the organization believes in outsourcing, its first cousin, subcontracting, should be acceptable. On the one hand, asking providers to identify subcontractors gives the project team the opportunity to assess the subcontractors. On the other hand, it may force the provider to make choices prematurely before they have sufficient knowledge and unnecessarily limit their subcontractor choices.

Request for Innovative Ideas

While the RFP should ask the providers to concentrate on the important issues, it should also ask providers to list any innovative ideas that would differentiate their services. In fact, many innovative ideas will come from the proposals, and they can be explored later with the finalist provider firms and perhaps incorporated into their final proposals and the contract.

Further, innovative proposal information also "educates" the project team on what terms are possible beyond what they initially envisioned. Finally, this also decreases the knowledge gap between the project team and the providers, which will be important to leveling the playing field in later negotiations.

Communications, Meetings, and Information

Communications with providers must be clear and without favoritism. Any important information discussed with one provider should be made available to the others. This allows all of those bidding on the contract to evaluate the same information. Typically, a bidders' conference is held following the delivery of the RFP. Thereafter, it takes an effort to share information fairly and timely. For example, if an error is discovered in either the RFP or in detailed information shared later, all providers should be made aware of it.

Complex outsourcing initiatives require much investigation by the providers. The operations will be visited, interviews will be held with employees, costs and performance will be explored, personnel files will be reviewed (if employees are expected to be transferred), and other factors of production being transferred will be examined, and so on. The project team should let it be known in the RFP which individuals and information will be made available and when. The earlier the availability, the better. If important individuals or information are withheld, the providers may put restrictions on their proposals. This should be avoided wherever possible.

In general, more information is shared when the outsourcing involves functions and processes that are closer to the core competencies, involve complex transactions, and/or a strategic partner relationship is being sought. In these cases, the project team should be prepared to devote substantial time to answering questions, so the providers can begin to understand company-wide strategies, objectives, cultures, strengths, weaknesses, threats, risks, and so on. This information is necessary so the provider can begin to understand its role and how it can make a positive impact on the outsourced area and the organization as a whole. These roles and impacts are then described in the proposal.

This is also a good time to update the employees. The project team should indicate that requests for proposals are being mailed out and to whom. Generally, the list of providers would include some provider names that employees might recognize and respect. This would be a good time to outline the scope of the outsourcing and the provider qualifications being sought. The communication might ask for any information the employees have on any of the providers, as well as any employee reaction to any of the providers.

At this point the project team might also restrict internal communications with the bidders—only the project team should be talking to them. Having said that, the employees should be told of the anticipated formal provider due diligence and how they might be asked to be involved in this process.

Another Reason to Outsource: Commercially Exploit Existing Skills

If an existing function's or process's performance is above average to exceptional and at least above desired levels, and the services may therefore be marketable, the organization could consider outsourcing the unit. This would be attractive in situations where the unit has well-developed skills and unique technologies, but with broader market applications in which the organization is unwilling to invest.

A joint venture could be set up with a partner to commercially exploit the unit's special skills and technologies. The joint venture partner could be an outsource provider who doesn't have the internal unit's industry knowledge, special skills, or technologies but does have the desire to enter that service niche. The partner would also need to have the capital, marketing, distribution channels, and other infrastructure to support the venture.

Through outsourcing, an organization can capitalize on its existing knowledge, skills, and technologies, turning it into a new revenue generator.

Chapter 15

Comparing and Evaluating Proposals

Restate All Proposals in Common Terms

If the RFP was prepared well, the proposals that arrive should be fairly easy to compare. Still, they will come in different formats—using terms unique to the provider, showing innovative approaches not considered in the RFP —and the details may not necessarily be comparable. Although this makes the evaluation somewhat harder, it is also beneficial. The objective is to choose the best provider, and this will happen only if the best providers are able to differentiate themselves. Having said that, evaluators can chase their tails for days and weeks if they don't try to restate the proposals in common terms.

A simple way to do that is to develop a matrix of the requested elements that were in the RFP (see Exhibit 15.1). Then for each element, restate each provider's response to it (in common terms) in the provider's columns to the right, simultaneously highlighting the narrative covered in the proposal, and noting the specific page number of the proposal in the matrix (for quick reference). This allows effective comparisons.

This exercise also forces reviewers to determine that all of the elements have been covered or to notice an omission and determine why it happened. For example, the provider didn't cover a particular point for a reason (perhaps they didn't want to give the requisite number of industry-related references because they either didn't have that many or some would have made unfavorable comments).

PROVIDER: Sodexho Marriott Services (for-
                   merly Marriott Health Care
                   Services, a division of Marriott
                   International, Inc.)

CUSTOMER: Allegheny University Hospitals
                   MCP

SCOPE: Nonmedical services

LOCATION: Philadelphia, Pennsylvania

REASONS TO   Allegheny's reasons to out-
OUTSOURCE: source included improving cus-
                   tomer service and reducing costs.

CONTRACT:
   Duration: 1994–1996
   Type: Fixed fee

Allegheny University Hospitals MCP is a group of full-service hospitals headquartered in Philadelphia. The company has approximately 2,200 employees. None of the Allegheny employees were terminated as a result of this outsourcing.

Sodexho Marriott Services was spun off as a publicly traded company by Marriott International as of March 31, 1998. Sodexho, headquartered in Bethesda, Maryland, has approximately 100,000 employees worldwide. It serves more than 1,000 hospitals and nursing homes in North America, including the National Institutes of Health, Stanford University Hospital, Detroit Medical Center, Cleveland Clinic, and St. Elizabeth's Medical Center (Boston).

At Allegheny, Marriott assumed responsibility for nonmedical services, and, as a result, patients feel more like customers than patients. When patients and their families enter the hospital lobby, they are immediately greeted with smiles and offers of assistance. If needed, hospital employees escort patients and their families to their destinations.

Families waiting for loved ones can relax in the "family focused" waiting area. Here, visitor coordinators make family members feel welcome and valued and provide them with coffee and magazines upon their arrival. Coordinators also serve as a link between patients' families and the medical team. For example, coordinators update family members if surgery is delayed, or, if a doctor wants to schedule a meeting with family members, they make the arrangements and ensure that contact is made. Visitor coordinators also schedule times for family members to visit the intensive care unit, thus freeing up nurses from this "gatekeeping" duty. Above all, these coordinators are good listeners, lending an ear to family members with questions or concerns.

Historically, during a typical three-day stay at the hospital, patients may have interacted with fifty to sixty different hospital employees. Under the hospital's new customer service approach, a single multiskilled employee is assigned five to eight patients and handles most of their nonmedical needs. Marriott has cross-trained these employees in a variety of nonmedical, nonlicensed skills, such as completing meal forms, transporting patients, and cleaning hospital rooms. Service partners also act as service liaisons for patients, taking care of requests such as supplying patients with additional pillows or linen, distributing patient mail, and ensuring comfortable room temperature levels.

Marriott has introduced an integrated communications center known as the service response center. It is designed to improve responsiveness to patient and staff needs by providing a single point of contact for non-clinical support services (e.g., environmental, food and nutrition, linen, security, biomedical engineering, and maintenance, as well as answering questions about in-room television service and requests for directions to the institution). Employees or patients can place one call to the service center representative, trained in customer service, who coordinates with the appropriate departments for problem resolution. Service calls are entered into a computer to track their status, enabling staff, even during shift changes, to quickly determine which requests are outstanding and which have priority. In response to service calls, an appropriate staffer is notified via pager that his or her assistance is needed. These pagers hold up to eighty characters per message. A follow-up system confirms when services have been rendered and determines whether additional services are required.

Another innovation is an infrared counting system, which monitors the service needs of public rest rooms; to assist with staffing and cleaning schedules, it also gives a numerical count of individuals using specific rest room facilities. A menu bar, installed on the bathroom wall, also permits users to access services and send messages such as "towels are running low," "need toilet paper," "restroom requires cleaning," or "customer needs assistance." This system provides improved service and response time for customers.

The results of the outsourcing initiative are that:

- Patient surveys indicate a 15 percent improvement in customer satisfaction with nonmedical services.
- Employee surveys reveal a 12 percent improvement in employee satisfaction.
- Cost reductions have run into millions of dollars, including better productivity and new waste management and recycling programs.
- Compared to industry standards of four days, routine maintenance takes less than one day, despite a 20 percent increase in the number of requests.

Exhibit 15.1 Restating Proposal in Common Terms

Provider Proposals

Information Specifically
Requested in the RFP

When this has been done for each RFP element, the project team should go back to the proposals and read the nonhighlighted areas to see if there are important proposal points not covered in the RFP that should be added to the matrix. Most of this nonhighlighted part of the proposal will be boilerplate and marketing puffery, but occasionally there is a pearl to be found. These are typically elements that should have been in the RFP but fell through the cracks or innovative ideas that really add value to the process.

Qualifications Evaluation

As discussed in Chapter 13, the team set forth the criteria for provider qualifications. Now it's time to evaluate the proposals against those criteria (see Exhibit 15.2). To begin this process, refer to the matrix of RFP elements and proposal responses, restated in common terms. If the RFP clearly outlined which qualifications were desired, then the evaluations should be straightforward. If the desired qualification level is 100 percent, then each provider's qualifications for each criterion can be stated as a percent of that ideal.

If after looking at the RFP again, the reviewer finds it was either unclear or incomplete, the missing criteria should be added to the provider qualifications column and the reviewer will need to dig out of the proposals any references to these criteria. This will require follow-up in subsequent interviews and the due diligence phase.

In the qualifications evaluation, a few cautionary points follow:

■ *The objective is to evaluate the providers' qualifications, nothing more.* The reviewers aren't deciding the short list, aren't selecting the final candidate, and aren't even deciding to outsource. While their evaluation will later help these decisions be made, they should try to eliminate this from their thinking.

■ *Sometimes what we think we know about a provider going into a qualifications evaluation exercise, based upon prior experience, reading, hearsay, and so on, may not be true.* As American humorist Will Rogers said, "It isn't what we don't know that gives us trouble, it's what we know that ain't so." Accordingly, it's important to look for ways to prove or disprove in the proposals what we believe to be true.

■ *Providers want to be seen as "qualified" for every RFP element, and they are "selling" in the proposal.* That combination means that the reviewers must

Exhibit 15.2 Evaluating Proposals

[*Provider Name*] Provider Qualifications	Raw Score*	Weighting	Weighted Score

*The raw score should be the reviewer's evaluation of the provider's qualifications, as a percentage of a 100 percent perfect match with the expectations.

look to disprove what is in the proposal. Sometimes you must read between the lines. For example, be careful to note obfuscation, which may be, for example, covering a lack of the desired experience in a particular niche. This will also require follow-up in subsequent interviews and the due diligence phase.

■ *The reviewers should be looking at qualifications without bias (independently of other issues).* For example, if one of the reasons to outsource is to reduce costs, there will be a natural bias in favor of the lower-cost bidders. As a result, reviewers may rationalize certain qualification criteria. The project team should guard against any such bias entering into the evaluation.

In this example, that bias can be largely eliminated if the qualifications reviewers are not given a copy of the cost section of the proposal. Also, if one of the providers is well-known to key decision makers, the providers' names could be deleted from the qualifications section of all of the proposals and can be reviewed separately. Take care to eliminate, or at least mitigate, bias.

■ *The reviewers must do their evaluations independently of each other—and other influences.* In a group setting an influential individual can sometimes sway the group. The project team should guard against this by asking each reviewer to come forward with their evaluation for tabulation before group discussions begin.

If there are questions of fact or interpretation about the providers' qualifications, a project team member should be assigned to contact each of the provider's representatives to get clarification. This investigator should take copious notes, confirm the key points in short letters to the providers, and send copies to the reviewers.

Then the reviewers should meet to discuss each provider's qualifications and their individual evaluations of them. Where there are differences of opinion, they should be openly discussed. Then each reviewer's evaluation can be finalized, retabulated as a group, and finalized for each provider —for each criterion. Then the provider's overall qualifications can be calculated based upon the preset weightings (set when the qualifications criteria were prepared) for each criteria.

Performance Commitments

Each provider should have been asked in the RFP to confirm that the requested provisions can be delivered, to specify what they will not deliver, or to propose reasonable alternatives. that would improve the desired result. Have they done so?

Why is this important? First, the evaluators can rate the providers' confidence level. If there are clear confirming statements, this is probably a confident provider who understands the RFP. If the statements ramble, touching indirectly on the issues and failing to confirm the requested services without offering alternatives, this may be an inexperienced provider to avoid.

Second, when the contract is drafted, key elements of the proposal could be incorporated by reference so the proposal's commitments don't get lost in the legalese. After all, the proposal is what initially sells the deal, so the providers must be held accountable for their commitments (and claims).

Price Comparison and Evaluation

In evaluating the proposal pricing, reviewers should seek to understand its underlying assumptions. The differing prices in the proposals may be caused by a number of different factors, for example:

- They have different cost structures (operational and capital).
- They have different unused capacity levels, and thus different needs for new business.
- They have different risks, short-term and long-term.
- They have different profit motivations and requirements.
- They have different understandings of the problems and the scope, or both.
- They have different assumptions about solving the problems and accomplishing the scope.
- They have different perceptions about the market's existing pricing environment.

One question to be asked is this: what are the cost drivers and dynamics in the providers' industry? All providers don't have the same cost structures because, for example:

- They are at different points on the experience (learning) curve.
- They have different scale of operations (for example, size).
- They have different processes of operation.
- They have different performance levels.
- They have different quality of management.
- They have different factors of production at different costs.
- They have different value chains and levels of controls over them.
- They have different costs of capital.
- They have different overall economic forces (for example, inflation and currency fluctuation).
- They have different institutional forces (for example, government regulations and unions).

If the lower pricing is based upon an overall lower cost structure, the team should explore the provider's specific competitive advantage. Having this information gives a basis for understanding the lower price. But the team needs to probe a bit further and determine that the lower cost structure won't disappear in the near term—for example, because their technology is becoming obsolete or their favorable union contract is about to expire and the union expects major wage and benefit increases. If the competitive advantage is not sustainable, there will be significant upward pricing pressures during the contract term and at the time of renegotiation.

Does the provider really need or want new business? In component parts outsourcing, manufacturing capacity is measurable. In service businesses, however, if labor is both necessary and scarce and the provider is operating near capacity, new business may not be a priority. In either case, the provider could probably handle the new business at a premium price, but otherwise may not be worth it. On the other hand, if the provider has been losing market share and thus has excess capacity, they might fight fiercely and price aggressively for the business.

Different providers have different profit motivations and requirements. An industry leader may expect a premium price for the well-established, long-recognized service they deliver. An industry newcomer may expect to discount the price for their somewhat unproven service. A publicly traded provider may have profit expectation pressures from Wall Street, while a private company provider may be willing to look at a longer term profit yield, over time, on their investment in services.

Another question to ask is whether the provider could have misunderstood the problems or the scope, or both. For example, one proposal may have a price 25 percent or more below the others. In comparing price, the evaluator needs to analyze the provider's assumptions. Compare the scope section of that proposal to the other proposals to see if there are differences in scope. Did the low bidder do any due diligence on the organization and areas to be outsourced? If not, it may be that they don't understand the issues and problems. Acceptance of this type of proposal is like watching a train wreck in slow motion—it *will* happen as soon as the provider wakes up.

Does the provider have "better ideas"? Ideally, the provider has done sufficient due diligence on the operations to be outsourced and has arrived at a better way of operating. Remember that this is a big reason for outsourcing—to reap the benefits of the provider's expertise. The proposal should give the basis (but probably not the proprietary details) for their better ideas, and this can be probed further in subsequent discussions.

Not all providers have the same understanding of the market's existing pricing environment. Providers who submit a lot of proposals generally have a better feel for the market, whereas a provider who is more selective in responding to RFPs may have less feel for the market. Providers who sell on price generally have an excellent feel for the market's pricing, but providers who differentiate their services other than on price may not. It is helpful to determine if providers' price quotes are consistent with their marketing and sales reputations.

If there are questions of fact or interpretation about the provider's pricing, the team should get clarification, and a project team member should be assigned to contact each of the provider's representatives for this purpose. As in the previous case of investigating qualifications, this individual should take notes, confirm the points in a short letters, and send copies to the reviewers.

If everything goes well, the evaluation will reveal a rating for each provider's price quote. If the lowest is 100 percent, each provider's pricing can be stated as a percentage of that ideal.

Make or Buy Financial Decision: Update

As outlined in Chapter 12, the project team has determined each of the elements in the make or buy decision model except those relating to the providers' proposal pricing, because this information was not then available at that time. Now that it is available, the make or buy model can be completed and the results evaluated.

The project team should insert each provider's proposal price into the "buy" calculation (see Chapter 12) for each year in the proposed agreement. The final calculation is then made to determine the net present value of the "buy" cash inflow and outflow streams for each year, represented by the "Total Buy, to be Present Valued for Comparison to the Make Option" line for each year. (The present value of the "make" cash inflows and outflows, represented by the "Total Make, to be Present Valued for Comparison to the Buy Option" was calculated in Chapter 12.) The following table shows the calculation.

Year	Make	Buy
1999	$ AAAA	$ VVVV
2000	BBBB	WWWW
2001	CCCC	XXXX
2002	DDDD	YYYY
2003	EEEE	ZZZZ

With this information the project team can draw reasonable conclusions about the financial viability of outsourcing a particular component part, individual position, function, or process, both now and in the future. If the present value of the *make* cash flows is more, the financial analysis indicates that outsourcing will *reduce* costs over the anticipated contract period. If the present value of the *buy* cash flows is more, the financial analysis indicates that outsourcing would *increase* costs.

The financial implications of the make or buy decision are only a part of the final decision. A rule of thumb that might be considered is this: if the present value of the internal unit's make cash flows are not at least 10 percent less than the present value of the buy cash flows, the organization should seriously consider outsourcing. In all probability, the other benefits (for example, innovations) to be derived from outsourcing, many of which cannot be quantified in the present value calculation, will more than make up for the 10 percent difference.

Decision Time

At this point the project team has enough information to decide whether to proceed with outsourcing. It has the providers' qualifications, pricing, and the make or buy financial analysis. Generally, this information is as positive about the providers and their proposals as it will ever be. Later due diligence may uncover something that causes the project team to question some of the providers' qualifications, and hidden provider costs may come to light. Without negotiating the price down, which may be a valid strategy, the project team should assume the information isn't going to get any better.

Based on this information, does it make sense to continue to pursue outsourcing? This is not the final decision to outsource, only whether to proceed with provider selection and negotiations. Think about the reasons to outsource. Does the information lead the project team to believe that the providers can bring the benefits to satisfy those reasons at a reasonable cost?

This may be the time for the project team to meet with senior management to review their progress and findings. They can discuss their analysis of the proposals as compared to:

- The proposal
- The evaluations of the proposals
- The make or buy financial analysis results

Then the project team should make a recommendation on whether to proceed.

Another Reason to Outsource: Acquire Innovative Ideas

As author Joel Arthur Barker has put it, "So where is the strange logical place for innovation to come from? The edges. The fringes. Where there are outsiders who do not know that it cannot be done. . . . You must have tolerance and patience. You must be open to surprise from the most unlikely of sources. Only then do you increase the likelihood that you will hear the paradigm shifters when first they speak. And it is hearing them the first time they speak that carries all the leverage."[1]

Providers don't know your business as well as you know it, and that's a good thing. First, they can see the craziness (for example, non value-added activities, bureaucratic policies and procedures, and ineffective personnel) in your business that you could never see because you are buried in the organization's paradigms or the industry's paradigms of how things are done. Second, when fresh eyes observe the craziness, it invariably triggers suggestions for im-

[1]Joel Arthur Barker, *Future Edge, Discovering the New Paradigms of Success* (New York: Morrow, 1992), page 70.

provement. Some of these suggestions may be off the wall, but many are on target. If you open your mind to such suggestions, you can enjoy a blinding flash of the obvious, shared at no cost by providers. Third, providers have every incentive to help you improve your business, because what helps you helps them (what increases your volume increases their volume, for example).

Innovation is critical to competitive advantage. Who would have believed that the Japanese economy, devastated by World War II, could have become one of the world's leaders? The Japanese relied on quality and innovation. It is so easy to think that "our way" (our current products, services, processes, and so on) is just fine and there is no need to change. But refusing to change is just as risky as innovating. Outsourcing allows us to receive innovative ideas about our business from intelligent, well-meaning professionals—our provider. And because it comes at low cost, it's much less of a gamble than some other sources of innovation.

Chapter 16

Provider Selection

The Relationship Team

By now, the organization has reviewed the proposals, found several to worth pursuing, and expects that outsourcing might actually occur. Accordingly, it needs to begin preparing for the transition of resources and the management of the provider relationship. If it has not already done so, the organization should decide who will be involved.

The key position is the relationship manager—the person who will deal directly with the provider's account manager. The relationship manager is typically the former head of the unit being outsourced, and while this is the easy choice—in that it avoids confrontation, termination, severance, and so on—it may or may not be the right one. The skills needed to manage a provider are different from the skills needed to manage the people and technical issues of an internal unit.

Organization/provider relationships are arm's-length relationships. Each party has similar—and dissimilar—objectives. The long-term success of outsourcing frequently depends on the people involved and the quality of their relationships. The people will be tested in building the relationship, as unforeseen problems arise, as employee feelings are hurt, as perceptions of unfair advantages emerge, and so on. Does the proposed relationship manager have the necessary skills to build and maintain the relationship? If not, then the search for a qualified relationship manager should begin immediately, internally if possible, but externally if necessary.

For large, complex transactions, the relationship manager may need the help of technical specialists. These individuals are often selected from the outstanding technicians in the internal unit. This group, referred to as the relationship team, would be dedicated full-time to these activities.

PROVIDER: SPS TeleServices

CUSTOMER: Eddie Bauer, Inc.

SCOPE: Sales, order management and
                   call center customer support

LOCATION: Asheville, North Carolina, Sioux
                   Falls, South Dakota

REASONS TO   Eddie Bauer's reason to out-
OUTSOURCE: source was fairly simple—it
                   needed assistance in handling
                   the huge spikes and fluctuations
                   in call volumes for their catalog
                   orders, especially during the holi-
                   day season.

CONTRACT:
   Duration: 1996–2000
   Pricing: Variable, based on length of
                   call

Eddie Bauer, headquartered in Bellevue, Washington, is an upscale retail catalog company recognized for its high-quality customer service. In its seventy-eight-year history, Eddie Bauer has evolved from a single store in Seattle to an international company with more than 500 stores and 120 million catalogs.

SPS, headquartered in Riverwoods, Illinois, has approximately 4,000 employees. SPS provides call center-services for many corporations, including Ameritech, IBM Global Services, Motorola, Goodyear and Southern California Edison. SPS operates four call centers and handles over 60 million customer contacts annually.

The original Eddie Bauer agreement was to handle one million inbound catalog order and service calls from Eddie Bauer's customers and to provide support services to Eddie Bauer during the seven weeks preceding Christmas, from 3 A.M. to 11 P.M. Pacific time.

This is when Eddie Bauer's call volume traditionally exceeded its own call center's ability to handle the volume. One of the key objectives was for SPS to be able to match Eddie Bauer's call center's performance, especially in the customer service area. Other service levels measured included sales percentages and, when needed, customer support and disaster relief. In order to deliver this performance, it was imperative that SPS employees understand Eddie Bauer's culture and deliver a high level of customer service. SPS put its 550 assigned employees through an intensive forty-hour classroom training program and a forty-hour on the job-training program.

As a result of this outsourcing initiative, SPS has:

- Handled a 20 percent higher call volume than had originally been projected (which increased Eddie Bauer's sales).
- Handled unplanned volume increases due to inclement weather at Eddie Bauer's location, sometimes by as much as double the anticipated volume.
- Met and exceeded Eddie Bauer's performance levels, especially in customer service.
- Signed a long-term agreement and expanded its call center support to twenty-four hours a day, seven days a week.
- Became Eddie Bauer's exclusive call center outsourcing partner.

For smaller, less complex transactions, the relationship manager might be dedicated full-time (to one or several contracts), and the rest of the group participates only part-time, as needed. In the transition phase a senior member of human resources should spend a significant amount of time working with the relationship manager on the transition plan, dealing with the many "people" issues involved.

If any of these people to be assigned to the relationship team have been identified, they should now be added to the project team as observers and advisers, and attend all meetings with the provider candidates. Further, they should review the project team's work to date, and become familiar with the details of their investigations. Finally, the relationship team should begin developing a transition plan (see Chapter 19), which will be used if a provider is selected.

Due Diligence on Providers

If all of the claims in the providers' proposals were complete and accurate, there would be little need for due diligence. But proposals are "sales" documents intended to position the provider in the most positive light and omit or hide any possible negatives. It is not suggested that providers make outlandishly false claims, but there are seldom "black and white" measures in describing on-point experience, expertise, qualifications, etc. In fact, there are many shades of color separating black and white, with many subtle word choices, interpretations and judgments made. Providers always keep the positive positioning objective in mind.

Also, proposals are meant to get the provider onto the short list. The thinking goes that the top gun professionals can then be brought in personally to show their expertise and close the deal. So claims may be stretched slightly, and a well thought out due diligence exercise is imperative. Let's go back to the RFP/proposal comparison matrix. Focus only on the top several, and think about these questions:

- Which of the elements and related proposal claims have set the leading providers apart from the competition?
- How could those claims be tested?
- For each element that should be tested, which test would yield the best result?
- How does the cost of the test affect our decision?
- Should the claims be tested now or later?
- Who is best qualified to do the testing?
- Where should the tests be conducted?

The tests of the providers' claims should generally be what might be called overstatement tests—that is, they determine whether the claims are supportable and not overstated. In testing, there are many different options:

- Observation of their existing operations
- In-depth technical interviews with the key personnel to be assigned.
- Role-playing with the key personnel to be assigned.
- Examination of the resulting product/service.
- Reference checking on a test basis from a complete customer list.
- Review of relevant documents and independent reports.
- Discussions with suppliers.
- Discussions with former customers.
- Discussions with former employees
- Discussions with competitors.
- Discussions with knowledgeable consultants or advisers in the industry.
- Actual test runs through their process.

In the tests involving discussions, there is the opportunity to also test for omission—testing to see if information was not shared in the proposal (generally of a negative nature) that might be relevant to the decision. This involves asking open-ended questions such as these:

- What are the provider's weaknesses?
- Has the provider suffered any recent disappointments?
- Is the provider losing market share, and if so, why?
- If you were running this provider's operation, what would you change?
- Who are some of the provider's former customers that we might talk to? What might they tell us?

Due diligence can be time consuming and costly, but a poor provider selection carries a far greater long-term cost and risk.

The Short List

It is a waste of time to keep fielding calls from all of the providers who proposed or to keep discussing their candidacy. So it makes sense to cut the field to two or three providers—the short list. Still, the objective should also be to maintain keen competition between these groups. Irrespective of their short-list ranking, they should feel they have a real chance to win— otherwise they shouldn't be on the short list.

If the project champion hasn't been attending all of the team's meetings so far, that person should start now. The project champion should support the project leader in meetings and decision making, bringing a senior manager's experience for the team's benefit. This will also give the project champion exposure to the short-list candidates, which will be helpful in making the final presentation to senior management.

To cut the field to the short list, the project leader should call a meeting of the project team. The project team members who reviewed the providers' qualifications should make a presentation of their findings and the final ranking. Likewise, the team members who reviewed the providers' pricing and prepared the make or buy calculations should present their findings and the final ranking of the providers. It is necessary at this point to remember two things about the providers' price: (1) it can be negotiated, and (2) unless the organization's survival depends on a very low price (its reason to outsource), it should not be the primary issue.

Considering the relative importance of qualifications vs. price, a discussion of each provider's overall merits is held. This is also the time to discuss the benefits each provider can bring that couldn't be quantified or measured. Generally, after this combining of criteria, the field will quickly narrow by at least 50 percent. If there are still several provider candidates bunched for the final spot on the list, more detailed discussions can be held before taking a vote.

This is also a good time to update the employees as to the outsourcing initiative's progress. The project team should say that the proposals have been received and evaluated and the list of possible providers has been cut to the short list. Generally, the short list provider names should be announced. This would be a good time to list the innovative ideas included in the proposals, so as to get support for the strong capabilities providers are bringing to the table. The project team might ask for any information the employees have on any of the short list providers.

The project team might also repeat the restrictions on employee communications with the bidders—only the project team should be talking to them. At this point, if they didn't before, employees will begin to understand that outsourcing may well become a reality. As Ralph Waldo Emerson, American essayist and poet, put it, "People only see what they are prepared to see." With each successive communication, the employees should be seeing that the outsourcing train is rolling down the tracks. The project team needs to watch out for resistance and be prepared to counsel the resisters.

Short-List Contenders

This is the point at which the project team gets familiar with the provider's proposed account team. This interaction generally takes the form of a formal presentation by each provider's team, followed by a question and answer period. The provider should be able to bring in their choice of presenters, with the stipulation that their lead account representative and that individual's immediate superior will be active participants on the presentation team. All of the presentations should occur within a two-day period.

To achieve comparability in the presentations, the team may choose to do a structured question and answer session using the same questions for each provider group so as to allow some comparability in the presentations. This is a good time to pose those open-ended "what if" questions, questions that help the participants measure the compatibility of cultures, personal chemistry, and so on. Some examples of open-ended questions might include:

- What are some of the issues our industry is facing now?
- What happens if we want our lawyer to draft the contract?
- What happens if we want you to employ most of the people in our internal unit?
- What percent of our contract's services will your company deliver directly, and what percent, if any, will you subcontract to others?
- What are some of the challenges we will face in transferring our factors of production to you?
- How can we make this transition seamless?
- When problems arise, how do we solve them?
- What happens if a number of our people complain about the services performed by one of your key people?
- What happens if we double in size, through growth or merger, during the contract period?
- How can our staffs interact seamlessly, including the internal customers, in such a way that cutting-edge knowledge can be shared both ways to encourage innovation?
- How can we ensure that contract change orders are not really for services that we are paying for in the base charge?
- How do you expect each of the different elements of your costs to change over the contract period, and why?
- What happens if your account manager gets hit by a bus?

- Could you describe the most challenging client situation you've been involved with and how it was resolved?
- Approximately what percent of your outsourcing revenues would our contract consist of?
- What elements in this contract do you think will be profitable?
- What happens if you determine that our contract is not profitable?
- How do we build this relationship in positive ways?
- How should we maintain sufficient independence so we are not locked in to your services at the contract termination?
- How would you describe your company's culture?
- What is your company's vision for its future?
- What functions or processes do you outsource, and to whom?

This is a good time to probe the innovative ideas presented in the provider's proposal. Typically, this is the meeting in which their big guns show up, but questions should be addressed to the individuals who will actually be assigned to the account. The presenters should also be given an opportunity to ask questions of the project team. Plenty of time should be allowed for this to occur and for the project team to meet immediately thereafter to debrief. Formal presentations should not exceed half an hour. The question and answer session should not be less than one hour, and the debriefing session should be the same length. The debriefing session should include open discussion and debate about the presentation, expressions of any concerns, and a list of any final questions for follow-up by the project leader with each provider. Handled properly, this is a high-energy exercise, and it is difficult to do more than two of these presentations, question-answer sessions, and debriefings in one day.

Confirming That the Proposals Are Final

Before making the final cut, the project team should first have *each provider* confirm their proposal, so that it is no longer subject to due diligence. The project team should be confident that before further effort is invested, this provider has all the facts and is prepared to move forward with the RFP,[1] its due diligence, the resulting proposal, and the formal presentation as the

---

[1] In this context the RFP includes subsequent correspondence (e.g., amendments and notes from telephone inquiries).

foundation of the negotiation. The project team doesn't want to march down the negotiating trail only to discover that there was an irreconcilable difference resulting from a misunderstanding.

Likewise, the provider deserves to be treated fairly before investing any more time and money. The project team should have completed its evaluation, its due diligence on the provider, and had any questions or concerns answered. The provider should be confident that the project team has all of the information it needs to negotiate, with the RFP, the resulting proposal, and the formal presentations as the foundation of the negotiation. The provider also doesn't want to discover an irreconcilable difference.

Selecting the Prime Candidate

After the presentations and proposal confirmations, there is generally a clear ranking of the providers in each team member's head. The project leader might let a few days pass and then take a poll of the team member's rankings. The team can then meet to hear the vote, confirm and explain their vote, and hold a final debate. Then a show of hands generally confirms the choice of a prime candidate. *But no announcement is made at this time.*

Before any announcement, the key terms of the transaction should be reduced to writing in what is commonly referred to as a "term sheet," a "memorandum of understanding" or an "agreement in principle" (hereafter referred to as a term sheet). The next chapter covers some of the issues to be addressed in negotiating a term sheet.

For expediency, this effort is generally only undertaken with the unannounced prime candidate. If the prime candidate believes this is the case, however, the organization could lose significant negotiating leverage. If the top two contenders are close in rank, term sheets could be done with both in order to maintain the maximum negotiating leverage. But those involved should recognize that this potential leverage comes at a real cost in both project team time and money (for example, advisers' fees).

In preparing for the negotiation, the project team should develop and document their list of issues to be negotiated, rank those issues by importance, and draft the list of questions that will be used in the negotiation. The project team should also anticipate and list the provider's issues that may have been raised in the previous discussions. This is better done now, while it's fresh in everyone's mind, and not several weeks later, when negotiations are set to begin.

Another Reason to Outsource:
Give Employees a Stronger Career Path

Most organizations care about their employees. They recognize that one of their key assets is their people (and this is especially true in the labor-intensive service industries). They also recognize that employees who don't have a defined career path, with an opportunity for advancement, will not likely stay with the organization. Turnover is costly, both from the obvious loss of productivity, but also from the more hidden risks (for example, lower quality and future service claims, less expertise, and missed opportunities).

Now let's look at those employees who staff noncore competency areas of the organization and represent some of the lower paying positions, such as the janitorial staff, the cafeteria staff, the loading dock workers, the truck drivers, the security staff, the mail room staff, the secretaries, and the payroll clerks. Moving up the pay scale in the organization, but still noncore, look at the accountants, systems operators, programmers, internal auditors, purchasing clerks, and other administrative and staff (vs. line) positions and functions.

Can the organization really offer these people a career path and the training and development necessary to achieve their career potential? They might get an annual raise for awhile and perhaps be promoted once or twice as more senior staff leave, but there is a clear ceiling to their compensation and advancement. No matter how well the employee performs, the top level they can achieve is probably the head of their function, and then only as the more senior people ahead of them leave or retire.

At the same time, the providers who specialize in these administrative and staff functions have expanding needs for these same people. Such providers will be quite pleased to offer positions (and career paths) to the capable staff you have developed. Providers such as Service Master (janitorial) Pitney Bowes (mail processing), Guardsmark (security), Ryder (logistics), the large public accounting firms such as Deloitte and Touche and Price Waterhouse (accounting and internal audit) and the large IT providers, such as CSC, IBM-ISSC, and EDS (systems operators and programmers), want to do business with you and hire capable employees for their expanding businesses—your employees.

Outsourcing gives your employees the chance for career opportunities similar to yours, and the training and development necessary to achieve it.

Part Six

Negotiating Terms

Chapter 17

Negotiations

Overview

The outsourcing initiative up to this point has been like a doubles tennis match. The team planned, trained, studied the statistics to set strategy, and then served the ball (in the form of an RFP). There followed a series of volleys (sharing information—bidders' conferences, interviews, and so on). Then the playing partners served the ball (in the form of a proposal), followed by a series of volleys (sharing information—due diligence, presentations, and so on).

Now that the teams have settled into the match, it's time to pick up the pace and start competing (in the form of negotiations—to structure the relationship, identify the key business and legal issues, and negotiate their resolution). Here the volleys will gain intensity, because the objective is to have a memorable match that the reporters (lawyers) can write about tomorrow (the term sheet and the contract).

Each of the key terms that will be in the final agreement should be addressed, negotiated, and documented, so that later, all the lawyers have to do is add the contract legalese that makes the agreement enforceable. This is not to suggest that the lawyers have not been involved up to this point, only that these discussions are focused on the key terms, not the words.

This is when the detailed issues nobody has wanted to deal with should be negotiated, for example:

- What services will the provider perform?
- What responsibilities will the organization retain?
- On what terms will the provider employ transferring employees?

- Which employees and which pieces of equipment are going and which are staying?
- What decision rights are being transferred and which are staying?
- Which performance standard will be used for each service?
- What will happen if each performance standard is not met (for example, liquidated damages)?
- How will changes in volume trigger price changes?
- Which cost of living algorithm will be used in the calculation?
- What will be the terms for terminating the relationship?
- What termination assistance will the provider deliver and how much will the provider be paid for that assistance?

Like tennis, this exercise should be conducted with intensity, but also with dignity and grace. This is where the team member(s) who have negotiating experience should stand up and be counted. This is also a point at which the help of experienced outsourcing advisers and lawyers is particularly important.

A final word about this negotiation: in the future this playing partner will be a business partner. Just as in good sportsmanship on the tennis court, in which you wouldn't cheat or get angry at your playing partners, so goes the negotiation. If there is a win–lose strategy to the negotiation, it will almost certainly result in a lose-lose result in the relationship. As the American financier Marvin Levin once put it, "If you are planning on doing business with someone again, don't be too tough in the negotiations. If you're going to skin a cat, don't keep it as a housecat."

Principled Negotiating

Perhaps the finest book ever written on negotiating is entitled *Getting to Yes*.[1] Although it is well-written, insightful, and to the point, these are not the qualities that make it so valuable. Unlike many other such books, which focus on winning at positional negotiating, what makes this book special is its proposed approach: *principled negotiating*. This approach, developed by the Harvard Negotiating Project, advises the reader on how to

---

[1]Robert Fisher and William Ury, *Getting to Yes: Negotiating Agreement Without Giving In* (Boston: Houghton Mifflin, 1981); *Macmillan Executive Summary Program,* Macmillan Book Clubs, Inc., October 1985, page 3.

look for mutual gains, and, in cases in which interests conflict, tells how the sides should search for objective standards, independent of either side's will.

In the traditional positional negotiating, each side takes its position on what it wants out of the deal. Because each side knows that, through negotiating, it will have to give in on some of the issues, it takes extreme positions to allow room for compromise. Each side tries to squeeze the other and takes positions like the nineteenth-century railroad magnate Collis Huntington took when he said, "Whatever is not nailed down is mine. Whatever I can pry loose is not nailed down." This attitude dramatically reduces the chance of making a deal that both parties will be happy with, and it is time consuming to complete. And while it might work in certain negotiations, such as selling cars or houses, in which the parties may never see each other again, it doesn't work well when the parties must work together going forward, such as outsourcing.

According to Fisher and Ury, under the principled negotiation method, the deal is approached entirely differently.

Principled negotiation or negotiation on the merits, can be boiled down to four basic points:

1) Separate the people from the problem
2) Focus on interests, not positions
3) Generate a variety of possibilities before deciding what to do
4) Insist that the result be based on some objective standard

These four propositions of principled negotiation are relevant from the time you begin to think about negotiating until the time that either an agreement is reached, or you decide to abandon the negotiations. This period can be divided into three stages: analysis, planning, and discussion.

During the analysis stage, you simply try to diagnose the situation. . . . You will want to consider the people problems of partisan perceptions, hostile emotions, and unclear communication, as well as to identify your interests and those of the other side. You will want to note options already on the table and identify any criteria already suggested for agreement.

During the planning stage, you deal with the same four elements again, this time generating ideas and deciding what to do.

During the discussion stage, when the parties actually com-municate back and forth, looking toward agreement, the same elements are the best subjects to discuss. Differences in percep-tion, feelings of frustration and anger, and difficulties in com-munication can be acknowledged and addressed. Each side should come to understand the interests of the other. Both can then jointly generate options that are mutually advantageous and seek agreement on objective standards for resolving opposed interests."[2]

This style of negotiating can be used effectively in the various nego-tiations with a provider in an outsourcing initiative, including later prob-lem solving and contract renegotiations.

Preparing for Negotiations

The negotiations should not begin until the following have occurred:

- The project team (or its delegate) is prepared to negotiate.
- The negotiation strategy has been well planned.
- The provider has completed its sales process.
- The ground rules for the negotiation have been set.

In analyzing the proposals, oral presentations, and due diligence, the project team should have developed and documented its list of issues for negotiation, ranked those issues by importance, and drafted the list of ques-tions to be used. The project team should also have identified issues that might be on the provider's mind.

In thinking about the issues in order to plan the negotiation, the proj-ect team should identify what it wants out of the negotiation. What is iden-tified is a range of alternative solutions for each issue. It is a preliminary range and can be readily revised as the provider introduces new informa-tion during the negotiations. It sets forth the ideal solutions, what solutions would be satisfactory, and what provider-proposed solutions would break the deal. All of the issues or solutions will not be deal breakers. Likewise,

[2]Fisher and Ury, *Getting to Yes.*

the project team should think about the provider's issues and alternative solutions and how they might be satisfied. The project team should also look for independent standards that might support these solutions. The key is to think about alternative solutions, not just one rigid position.

The provider's sales process should be completed before negotiations begin. This can be difficult if the provider has gotten the ear of a decision-maker and enthusiasm for outsourcing is high. While delays can kill outsourcing before it begins, impatience can kill it down the line. Rushing to negotiate invariably gives the provider an unfair advantage. Once the hype has cooled the real issues can be addressed. Falling prey to impatient negotiating creates a poor deal for the organization, which will hurt the long-term relationship.

There are entire books written on negotiating tricks and strategies. John F. Kennedy said, "We cannot negotiate with those who say, 'What's mine is mine, what's yours is negotiable'." The team might review some of them, not to use their tricks but to recognize if the provider is using them. Don't let the other side play those tricks, and if they try to do so, confront them on it. Remember the old saying, "Don't wrestle with pigs; you get dirty and they enjoy it."

The project team is encouraged to use the principled negotiation approach (previously discussed) and should advise the provider of its intention to use this approach prior to the negotiations beginning. There are several reasons for using this approach:

- The principled negotiation method is the fastest, most effective method.
- The provider negotiates outsourcing agreements frequently, so it would be more difficult to match wits against their usual negotiating strategies; this levels the playing field somewhat.
- The provider should learn to use the principled negotiation method now, because you will want to use it later in problem solving.
- If the provider cannot negotiate with this method now, when they are trying to get your business, they won't use it later in problem solving. So this is a test.

In the negotiations the two parties are represented by persons who are authorized to negotiate—by decision makers. If the project team doesn't have that authority, either one of its members needs to get it or the project champion (who should have that authority) must attend the meetings. Each party should confirm who has the authority to negotiate. Others, such as outside advisers and legal counsel, should also be present.

Negotiation Levels

Think of the negotiating process as a funnel (see Exhibit 17.1), in which the issues are placed in the top, and slowly, through analysis and discussions, the issues are addressed and agreement is reached at the bottom. Which issues are addressed when? There are many different approaches. Experience shows that it is easier to gain agreement by dividing the issues into parts: the broader business issues (addressed first) and the detailed contract issues (addressed later). There is a much greater chance of reaching agreement in common business language than in legalese.

First, there are the high-level discussions, represented by the term sheet negotiations, in which agreement is sought on the parties' interests

Exhibit 17.1   The Negotiating Funnel

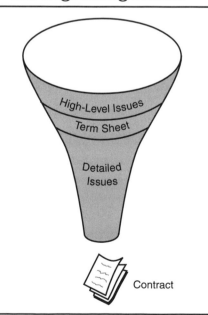

and the basic business terms of the transaction. This sets the framework for the subsequent contract negotiations, which take up the details. For example, in addressing the pricing issues in the high-level discussions, the parties might reach agreement on the pricing model to be used, how the changes in the business should adjust price, and the cost of living algorithm to be used, without actually discussing the dollar rates.

Allen Klein of Shaw Pittman Potts & Trowbridge, one of the leading law firms involved in complex outsourcing transactions, suggests that the organization first prepare a draft term sheet. This is done for purposes of (1) getting these issues on the table, (2) requesting a formal provider response to each point in the draft term sheet, and (3) then holding the high-level discussions. Others may prefer to hold the discussions first, then prepare a term sheet summarizing them. Either way, negotiations should not be handled piecemeal. The term sheet issues are highly interrelated and both parties' views must be on the table at the same time.

The objective is to get agreement on the big issues in general terms. Then many of the smaller issues will become less important to each side, making these detailed discussions flow more smoothly. If the parties can reach agreement on these big issues, experience shows that 50 percent of the remaining issues will be throwaways, 25 percent will be of a minor nature, requiring little negotiation, and the last 25 percent will require real negotiation (for example, setting the dollar rates). This can speed agreement and reduce endless debate over minor points.

The term sheet should generally include the following high-level discussion points (generally in a document of twenty-five to fifty pages, for complex transactions):

- Scope of services
- Performance standards
- Pricing
- Factors of production
- Management and control
- Transition provisions
- Billing and payment terms
- Termination provisions
- Other issues (examples):
  - ▲ Contract term
  - ▲ Confidentiality
  - ▲ Warranties/indemnities

▲ Limits of liability
▲ Use of subcontractors
▲ Third-party licenses

Second, there are the contract negotiation discussions. These relate to both detailed issues (for example, setting the dollar rates) and contract wordings, as described in the next section.

Face-to-Face Negotiations

In first-time outsourcing agreements the parties are generally new to each other and the people are on their best behavior. Having said that, it is important to know the person you will be negotiating with. As the American psychologist and philosopher William James once said, "Whenever two people meet there are really six people present. There is each man as he sees himself, each man as the other person sees him, and each man as he really is." Negotiations tend to move along more effectively and efficiently when it is the last two who are talking.

Using the principled negotiation method, each side should be asked to identify for discussion the five to ten business issues that form its perspective, within the agreed-upon framework (e.g., interests and high level discussions) that are critical to moving forward. This framework can be posted on flipcharts, hung on the wall, and focused on. If each party can relate its issues to the framework (what's on the wall), they are not likely to become fixed in their positions.

After the issues have been addressed, the possible solutions can be identified. The parties can identify alternative means of resolving the issues, articulating the advantages and disadvantages each party sees in each alternative. As the negotiation progresses, both parties should try to develop even more solutions as they work through each issue creatively. Finally, wherever possible, independent standards that can be introduced should be identified. This adds to the "fair play" environment that will bring about the fairest final resolution in the fastest time.

While smaller deals might take just a few days, negotiating the term sheet for a complex deal can take weeks and the contract can take even longer. The project team should be patient and let the negotiation progress at its appropriate pace.

Principles of Fairness

Both the organization and the provider should keep the following points in mind as they enter negotiations:

- You deserve to get the service you need (to satisfy the reasons to outsource), which the provider agrees to deliver.
- The provider deserves to get a fair price for that service.
- You deserve fair market value for the assets transferred to the provider.
- Mistakes will occur on both sides, so plan for it in the contract.
- The final deal must be seen as a win-win deal at the end of the negotiation *and* throughout the contract term both sides should feel that the negotiated terms were reasonably fair.

The organization has reasons to outsource, and both parties have it in their best interest to satisfy those reasons. If the organization's service needs involve innovative solutions and greater flexibility, then both parties should focus the negotiation on what it will take to meet those needs.

The provider's price in the proposal was tested in the competition. If the proposals were reasonably comparable, the organization understands the market's pricing. The organization may believe the provider's price is too high, and it should explain, by reference to supporting information (for example, a technical adviser's study or the other proposals to the extent they are not confidential), why it feels this way. If the provider understands how the organization arrived at its conclusion, it can then explain the basis for its pricing—perhaps it was intending to do more than the other providers planned to do, but the proposal wasn't sufficiently clear, and now they can show that. In any event, the parties should focus on a fair price. One thing is assured: if the provider doesn't have a fair price, the organization's chances of getting the service it needs are dramatically reduced.

When assets are transferred to the provider, values will be negotiated for those assets. The organization deserves the fair market value. What values are in its accounting records are irrelevant to fair market value. For example, the organization cannot expect the provider to accept somewhat obsolete equipment and pay more than its fair value, even if the organization will take an accounting loss because of an unrealistically long useful life used in depreciating the equipment. On the other hand, if accelerated depreciation was used originally, the fair market value may exceed the book value, with the organization recognizing a gain. In such cases, the parties may decide to transfer the equipment at book value and adjust the contract price for a gain or loss. If asset values are significant, an independent appraiser, recognized and accepted by both parties, can be very helpful.

If mortals were perfect, contracts would only be a few pages long. Since they aren't, the contract will need to cover the risks of what could go wrong for each party. What happens if the provider doesn't perform as promised? What if the organization doesn't pay as promised? These and other points should be negotiated to get an enforceable contract. By covering these risks, however, the parties should not create an atmosphere of distrust (for example, that either believes the other is intending to take advantage).

Because it is in both parties' interests to have a long-term relationship, it is in both parties' interests to negotiate a fair deal. The organization wants consistent, high-quality service. It doesn't want to go through another time-consuming competition every few years or be forced to switch providers. The provider wants a stable long-term revenue stream it can manage to a profitable result. Any competition, whether it be a recompetition for the existing contract or new ones to replace the lost contract, are costly for the provider. Providers generally want to keep every profitable customer they have.

Decision Time

When the high-level discussions are completed and the term sheet is drafted, the organization should make the final decision to outsource to the prime candidate provider, in which case it would proceed with final negotiations and drafting the contract. Very seldom do the negotiations break down after the term sheet has been completed.

This would be the appropriate time for the project team to meet with senior management to review their progress. They can present their analysis of the make or buy decision, the negotiations, how the reasons to outsource will be satisfied, and outsourcing's anticipated effect on the business. The presentation should be led by the project leader and the project champion. Having the outside adviser attend may be helpful as well, if questions arise about outsourcing in general. But this is not a time for reviewing individual negotiation points (as that wouldn't be fair to the provider who has been negotiating in good faith with the organization's authorized negotiator). It is, instead, a high-level review of the overall deal.

The project team should now make a recommendation on whether to proceed. Senior management should either approve the recommendation or give guidance. If the unit to be outsourced has a close relationship to the board of directors (e.g., Internal Audit), then the CEO, the project champion, or the project leader may need to get their approval.

Another Reason to Outsource:
Increase Commitment and Energy
in Noncore Areas

Fear is a powerful motivator. It is unlikely (and unwise) that any organization will outsource all of its noncore competency areas in one fell swoop. So when the first and second outsourcing initiatives prove successful, what do you think the rest of the employees do? They kick it into gear. They are thinking, "there but for the grace of God go I," and try to show that they can beat any potential outsource provider's performance. This renewed commitment and energy improves performance.

But this is more than about fear as a motivator. We now understand that any noncore area, irrespective of performance, should be considered for outsourcing. Improved performance may delay outsourcing, but it shouldn't eliminate its possibility. If for no other reason, outsourcing enhances management's effectiveness by allowing it to focus on what it does best. No, the renewed commitment, higher energy, and improved performance do three important things:

■ In the short term they help improve the organization's results.

■ More importantly, in the long term, the employees themselves improve their skills and results, so that when outsourcing does occur, they are more attractive to the outsource provider as potential employees, and can move forward in their careers with the provider.

■ If performance improves so much that the current employees can compete with potential providers, they should allowed to compete. If they win the contract, then they can be spun off into a separate business, of which they own all or a significant part.

Outsourcing allows the organization (and the employees not outsourced) to benefit while the organization progresses toward further outsourcing initiatives.

Chapter 18

Contracts

Overview

The project team should keep in mind that the objective is to arrive at an enforceable contract. Outsourcing contracts can generally be divided into four sections (each of which might need twenty to thirty pages to cover the terms, with lengthier appendices as needed):

1. Scope of services
2. Performance standards (service-level agreements)
3. Pricing schedules
4. Terms and conditions

The scope of services section gives a map of the services that will be performed by the provider. The performance standards section describes the minimum service levels to which the provider will perform and the consequences of failing to do so. The pricing schedules section describes what the provider will be paid for the services. The terms and conditions section contains the deal's basic business and legal terms, including such things as the ownership of the factors of production, provisions for management and control, transition provisions, billing and payment terms, and contract term and termination provisions. Obviously, a lawyer must be involved in drafting the contract.

For complex transactions there will be appendices; one example would be listing specific factors of production that are being transferred. As was suggested in Chapter 15, key elements of the provider's proposal could be incorporated by reference so that the proposal's commitments don't somehow get lost in the legalese and the provider is held accountable for its commitments and claims. This assumes that the commitments and claims in the provider's proposal are clear and unambiguous, which may not always be the case.

Scope of Services

The scope of services is negotiated using the RFP, the proposal, and the subsequent discussions as the foundation. What services will the provider perform? Are there particular methods or processes the organization feels are critical to the provider's performance? What activities and decision rights will be retained by the organization? As a test, the team might consider having the provider talk the group through a day, week, month, and year of their services, outlining what they will be doing and what the deliverables are. How does this compare to the well-understood activities that were identified and analyzed? What about the deliverables required? They might also reverse the exercise and have a knowledgeable employee from the unit being outsourced talk the group through their deliverables activities.

There will be differences to be addressed, negotiated, and accepted. These preliminary differences of scope are not necessarily bad, as long as results at least meet expectations there are no unfair charges, and, having been identified at this point, they are agreed to. Unless the team has suggested that the organization retain certain decision rights, how the provider performs the activities should not be of great issue. Having said that, organization oversight is important (see the Management and Control section later in this chapter). Remember, the provider is being brought in because they will do things differently—much better.

The resulting list of services, functions, and activities should be reasonably comprehensive, yet it should not fall into the "task" level details trap. A balance should be struck between the desire for specific and precise language and the need for flexible language. Precise language brings comfort in setting forth exactly what services will be delivered. But broad, flexible language is necessary because no list resulting from specific and precise language can ever be complete or remain accurate when the business environment changes.

Performance Standards

Chapter 11 discussed how the team explored the specific standards to be used and the expectations for improvement. How does the provider's proposed standards compare? There will be differences, and now is the time to negotiate the details.

Ideally, the contract should specify, with as much precision as possible, a standard for each significant activity that is being performed—and perhaps more than one standard, if the activity is directly related to the reasons to outsource. For example, if a particular activity had a significant impact on both quality and cycle time, and these were the reasons to outsource, then the performance of this activity should be measured against both standards. The provider should regularly report its measures and be subject to audit.

What happens if the provider fails to deliver on its promised performance? The problem should be confronted, and the provider's remedies might include such things as a thorough investigation, a cure of the problem, and a promise not to have the problem recur. Obviously, if there is consistent failure, the organization must have the option of early termination. But what if the failure is inconsistent but still damaging? Unless the service scope is very much a commodity service and easily transferred to another provider, then realistically termination is only an option of last resort. For this reason, many agreements contain liquidated damages, which should be negotiated.

Liquidated damages are typically tied to the frequency and/or severity of the failure. These damages should be designed to encourage the provider to deliver what is promised, and to ensure that the organization pays only for the level of service that is actually being delivered. If every performance measure carried the same small damages for failure, the provider would simply build this into the price. The team should concentrate on the damages to the business that would require liquidated damages. It should try to set up either increasing damage amounts for a pattern of increasing failures or a significant and meaningful "cliff" of failure and damages that the provider will not want to go near.

The provider may try to negotiate performance incentives such that they receive a bonus for exceeding certain performance standards. This may seem logical, given the liquidated damages for failure, but the real test is whether the provider really adds any value to the organization (lower costs, increased revenue, greater customer satisfaction, and so on) by exceeding performance standards. If not, the organization would be paying unjustified fees. Moreover, some suggest that in order to ensure that the customer always gets the service it contracted for, no bonuses be paid during any period in which there are service-level failures.

Pricing Schedules

Price is negotiable. In fact, one of the greatest benefits of the open RFP competition is that the market has made it easier to evaluate the fairness of the provider's pricing. The project team should use this information to cut the best, fair deal that can be made.

The assumptions will need to be established by considering historical trends and future projections. The basis for these projections was established when the project team projected future costs, as outlined in Chapter 10. The contract should set forth the basic pricing model, how it works, and the negotiated price for the baseline assumptions (initial services).

The basic pricing model or algorithm is as important as the day-one price. The ideal pricing algorithm provides a fair price without renegotiation as the volume of services consumed changes. The contract should also contemplate the renegotiation of pricing as business conditions dictate.

The key to achieving this flexibility is to negotiate the framework for handling these changes in a fair, open environment. This goal demands that the subsequent adjustments can be made without lengthy renegotiations and without either party having an unfair advantage in pricing the adjustments. The parties should set the framework for:

- Handling changes in the organization's business, such as:
  - ▲ Volume changes
  - ▲ Scope of service changes
  - ▲ Institutional changes (for example, new regulations)
  - ▲ Environmental changes (for example, new or closed location)
  - ▲ Structural changes (for example, acquisitions, dispositions, and additional outsourcing)
- Handling changes in key pricing terms, such as:
  - ▲ Cost of living adjustments
  - ▲ Foreign currency translation
  - ▲ The organization's option to obtain out-of-scope services from third parties, with appropriate cooperation from the provider, where that cooperation is necessary to such services

In any event, the pricing algorithm should be simple. The parties should take care not to create an administrative nightmare in which excessive time is spent tracking changes and repricing for them. It might be useful, for example, for volume changes, to set forth dead bands around the baseline volume (for example, plus or minus 10 percent) within which no additional charges or credits will occur. Beyond the dead bands, the best approach is to limit the extent to which the different volumes must be repriced later, by agreeing to a unit based or similar algorithm that automatically adjusts for the volume changes.

The framework for pricing changes should also consider economic reality. As discussed in Chapter 10, the team should have analyzed the nature of the costs and how they vary with changing business conditions. A 15 percent volume increase or decrease does not change the provider's costs by 15 percent because some of the provider's costs are fixed, not variable. For this reason, a marginal pricing arrangement should be calculated based upon an analysis of the anticipated costs.

The framework for other changes, such as scope, locations, and regulations, can be more challenging. First, to take a scope change example, every scope change doesn't necessarily change the amount of work. Second, even if a scope change appears to change the amount of work, it may or may not create a net cost change. Third, even if there is a short term cost change, it doesn't necessarily mean there should be a pricing change. The contract should set forth how the analysis of scope, cost, and pricing changes should be conducted and develop a reasonable pricing method for such changes. The provider will look for opportunities to increase scope and fees. If it can be demonstrated by analysis, then the provider deserves higher fees. On the other hand, many providers will look carefully at their costs and pricing, with an eye toward providing value-added services, without always charging extra for every change. As British prime minister and novelist Benjamin Disraeli said, "Next to knowing when to seize an opportunity, the most important thing in life is to know when to forgo an advantage."

If the pricing terms call for cost of living adjustments (COLA) or similar index-driven adjustments, this should be set forth. But caution is necessary. On the surface, the use of a COLA and other indices have some logic. But what counts is whether the provider's costs really vary with the indices. Do providers' costs go up if properly managed, and if they do, do they go up in comparison to a COLA index? If so, which one? The project team should not assume the answer to any of these questions.

There are variations to the standard COLA adjustment. For example, the organization may want the provider to:

- Defer the impact of COLA changes for six to twelve months, so that new budgets can reflect the change.
- Protect the organization from minor changes by using dead bands.

- Share the COLA change impact (to encourage the provider to manage the costs).
- Place a cap on the annual change or the total change (or both) that can occur over the contract period.

The project team should do a sensitivity analysis (measuring the impact of incremental changes) for these questions and variations, because how the COLA is applied can have a significant financial effect over the length of a large outsourcing contract.

Factors of Production

Now it is time to get specific about who and what are going or staying. Specific lists should be made about which, if any, of the following are going to the provider:

- People
- Facilities (space and related services)
- Equipment
- Software
- Third-party contracts

With respect to people transferring to the provider, the contract also needs to address the terms upon which those people will transition. What salary and benefits packages will be offered to those employees? Resolution of the issue requires an understanding of how the current employees' current salary and benefits packages match up with the provider's standard package. Employee morale—that is, of employees who will remain with the organization as well as of those who will transition— must be taken into account.

Severance packages are typically given to outsourced employees. These can range from the standard severance that might be offered to any terminated employee to more generous packages that encourage the employee to either leave happily or join the provider and that support good overall employee morale.

For example, the more generous severance package might guarantee employment with the provider for at least six months (to give all employees a chance to prove themselves or time to look for another job) during which time the provider will not terminate except for cause. The provider will calculate the costs of these packages and the amount it is willing to bear. For example, if the provider only needs 75 percent of the employees, then the organization can expect to pay the six months of salary for the unneeded 25 percent of the employees, as well as the related severance packages, in the form of a higher price. This is the type of negotiating done in developing the contract.

Who will pay for the relocation costs of employees who must move to work for the provider? Who will be responsible for employment-related claims made before and after the transfer of employment to the provider? These and other "possible" future costs should be negotiated and resolved.

There is no inclusive list of nonemployee-related questions that should be addressed, but the following are examples of the types of details that might need to be negotiated. If the provider will use space in the existing facilities, what will it pay for the space, janitorial services, utilities, and so on? If certain pieces of equipment will go to the provider, will existing warranties transfer as well, and if so, at what transfer cost? What value will each piece of equipment carry? Will equipment leases transfer, and if so, at what transfer cost? Will existing software licenses transfer, and if so, at what transfer cost? Will existing maintenance contracts with third parties transfer, and if so, at what transfer cost?

The proposal was an "offer" to perform services. While these questions may have been addressed casually in the proposal, who pays how much can now be negotiated. If there are extra costs associated with transferring leases, licenses, contracts, and so on, who bears how much of those costs? For example, there may be a cost if a license is simply terminated, but a lesser cost if it is transferred. Should the organization pay these transfer costs (so as to avoid the termination costs) and the provider bear the ongoing license costs?

Management and Control

In the contract, the decision rights over the following areas should be addressed:

- Factors of production (decisions about the resources to be deployed)
- Processes (decisions about how work will be performed)

- Management (how operating decisions will be made and by whom)
- Strategy (how long-term direction will be set and by whom)

As the scope-setting and negotiating exercises are being performed, it is necessary to think about the decisions that will be required. Now is the time to negotiate who makes those decisions—the organization or the provider. Generally the provider will control the factors of production, processes, and most of management decisions. The organization will have oversight over these decisions and will control or share control over the remaining management and strategic decisions. But what does oversight mean?

The organization, for example, may want to have final approval over:

- The provider's account manager and key direct reports
- Any voluntary movement of personnel to other contracts
- Any significant changes in technology (that might too tightly lock the organization to the provider, for example)
- Any changes in the outputs (for example, report formats and frequency)
- Any changes in the processes (that could harm related organization processes, for example)

This is the time to negotiate not only the level of control, but also the procedure for making these decisions. For the more complex outsourcing transactions, procedures manuals may be developed as well, to set forth requirements for reporting, monitoring and meetings, change procedures (for example, for such things as scope and control), annual planning, and other important activities.

Transition Provisions

Outsourcing's success often depends on the transition, beginning with the announcement of a signed contract through the transfer of the factors of production to the implementation of operations. How the transition is executed can affect future costs for each party, the provider's future profits, and, most importantly, the fulfillment of the organization's outsourcing objectives (reasons to outsource).

The contract should identify the specific roles assumed by each party in the transition. For example, the employees being outsourced are generally important to the provider's future operations. How the announcement is made, what severance and benefits packages are offered, how each person is counseled on their future, and how the provider is described to them, are tasks the organization must perform well—or the provider will suffer later.

Likewise, how the provider handles its tense first meetings with employees, what salaries and benefits the provider offers, how it counsels each person on their new positions, and the career paths it presents, all affect the organization—its transition costs, the morale of the employees not being outsourcing, and its overall operations. It also affects whether outsourcing can be a future organization strategy. The provider must do these tasks well or the organization suffers.

Billing and Payment Terms

The specific terms of paying for outsourced services should be negotiated. A number of questions arise. Does the organization have any special needs in how it wants to pay for the services the provider will perform (see the discussion of financial engineering in Chapter 12)? Will there be any discount for early payments? Will the payments be monthly? What will the penalty be for late payment? What currency will payments for foreign services be made in? Will the organization be allowed to withhold payment for unsatisfactory service?

The provider wants assurance that it will be paid on time. If there are disputes, can the organization withhold payments? If so, how much? The provider doesn't want the entire payment held hostage if failures are minor or if the disagreement over a change order relates to a small percent of the amount due.

Termination Provisions

The parties should think about how the relationship would be terminated. This may seem odd, given that the relationship is just beginning. But just as legislators have passed laws on how to terminate a marriage even before one begins, so should the contract cover termination provisions.

Outsourcing agreements typically provide for termination:

- At contract expiration
- For cause

- For convenience
- Upon change in control

If the contract is not renegotiated, it expires at the end of the term. This could occur because either party wants to end the relationship. For example, at expiration the organization might believe that there are better providers, or it would prefer a type of service unavailable from the provider. The provider may not have found the relationship to be profitable or has found the organization's culture incompatible. The reasons are endless.

The typical termination for cause provisions permit a party to terminate the contract prior to expiring if the other party has breached the contract (not performed in accordance with its provisions) and such breach is material. Perhaps the organization did not pay for satisfactory service or the provider did not meet performance standards for several consecutive months.

The typical termination for convenience provision permits the organization (but generally not the provider) to terminate the contract prior to expiration in the absence of a provider breach, but only upon payment of a termination fee. Termination fees should be set forth in the contract. It is often easier to reach agreement up front than it is later when the organization wants to terminate the relationship.

Typically, outsourcing agreements contain provisions permitting the organization (but not the provider) to terminate the contract upon a change of control of the provider or the organization. In other cases, a termination fee is required.

Contract termination should always be viewed as the last resort, one to be used only when all other efforts have been exhausted. Continuing the marriage analogy, consider what happens when two people are thinking about divorce. Seldom will simply dissolving the marriage suffice to resolve the problems. Each marriage partner is also thinking:

- Who is responsible for these problems (blame apportionment)?
- How should I be compensated for being treated so unfairly (settlement)?
- How will I ever get through this difficult period, before and after the divorce (individual transition)?
- How will the family deal with this situation (group transition)?
- Who will do for me what my spouse did for me (replacement)?
- How will we split up what we have acquired (property transfer)?

These same questions will be asked in an outsourcing relationship. Seldom will simply terminating the relationship be enough to resolve the problems. If one party is to blame, should they bear more of the costs? As the relationship ends, will the provider's performance suffer? How will this affect the organization's operations and costs? How will the organization's employees, who work with the provider, deal with the change? Who will deliver the service in the future? How will the factors of production be transferred so the service can continue? Ending outsourcing relationships may be far more challenging than getting into them.

How the relationship will be unwound should be negotiated in the contract. While the parties cannot rely upon termination, or the threat of termination, to resolve problems, there should be a possibility of termination in appropriate situations in order to reinforce the parties' discipline during the contract.

The negotiations should include the termination assistance provisions. The provider should be responsible for a smooth transition of its operations either to the organization or to another provider, whatever the reason for termination. The contract should address:

- What assistance will be given
- Who will give the assistance
- When the assistance will given (for example, start and end points)
- Where the assistance will be given
- How the assistance will be given
- What the provider's compensation will be for such assistance
- What factors of production will be transferred, at what cost
- What the payment terms will be for such compensation and the cost of any transferred factors of production

The assistance should be broad enough to cover planning and executing the transition and specific enough to review procedures manuals with the new service providers and answer their questions. The provider's assistance should include the transfer of the factors of production. For example, the organization or its new provider should have the right to interview and offer positions to key provider operating personnel on the account, license key provider operating software, and purchase the equipment necessary to continue the service.

Once a decision is made to terminate, the transition planning should begin. The transition will continue at least several months past the termination date, until the new provider is operating smoothly. The provider deserves a fair compensation for this assistance.

In cases of termination for convenience, the contract should set a framework for termination payments. If the provider terminates, the organization will have unexpected costs (for example, such things as rerunning the competition process and transferring the factors of production) that should be borne by the provider. If the organization terminates, in addition to unexpected provider costs that come with winding down, there will likely be unrecovered provider start-up costs that the provider will expect to recover upon termination. These should be negotiated. Some providers also seek contract provisions entitling them to recover lost future profits, although organizations generally resist this.

Other Contract Issues

Because contract law varies by jurisdiction and, the contract should include the technical language that makes the agreement enforceable in the jurisdiction that will govern the validity and construction of the contract. The organization should have its lawyers prepare the contract and have its location be the governing jurisdiction. This is done for several reasons:

- The organization is more familiar with the contract wordings if its lawyer prepared them, and can thus can better evaluate suggested changes.
- The organization is more familiar with the local laws, and thus can better evaluate suggested changes.
- The organization's document provides the foundation from which it can negotiate; consequently, it is easier to make concessions than to get them from the other party.
- Using the provider's standard contract may appear to be cheaper but may be riskier, as the foregoing advantages now lie with the provider.

Details of the decision rights to be assigned, the contract length, and the termination date were covered in Chapter 9. There are many other issues that the typical outsourcing agreement addresses, including intellectual property rights, confidentiality, warranties, subcontractors, foreign currency translation, dispute resolution, provider insurance, *force majeur,* and limitations of liability. The importance of using an experienced outsourcing attorney from the initiative's inception cannot be underestimated.

Announcing the New Relationship

The announcement to all employees (not just those directly affected) that a formal contract has been signed should be coordinated with the provider. This announcement launches the transition phase of the initiative (see Chapter 19) and the employees now know where they stand. To use an analogy, at the end of a concert, the audience stands and, by its ovation, encourages the artist to perform an encore. After that piece is played, they may remain standing and applauding, hoping for another encore. Then an announcement is made, such as "Elvis has left the building," and the concert is really over. In the same way, the announcement should bring closure to the employees—their activities have left the organization through outsourcing.

The provider should be asked not to make any announcement until the organization makes its to the public first. The announcements should be made in the following order:

1. Employees directly affected
2. Other employees
3. Losing bidders
4. Public

In making the announcement, further guidance is provided in Chapter 19 under "Communications."

The project team should also be sensitive to the employee population as a whole. They may be concerned that this is the first of many outsourcing initiatives (and it may be). It is particularly important that the employees conclude that the outsourcing initiative was performed in a fair and open manner, with appropriate employee involvement, and that the employees directly affected by the result were treated fairly and sensitively.

The losing bidders will have invested significant amounts of time and money in this competition. They deserve the project team's thanks. They also deserve an explanation of why they were not awarded the contract. This may seem to be a waste of time, but it is an appropriate investment in case the project team wants the losing bidders to be involved in any re-competition in future years.

The organization's public announcement, often coordinated for simultaneous release with the provider's announcement, should concentrate on the reasons to outsource but can also include the basic terms of the agreement. The announcement should thank the employees directly affected by the initiative for their contributions.

Part Seven
Transitioning Resources

Chapter 19

The Transition Process

The Relationship Team Takes Over

Up to now, the relationship team has generally been serving in a consulting role to the project team. Now the roles should reverse. The relationship team will have to live with the results of the transference of the factors of production to the provider. Accordingly, it should now assume primary responsibility for the initiative.

The project team should return to their daily activities, with the exception of the project leader. The project leader should be an active member of the relationship team through the transition's completion. The project leader performs a valuable role by assuring that the project team's acquired knowledge is transferred to the relationship team. The project leader will consult with the relationship manager and employ the project team's resources (for example, specific project team members), as necessary, to assist in the transition.

Just as important, the project leader attends all meetings with the provider during the transition. This ensures that previous provider commitments (and their interpretations) don't fall through the cracks or get reinterpreted to the organization's detriment. At the outset, the relationship manager cannot, and should not, be expected to know and understand every nuance of the agreement, or why certain actions (for example, contract clauses) were taken. This is where the project leader guides the relationship manager.

The project champion's role stays the same—senior management's representative in guiding the relationship team to a successful completion of the initiative. Having said that, it is also important to update the executive to whom the relationship manager will report. This responsibility falls to the project champion. It is useful to remember that this executive may not be thrilled that the outsourcing occurred in the first place. That's why it is the project champion's job to assure that the executive is comfortable with the initiative and will support it. Any problems here should be handled by the project champion and the CEO (or COO, if one exits), not by the more junior relationship manager or project leader.

Until the initiative is completed, the key players are as follows, in descending levels of authority:

- Project champion
- Executive (to whom the relationship manager will report)
- Relationship manager
- Project leader

At the same time, the relationship manager's role should be established. This will enable the provider to recognize and accept the relationship manager as the decision maker to whom the provider reports.

Transition Roles

Outsourcing's success often depends on how the transition is implemented beginning with the announcement of a signed contract through the transfer of the factors of production to the implementation of operations. This is where the best-laid plans can fall apart.

In the term sheet and contract, the specific roles for each party in the transition were identified, what will be done, how it will be accomplished, where each will be done, and when each will be accomplished. Now it's time to make the final statements of how those roles will be executed. Up to now, the account manager had very limited access to the organization, and then only through the project team. That has to change now. Together with the relationship manager, these two should begin to build the type of relationship that can weather the storms they will face.

The relationship manager should have developed a transition plan to smoothly move the factors of production to the provider smoothly. The provider, likewise, will have a transition plan. Together, the relationship manager and the provider's account manager should mesh the two plans into one that includes effective "change management" techniques, because outsourcing can both transform the organization and the way employees look at it. Up to this point, both parties have been negotiating. Now they should collaborate to execute a single plan.

The parties should have the full cooperation and involvement of the human resources function, or an outsource adviser, in counseling the employees directly affected by outsourcing. Most large providers have a human resources function that will contribute to the transition as well. Together, they should also be responsible for implementing tightened security where it is needed to protect those employees and the organization's other valuable assets. The following are examples of issues that should be addressed:

Communication Issues

- How and when will the employees directly affected by the outsourcing initiative be advised?
- How and when will the employees unaffected by the outsourcing initiative be advised?

Human Resources Issues

- What will be offered to each of the employees who:
  - ▲ Will be asked to remain with the organization in another capacity?
  - ▲ Will be asked to move to the provider?
  - ▲ May be asked to move to the provider?
  - ▲ Will be terminated?
- How will the offers be presented?

Transition Issues

- How and when will the employees, who will move to the provider, do so (for example, in a staged transition or one-time transition)?
- How and when will the other (nonemployee) factors of production be moved to the provider?

These issues are covered in the following sections of this chapter.

Communication Issues

If the project team did its job in communicating with the employees as the initiative evolved, then the employees learned of the initiative's progress at the following points:

- When the project plans were completed
- When the costs and performance analyses were ready to begin
- When the requests for proposals were prepared
- When the short list candidates were selected
- When the contract was completed

The goal was to avoid surprises or rumors which could trigger stress and discontent. It will be hard to say whether the project team succeeded, because this is a high stress time for employees, irrespective of the project team's success. The true measure of their success will be how quickly the employees accept the change and move forward.

The CEO, preferably (or if not, the same person who announced the outsourcing initiative at the beginning), should announce that the outsourcing contract has been signed. The announcement should not be made on a Thursday or Friday, as there are important follow-up meetings that should be held in the next few days. The announcement should be crafted with care and delivered to all employees in the affected locations. As Andy Grove, chairman of Intel Corporation, once said, "The worse the news, the more effort should go into communicating it." The project team should also be recognized for their outstanding efforts and results.

Further, the announcement should be delivered in person in a presentation to those employees who will be directly affected by it. John Morley, British statesman and writer, once said, "Three things matter in a speech; who says it, how he says it, and what he says—and of the three, the last matters least." The CEO should be sincere and compassionate, yet optimistic and upbeat in making the presentation.

The announcement to those directly affected employees should be short, but a period for questions should immediately follow. In the presentation, the CEO should:

- Announce that the outsourcing contract has been signed.
- Reveal who the provider is, and speak favorably about the provider.
- Indicate how this will affect the employees, including their probabilities for future employment with the provider, severance packages, and so on.
- Thank the employees for their years of service.
- Set up the subsequent meetings to be held (see below).
- Reiterate the reasons for outsourcing.
- Set forth the timetable for the transition.

- Describe any of the key terms in the contract that differ from the term sheet announcement (which was previously shared with the employees).

The account manager and his or her superior should represent the provider and should participate as appropriate (for example, to answer specific questions).

Within twenty-four hours of the announcement that the contract has been signed, there should be a series of meetings to explain in more detail the answers to the employees' questions. These would include:

- A meeting with the organization, for each individual employee directly affected by the outsourcing for counseling
- A meeting with the provider for all employees as a group who will be, or may be, offered positions with the provider
- Meetings with the provider for all employees individually who will be offered positions or interviews with the provider

When meeting with the individual employees, the organization should be able to explain which option (or options) is available (for example, to stay with the organization in another capacity, to accept an offer from the provider, to interview with the provider, or to be terminated). Meeting with the employees first allows the employees to meet with the provider with an understanding of what will happen to them, irrespective of the provider.

In the meetings with the provider, any employee who will be made an offer—or who will have a chance to interview—should have the benefit of learning everything that would be necessary to make an informed decision, including:

General Meeting

- Information about the provider, such as its history and how it operates
- Information about general opportunities for career development, training, benefits, and so on

Individual Meeting for Those Receiving Offers

- A written offer of employment and the period in which it remains open

- Information about the specific position to be filled (for example, a written position description), how the activities will change from the individual's prior position, to whom the position will report, and so on
- Information about specific career development, training, benefits, and so on
- The financial elements of the offer
- A face-to-face meeting with the new supervisor

Individual Meeting for Those Interviewing

- A personal interview with the hiring manager and the account manager
- The timetable for the provider's decision on their potential employment

In most cases, the provider's career opportunities, development, training, compensation, and benefits should be positive to the employees. They will see opportunity and want to accept the offer.

Human Resources Issues

The relationship team should be sensitive to what the employees are going through. Following this announcement, the reality is now beginning to sink in: change will occur. They are feeling discomfort and insecurity, and the organization should express confidence about their futures.

The organization should present to each of the affected employees, in writing, the financial and operational implications of the options it controls (for example, it doesn't control the provider's offer), including salaries and benefits continuance, severance benefits, and retirement implications. It is imperative that these terms be at least fair (and be seen to be fair by unaffected employees) and preferably somewhat generous. This should be the goal, whether or not there are opportunities of employment elsewhere in the organization or with the provider. These employees have served the organization well and deserve fair treatment as they leave.

The organization will have identified several people in the outsourced unit that it wants to keep. These may have been persons that will fill roles on the relationship team or that have skills needed elsewhere in the organization. While it may appear that these individuals are lucky to be staying with the organization, they may feel otherwise. After all, they still must go through the uncertainty of an involuntary change of position. That is why sensitivity and counseling are necessary here as well. The organization should be able to make their written offer of employment at the same time the contract announcement is made and schedule the meetings with their new managers to occur within twenty-four hours. Having said that, if the offer is not accepted, then the provider should consider these individuals for employment, and if no offer is forthcoming there, they should receive the same severance package as those employees who will be terminated.

The provider should previously have been able to identify the key employees who should be made an immediate offer, concurrent with the announcement, in order to improve the employees' chances of quickly accepting the change. This should have been accomplished by a review of the personnel files, a review of the organizational structure and their position descriptions, and discussions with the project leader, relationship manager, the executive to whom the relationship manager will report, and so on. It is very important that these key employees decide to go over to the provider in order to ensure a smooth transition.

Likewise, the provider should have been able to identify those employees it may want to hire (needing only to interview the individuals) and those it definitely doesn't want to hire. The organization should take care to see that the provider did not practice discrimination in making these decisions. Further, the organization should ensure that the provider has a fair interview process. This should help to manage the risk of lawsuits by disgruntled employees.

The group of employees that will be interviewed by the provider should be interviewed within twenty-four hours of the announcement. A decision on their offer should be communicated to them as soon as it can be —within forty-eight hours if possible. This group will suffer the burden of uncertainty the most, and accordingly, will need to be counseled. Obviously, the longer it takes to reach a decision, the less chance of hiring these people, because they will have entered the open market for employment.

The employees who will not be hired (either initially or following the interviews) will be the ones who will suffer the negative burden of outsourcing. While the organization is getting the gold mine (the benefits of outsourcing), this group will feel they got the shaft. Their career plans, their investment in moving up through the organization, and their existing security of compensation and employment will have all gone up in smoke. This may turn out to be a favorable turn in their lives, but now it's a harsh blow.

Worse still, they didn't get an opportunity to move to the provider so the rejection factor is doubled. David Kurtz, American educator and business writer, said, "The rate of unemployment is 100 percent if it's you who is unemployed." This group deserves special treatment, from in-depth counseling and outplacement benefits to a generous severance package.

The human resources function or an outsourcing team (or both) should assist the relationship team by counseling the employees directly affected by outsourcing. The counseling group will need to know what the provider is offering in order to answer questions employees may have (after the provider has made the offer) about:

- The salary and benefits packages that have been offered to the employees who are transferring to the provider
- The career opportunities, training, and development that have been offered
- How the employees' current health, pension, and other benefits compare to the provider's
- The relocation packages for employees who must move to continue employment with the provider

The counseling group should support the provider and encourage the employees to accept the provider's offer. It is in the organization's best interest to have its employees move to the provider so that the provider's services can start up without a break in service—and at least at the same performance levels.

With regard to salary and benefits packages, the counseling group should be able to support the provider's offer. Providers may offer different compensation plans that pay for performance using an adjusted mix of the compensation elements. For example, most of the organization's employees may have been on a plan that provided a base salary, plus a bonus in the 10 percent range, and a standard package of insurance and retirement benefits. This package was designed to meet diverse employee needs across an entire organization.

The provider, however, can tailor the compensation package to a specific niche of employees (competencies, performance measures, and so on). The provider thus better matches the compensation to the employees' needs and desires. To continue the example, the provider might offer 10 percent less in salary, a more suitable benefits package that costs the provider 10 percent less, and a "pay for performance" bonus of 20–40 percent (some of which should be guaranteed the first year, to keep the employees' existing base compensation whole).

These same employees would laugh at a similar plan proposed by the organization, because they wouldn't believe that the organization could accurately measure their bonus achievement. They fear unfair treatment. On the other hand, they will accept the fact that the provider understands their core competencies and special skills and can more accurately measure superior performance. This gives the employees faith they could earn and be paid the bonus. The provider has lowered fixed costs 20 percent and will pay any bonus out of the cost savings from the superior performance. The employees get a greater potential compensation, and one that is reasonably achievable.

With regard to the employees' future career with the provider, the counseling group should be able to support the provider's offer. The provider can offer the employees a career path and the necessary training and development to achieve their career potential. When they perform well, their opportunities for increased compensation and advancement are almost unlimited. The provider and the employees share the same core competencies and special skills, and the provider knows how to train the employees so they can, and will, perform well. Because the provider's entire business relies on these core competencies and special skills, instead of the small fraction your organization relies on, the opportunities for these employees' growth with the provider are much greater.

The provider will want to understand what severance packages the organization will offer to employees who do not accept the provider's offer. This will help the provider understand the financial package they are competing with. If the severance program is too rich, the provider may have trouble attracting any of the necessary employees.

Transition Issues

The list of potential transition issues is endless. As the relationship manager and the account manager combine their transition plans, they should try to identify any issues that may have been missed. They might ask questions such as:

- What flexibility are we building into our plan?
- What alternative plans should be considered?
- How will we know if the transition is being implemented poorly?
- Do we have a contingency plan in case unforeseen problems arise?
- How does the organization respond to failure, real or perceived?

Another question that must be addressed is whether to transfer the internal unit in one coordinated movement or stagger the transition over several phases. A variation of the staggered approach is for the provider to be asked to run a test, or run in parallel for some period of time. Delays can kill outsourcing initiatives, and speed is important, so a single implementation is preferred.

Staggered implementations might work if there is tremendous support for the initiative and the change isn't critical, but unless there are overwhelming reasons to do it in stages, this approach is best avoided. There are several problems with this approach: (1) the employees are caught in between two employers (how would you feel?); (2) any remaining powerful opposing forces will see one last chance (if they can sabotage the first phase they might yet kill it); and (3) the benefits of outsourcing will be delayed. The providers want to get started—let them.

In identifying the possible transition issues, it is advisable to concentrate on the factors of production and how the internal unit fits into the organization:

- People
- Facilities (space and related services)
- Equipment
- Hardware/software
- Third-party contracts
- Processes, functions, and activities, processing inputs and producing outputs

A number of the personnel issues were discussed in the Human Resources Issues section. Examples of nonpeople-related issues would include the following:

- How will the provider take full responsibility for the unit?
- How will the provider begin to use space in the existing facilities, or the unit will be moved to their facilities?
- How will any pieces of equipment transfer to the provider?
- How will existing warranties transfer to the provider?
- How will existing software licenses transfer to the provider?
- How will existing maintenance contracts with third parties transfer to the provider?
- How will interfaces occur during the transition?

The relationship manager and account manager should revisit the resource management, information management, and project management questions outlined in Chapter 5. As these issues are being discussed, other organization employees and stakeholders should be contributing as well, in addition to the human resources function.

First, and perhaps most importantly, the employees who will move to the provider should have a valuable wealth of knowledge, issues, and concerns. As soon as their status is settled, the relationship manager and account manager should interview them together. It is in that group's best interest, as the outsourcing front line, to get the transition right the first time.

Second, the internal unit's internal customers should be interviewed in order to get their concerns out in the open. This is the group that will be the most vocal if transition problems arise. They are the ones who are inconvenienced by any transition and burdened if it goes poorly. If the internal unit touched the customer, and the provider will now perform that activity, it may be appropriate to convene a focus group of external customers to get their input.

Third, if there are significant transfers of physical assets, then people such as plant engineers, maintenance personnel, building managers, architects, insurance agents, lessors, lien holders, financiers, equipment manufacturers' representatives, and moving contractors should be consulted. There are many nuances to moving physical assets beyond picking them up and loading them on the truck. Moving physical assets to the provider is something that may have not been contemplated in third-party agreements, so their representatives may need to contribute input as well.

Fourth, there will be others who should be sought out. Any internal unit employee who is not transferring to the vendor, but wants to cooperate, should be heard. Internal staff functions whose scope of service could be affected by outsourcing, such as controllers, internal audit, and information systems and technology departments should be consulted. They will address issues such as internal controls, performance auditing, and information access and security. Perhaps the provider has other account managers and executives who have made similar transitions for similar organizations, who might offer sound counsel.

Fifth, this is also a good time to update senior management on the transition plan and how it will be implemented. They want this transition to be implemented flawlessly, and may offer suggestions related to the transition plan's effect on other stakeholders, including the board of directors, suppliers, customers, and regulators, that could prove valuable. They will also want to know about suggested organizational policy changes that result from outsourcing.

One final point is important: there is a natural tendency not to want to let go, especially for those internal unit employees who now work on the relationship team. There will be some "buyer's remorse." There will be the "perfectionist" who wants to do just one more thing (many times) before turning over the reins. The process will never be perfect, and there will always be something else that could be done first. Yet the time has come. Like sending your child off to college or military service, you say goodbye with a tear in your eye. The organization must let go in order to enjoy the benefits.

The provider cannot start delivering those benefits until the organization lets go. While the relationship manager and the team have worked closely with the provider to review the transition plan, get the appropriate input, and play their roles, the primary transition role belongs to the provider. They must take the reins and drive the implementation forward. How the provider handles the transition and the inevitable obstacles will be a good barometer of the provider's quality and how it will perform.

Another Reason to Outsource: Generate Cash by Transferring Assets to the Provider

Tough times have hit, and you need cash. Now!

Remember the recessionary period of the late 1980s and early 1990s? Companies either in the real estate industry or dependent upon it were hammered by the combination of a soft market, deflated asset values, few liquid assets, and newly conservative bankers (who themselves were under attack by regulators) unwilling to lend them cash. Many of these companies were reasonably sound and could have weathered the storm but for a lack of cash.

Outsourcing allows us to sell assets for cash as part of a long-term service agreement. In situations like this, a strong, cash-rich provider can mean the difference between survival and failure.

A few words of caution: providers are not banks. If you need cash and cannot go to the bank (or financial markets), you can expect that your carrying costs will be significantly higher, to compensate the provider for accepting a risk that a bank would not. Further, the entire outsourcing transaction carries greater risk for the provider; thus their profit margins will be high. Finally, if you think that providers will pay you more than the market value for your assets, you are deceiving yourself. The provider may "allow" you more on the assets than the market value (just as a car dealer overvalues your trade-in), but you will repay the extra allowance, plus a finance charge, in your monthly outsourcing costs over the life of the contract.

Part Eight

Managing Relationships

Chapter 20

Performance Monitoring

Relationship Management

As a general rule, the organization doing the outsourcing will oversee the decision rights that have been transferred to the provider (see Chapter 9, under "Decision Rights"). In its oversight role, the organization, for example, may want to have final approval over:

- The provider's key personnel
- Any voluntary movement of these key personnel
- Any significant changes in technology used by the provider
- Any changes in the provider's outputs
- Any changes in the provider's processes

The organization is represented in the decision making by a relationship manager who is supported by technical specialists on the relationship team, as appropriate. The relationship manager's position is generally dedicated full-time to managing one (for complex transactions) or more contracts and providers.

To build the relationship effectively, the relationship manager and the organization should be active in monitoring and evaluating performance and in addressing issues. If this doesn't occur, the provider's performance is likely to suffer. This might happen because the provider takes shortcuts that are not caught and corrected. But the provider's performance is more likely to suffer because the provider cannot get answers to questions (causing delays or inappropriate assumptions to be made) or the provider's suggestions for organizational improvement (that affects the provider's performance) are not implemented. It takes time to manage the relationship.

PROVIDER: Greaver and Associates (G&A)

CUSTOMER: Roberts Ryan and Bentley (RRB)

SCOPE: Research director role (individual
                 activity level)

LOCATION: Towson, Maryland

REASONS TO   RRB was growing fast and the
OUTSOURCE: research role needed improved
                 performance. Historically per-
                 formed in part by different exec-
                 utives, it now demanded more
                 focus and new skill sets, includ-
                 ing a process orientation and
                 enhanced management skills.

CONTRACT:
   Duration: 1996–1998
   Pricing: Hourly fee

RRB is a U.S. executive search firm that provides retained executive search services to the insurance, financial services, and health care industries. Headquartered in Towson, Maryland, the firm has approximately thirty employees in three offices nationwide. As a result of this outsourcing initiative, one RRB executive was reassigned and no employees were terminated.

Greaver and Associates is a management consulting firm specializing in strategic, financial, and transformation issues for clients, including a significant practice consulting with organizations considering outsourcing. Having previously served RRB, it was clear that once the research director role was better defined and performing at optimal levels, the position should be insourced.

G&A's duties included the following:

- Manage the executive recruiters.
- Design and implement recruiting process changes as necessary.
- Coordinate the training and development of recruiters.
- Schedule search services to meet client's needs.
- Monitor progress on searches to ensure high-quality service.
- Review outgoing firm reports to clients for clarity, completeness, and accuracy.
- Act as liaison with the account executives.
- Evaluate performance and counsel recruiters.

As a result of this outsourcing initiative, G&A and RRB have:

- Implemented a structured, client-focused search process to better define the activities of retained search and increase accountability.
- Reduced search cycle times by 40 percent.
- Improved "completed searches with hires" results by 25 percent.
- Increased the consistency of search results across all searches.
- Dramatically improved the recruiter satisfaction levels.
- Shortened the communication cycle times with clients and sharpened the quality of those communications.
- Reduced the "number of recruiters per completed search" during a period of fast growth.
- Better defined not only the research director role but also the recruiter and account executive roles.

Oversight Council

Although the relationship manager and the account manager will be managing the relationship on a daily basis, they are not the only interested parties. The organization's internal customers who are receiving the services delivered by the provider are directly affected by how those services are performed. The executive to whom both the relationship manager reports and the provider's executive to whom the account manager reports are responsible to their organizations for each party's performance. In addition, the project champion has a vested interest in seeing that the outsourcing initiative is successful.

It is a good idea for these individuals to come together as a group, to act like a "board of directors" for this strategic alliance. The executive to whom the relationship manager reports should chair the meetings. In its oversight role, the oversight council would:

- Review the annual operating plans, and any major initiatives.
- Provide a forum for discussion of the major issues.
- Guide the two managers in making more effective decisions.
- Review the performance results—primarily exceptions to standards.
- Discuss recommended adjustments based upon these results.
- Review the contract terms and "change orders" to the contract.
- Act as an arbiter if problems arise.

While this group has no legal standing in the contract, that's not important. What is important is that there is an opportunity for the interested parties to come together periodically to provide this oversight role. Early in the relationship, perhaps in the first six months, the oversight council might meet monthly. This is the period, like the early months of a marriage, in which the roles are formed in practice and the relationship is developing rapidly. Most of the time, the relationship develops positively, but sometimes it doesn't. This is when the oversight council should act to get the relationship back on track. If this fails, they should look at the abilities of the personnel involved.

As the relationship and challenges settle down after the initial start-up period, the oversight council might reduce its meeting frequency to bimonthly. This might last for another six to twelve months. As the relationship becomes mature, the oversight council might again reduce its meeting frequency to quarterly. At this point, as the provider's performance is generally satisfactory and the problems are less frequent, the group should begin to focus on more strategic issues. For example, how can the provider's resources be brought to bear to effect even greater benefits for the organization?

Meetings

The relationship manager and the account manager should be meeting on a weekly basis to discuss any operating issues and on at least a monthly basis to review performance results. If these two are not communicating, the relationship will not develop. The monthly performance review meetings should occur in advance of an oversight council meeting. This would allow time for any performance problems to be investigated and appropriate adjustments to be recommended and implemented before being discussed at the oversight council meeting.

As often as possible, other members of the relationship team and the provider's account team should be involved in the operating meetings. This tends to build rapport among the troops, and team-building exercises should allow these two teams to mesh as one. Involving other team members in these meetings also improves the probabilities of successful transitions when personnel changes occur.

In the operating meetings, the following are examples of typical agenda items:

- Analyze performance results (see "Monitoring Performance Reports" below).
- Discuss performance issues.
- Analyze customer issues (for example, internal customer complaints).
- Review personnel issues.
- Discuss provider issues.
- Solve problems.
- Develop recommendations for changes.
- Plan new initiatives.
- Review any significant changes in the provider's technologies, outputs or processes.

■ Review proposed "change orders" to the contract.
■ Review the billings.

The objective in these operating meetings is to address problems and share in solving them. This strengthens the relationship.

Periodically, if the organization wants the relationship to develop into a strategic one, it should invite the provider's management team to participate in all or some of its key strategic meetings. These could include:

■ Senior management meetings
■ Strategic planning meetings/retreats
■ Performance improvement initiative meetings (e.g., reengineering and benchmarking meetings)
■ Board of directors meetings

Providers have a wealth of resources that can benefit the organization. But they need to know the organization's strategic problems and the organization's leaders who are discussing them. The provider's executives have great expertise in their areas of specialty. They are also intelligent businessmen and businesswomen, who have a breadth of experience with a number of customers, so they have seen "best practices" across a number of organizations and industries.

Perhaps more importantly, because they are not tied to the organization's way of doing things, they can find innovative solutions that couldn't otherwise be advanced. As English journalist and author G. K. Chesterton explained of any organization's executives, "It isn't that they can't see the solution. It is that they cannot see the problem." The organization may be unable to find the solution either because they don't see the big picture (missing the forest for the trees) or because advancing them internally would put someone's paradigm at risk (see Chapter 8 under "Transformation").

In their everyday activities, providers can see the nonvalue-added activities, the bureaucratic policies and procedures, and the ineffective personnel in the organization, thus triggering suggestions for improvement. But strategic partner providers can go beyond that. If the organization's executives will be open with its strategic challenges, providers will surprise and delight them with innovative solutions. After all, the provider has every incentive to help improve the organization's business, because what helps the organization grow and prosper will help the provider grow and prosper.

Monitoring Performance Reports

The contract sets forth the performance measures (see Chapter 11), deliverables, due dates, and other things that the provider is obligated to meet. Pravin Shah, an Indian management consultant, said, "Without a yardstick, there is no measurement. And without measurement, there is no control." Together, the relationship manager and the account manager should develop a reporting system that captures this performance information. These reports may be detailed for the operating meetings and summarized for the oversight council meetings.

The reports should be designed to report the actual performance, the performance standard, and the variance from standard. The reports should show the current period (see Exhibit 20.1) and the year-to-date cumulative information. This is the typical historical performance analysis. There will be some glitches in provider performance during the transition and in the first few months of the contract. Was the failure preventable or the result of factors beyond their control? This is when the relationship manager must set the tone for how failure will be addressed. As the old saying goes, "People should know what you stand for. They should also know what you won't stand for." Let the provider know how you feel.

The provider should also present a projection of future expected performance. James L. Hayes, former CEO of the American Management

Exhibit 20.1   Sample Performance Report— Current Record

Performance Measures	Performance Standard	Actual	Variance
Number of outputs	_____	_____	_____
Number of errors	_____	_____	_____
Number of on-time deliveries	_____	_____	_____
Number of days cycle time	_____	_____	_____
Number of outputs per employee	_____	_____	_____

Association, said it best: "Effective managers live in the present—but concentrate on the future." Intel uses an interesting 90/100/90 projection program for its managers that could be applied here. The manager makes a 90-day forecast each month for 100 percent of his or her key performance measures and is expected to achieve a 90 percent confidence (accuracy) level. This forecasting forces the managers not to just look at the past and apologize for poor performance but to take the actions to boost future performance.

The provider's projection reports force the provider to think seriously about the future in making the projection and being accountable for achieving it. They give the relationship manager an opportunity to react to the forecast in advance so that any adjustments can be made. This type of projection, when captured on a "stagger chart" (see Exhibit 20.2), provides excellent trend information, first showing the forecast for the third month in the future and how the forecast is refined each month afterward until it becomes actual. As importantly, it tells the relationship manager how well the provider is able to make forecasts.

Exhibit 20.2   Stagger Chart

Forecast Date	\multicolumn{12}{c}{Forecast Amounts}
	Jan.	Feb.	Mar.	Apr.	May	June	July	Aug.	Sept.	Oct.	Nov.	Dec.
January	B	C	D									
February	A	B	C	D								
March		A	B	C	D							
April			A	B	C	D						
May				A	B	C	D					
June					A	B	C	D				
July						A	B	C	D			
August							A	B	C	D		
September								A	B	C	D	
October									A	B	C	D
November										A	B	C
December											A	B

A = Actual Amounts

B–D = Forecast amounts, looking forward ninety days

Adapted from Andrew S. Grove, *High Output Management* (New York: Random House/First Vintage Books, 1983/1985), page 23.

The provider should produce the performance reports as information becomes available. Some information may be captured and reported hourly, daily, weekly, or monthly. If a provider's component parts operation's output is feeding the assembly line continuously, there are measures that should be made hourly. The manufacturer doesn't want to find out at month's end that there was a component parts quality problem that started on the tenth of the month and that thousands of its product units were finished and shipped in the intervening twenty days.

In certain cases, the organization may share in the performance measurement and reporting. In particular, the relationship team should routinely survey the internal customers to determine if they are satisfied with the service. If the provider has contact with the organization's external customers, there should be a mechanism to capture complaints or compliments. This information should be shared so the provider gets fast, appropriate feedback on their service. The account manager cannot review, see, or hear every single thing their personnel do, but the manager does want to give good service, so any feedback helps the manager judge how the service is being performed.

Regardless of who prepares them, the reports should be distributed, promptly reviewed by the relationship manager (or a delegate) and the account manager for problems. If necessary, immediate action should be taken. Otherwise, if routine reports have routine results, they can be reviewed in the weekly operating meeting or monthly performance review meeting, and appropriate action can be taken then. This feedback signals to the provider that the organization is engaged and should stimulate their excellent performance.

Few things frustrate a provider more than giving excellent service and seeing it go unrecognized. Worse still is when this slight is compounded and the provider's one foul-up brings down the wrath of the gods. To be sure, the relationship manager guards against poor performance, but that person must also recognize and appreciate outstanding performance. As Aristotle once observed, "In the arena of human life, the honors and rewards fall to those who show their good qualities in action." The relationship manager should see that the provider receives the honors and rewards that are due.

The relationship manager's monitoring should also include a review of the provider's progress against certain longer-term agreed-upon objectives. For example, the provider may have committed to upgrade certain technologies in year three. How is progress being made toward that objective? There is no need to wait until the provider has failed to meet that commitment before reporting that failure and taking action. Without that technology upgrade, the organization may lose ground against the competition. Further, the organization may have to plan for training and development requirements for its employees, in order to implement the new technologies.

Finally, the relationship manager should monitor the provider's training of its staff, especially in regards to any contact the provider's staff will have with the organization's customers. *The Washington Post* once reported that a gas utility had outsourced meter reading to a provider. The story related that one of the meter readers pepper-sprayed a customer's dog when it approached him while he was trying to read the meter. This episode created quite a stir, and the utility had to work very hard to overcome the bad publicity.

This being said, there is a fine line between monitoring and meddling. As Theodore Roosevelt, 26th U.S. President, said, "The best executive is one who has the sense enough to pick good men to do what he wants done, and self-restraint enough to keep from meddling with them while they do it." The provider was brought in to assume certain responsibilities, and certain decision rights were transferred to the provider. This was done because the provider could do these better than the organization. Accordingly, in the absence of performance failure and failure to cure the problem, the provider should be allowed to manage its own activities. The relationship manager only monitors the output.

Audits

The contract sets forth the rights of either party to audit the other's records. Such records might include the:

- Performance reports and underlying records
- Accounting records and supporting documents
- Special analyses and supporting documents

The relationship manager might ask its internal auditors, external auditors, or relationship team members to perform such an audit. For example, if the provider continues to report satisfactory performance in accordance with the contract yet the internal customers are screaming about noncompliance, then the provider's performance reports and underlying records should be audited. If the contract fees are based on cost plus pricing, then the provider's accounting records and supporting documents for the contract should be audited to ensure that overcharges are not being incurred. If the contract fees include gain-sharing elements, then the gain-sharing analysis and supporting documents should be audited to assure that the provider's claims of outsourcing gains have not been overstated.

The auditors should be counseled on how to conduct this type of sensitive audit involving a partner. The technical standards applied to internal audits shouldn't change, but the audit style and presentation may need to be more tactful. After all, this is a service provider with whom the organization wants to do business for a long time. As the American investment counselor Paul Rubin once said, "Auditors are people who go in after the war is lost and bayonet the wounded." Having been an auditor in the early days of my career, this offends me, and yet I recognize that overzealous auditors can be difficult to work with. The relationship manager should provide guidance here.

Personnel Replacement

The organization will want the opportunity to approve any new provider personnel assigned to the account. As was discussed in Chapter 13, there are a number of criteria that the provider and its personnel should meet. The project team had the benefit of interviewing the provider's key personnel (see Chapter 16) before the provider was brought in. The relationship team should have the same opportunity, and if the new person is the account manager or a key direct report, then the oversight council should be involved in the interviews as well. The relationship team should also check the references with prior customers. If either the interviews or reference-checking does not meet the organization's standards, the provider should be asked to submit another candidate.

Some would argue that the provider should not be allowed to voluntarily replace personnel by transferring them to other customer's contracts or to other positions in their organization. Clearly, there should be a minimum of voluntary turnover, and then only if the incumbent has been in the current position for several years. In this way, the organization doesn't lose the benefit of the experience that individual has gained. However, there is a strong potential benefit to allowing the provider to periodically rotate personnel, and that is bringing in a fresh perspective. If the proposed replacement has at least the same level of experience in the same position with the provider, has performed satisfactorily with previous customers, and passes the interview/reference checking test, then there should be no objection to the suggested change.

Other Changes

The relationship manager should review provider decisions that significantly change technologies, outputs, and processes. That is not to suggest that the organization shouldn't want the provider to make these changes. On the contrary, the provider should be encouraged to experiment and innovate.

The relationship manager's role is to make sure that the change does not damage the organization's flexibility to change providers later, if the need arises. For example, the relationship manager will want to review any significant proposed changes in technology because there is a possibility that it might bind the organization to the provider's technology, and thus to the provider. Even this wouldn't be a problem if the contract allowed other providers to operate the same technologies.

The relationship manager must also be sure that the organization can react effectively to the changes. For example, the relationship manager will want to review any proposed change in the provider's outputs or processes because they could have a significant impact on the organization's processes. Either way, the organization doesn't want to be surprised by the change, and the provider may not be aware of all of the implications such a change might bring.

Another Reason to Outsource:
Accelerate Expansion by Tapping Into the Provider's Capacity, Processes, and Systems

The market is booming! The CEO asks, "Why can't we turn out the products and services faster to benefit from this market?" The response: "We cannot build capacity fast enough to keep up with the market."

Most organizations have finite capacity and limited capabilities. Expanding capacity may require a new plant that would take several years to build. A major competitor may have just introduced a unique service made possible by advanced processes and systems that would take several years to design, test, and build. There just isn't time to do this! The market is hot now; who knows what it will be in several years? We could lose customers that might take years to recapture.

Outsourcing allows us to share the provider's capacity, advanced processes, and systems when we need them. We don't have to wait. By transferring the responsibility for production of certain products or product components or the performance of certain services to the provider, we can accelerate expansion now in order to keep up with the market, and keep our customers happy (and keep our customers).

Chapter 21

Solving Problems

Resolving Disputes

Even in the best of outsourcing situations, problems will arise. As the American essayist and poet Ralph Waldo Emerson said, "Our greatest glory is not in never failing, but in rising up every time we fail." Rising up means that the provider acknowledges the problem and fixes it. Sometimes the failure rests entirely with the provider, and they can report it, investigate it, and solve it. Such failures should become less frequent as the transition ends and the new operations smooth out. If this is does not happen, the relationship manager needs to get involved.

Other times the failure has roots in both the organization's and the provider's operations. Then the problem is worsened if both parties set out separately to investigate it. It is human nature is to seek the root of the problem in the other parties' actions or inaction. Then, when the investigation is over, it is easy to cast blame at the other party. This hardens positions on who is at fault, wastes time, solves nothing, and harms the relationship. It is in everyone's best interest to work together from the start to investigate the cause of the problem. Joint problem-solving will work more quickly and effectively and will also build the relationship.

Outsourcing problems can generally be segmented into one of four areas:

1. People
2. Process
3. Technology
4. All other

People problems can have many causes, from the loss of key people to poor performance to people not getting along well together. Process problems generally result from how the operations are set up; how decision rights, responsibilities, and authorities are distributed; and how the activities are defined. Technology problems generally relate to the acquisition, implementation, and maintenance of equipment or systems.

Because these problems can have root causes in either party, addressing the problems is a shared responsibility. Problems can be addressed at three increasing levels of attention:

1. Relationship team members and the provider's account team members
2. Relationship manager and the account manager
3. Oversight council

The obvious preference is for the problems to be shared and resolved at the lowest level, among the relationship team members and the account team members. These people should have a good working relationship so they can resolve the less significant day-to-day problems as they arise, without supervisor involvement. If such problems cannot be resolved at this level, or after initial joint investigation, they are more significant than originally thought, then they should be brought to the superior's attention.

At each level, the participants should use the preferred principled negotiation framework (see Chapter 17) in coming to agreement on the causes and solutions. This approach guides the parties in looking for several alternative solutions for mutual gains. Where interests conflict, it also encourages them to search for objective standards independent of either party. In this way, problems can be more quickly resolved before either side takes a firmly entrenched position. Then egos, pride, position and other human frailties become major obstacles to reaching agreement.

The relationship manager and the account manager can address these problems either immediately if significant, or if not, at their weekly meeting. Part of the relationship-building exercise between them involves agreeing on how to solve such problems and then successfully solving problems together within this framework. Significant problems should be addressed immediately, not only because they are hurting operations, but also because this allows time for the problems to be investigated and adjustments recommended and/or implemented before being discussed at the oversight council meeting.

The oversight council should decide what level of problems it wants to hear about (even if they were resolved at a lower level) and how it wants to address the problems that couldn't be resolved. For example, the oversight council may decide that it wants to know about any problem that is material (should be defined) to the contract, such as significant provider performance breakdowns, even if they have been resolved. In this way, it serves its oversight role in guiding the relationship manager and the account manager. Unresolved problems that come before the oversight council are typically either "people problems" (for example, disagreements between the relationship manager and the account manager) or significant contractual obligation issues that are unclear. These types of problems should be discussed in the oversight council; if the problem remains unresolved, outside judgment is needed.

American pharmaceutical executive and U.S. Secretary of Commerce Donald Rumsfeld said, "Success tends not to go to the person who is error-free, because he is also risk-averse. Rather it goes to the person who recognizes that life is pretty much a percentage business. It isn't making mistakes that's critical; it's correcting them and getting on with the principal task." An often seen outsourcing objective is to have a successful provider improve the operation by innovation and change. The provider will not be successful if they are constantly trying to avoid mistakes. Each person on the relationship team and account team should take Rumsfeld's observation to heart.

Third-Party Intervention

If the dispute cannot be resolved through joint problem solving and negotiation, then involvement of a third party will be necessary. This generally means one or more of the following interventions, in ascending order of formality and cost:

- Mediation
- Arbitration:
  - ▲ Nonbinding
  - ▲ Binding
- Judicial:
  - ▲ By a judge
  - ▲ By a jury

In using a mediator, the parties seek to introduce a trained facilitator. Some of the best known examples of mediators have been the involvement of United States officials in the search for peace in the Middle East. Henry Kissinger's famous shuttle diplomacy and President Jimmy Carter's Camp David accord are but two such examples. In an outsourcing dispute, the mediator might be an independent outsourcing consultant (not involved with either organization). The facilitator's job is set the ground rules and environment, improve communication, introduce creative solutions, and bring the sides to settlement. There is no authority given to the mediator to reach a conclusion.

Arbitration is a more formal hearing before an impartial third party or parties. It raises the position of mediator up a notch to a referee. Instead of bringing the sides to settlement, the arbitrator hears the arguments, reaches a conclusion, and issues a decision. In a nonbinding arbitration, either side may disregard the arbitrator's decision, but in a binding arbitration, that decision is final, and the parties are bound by it. Binding arbitration is used, for example, in the major league baseball free agency system to settle the player's salary when the baseball club and player cannot come to agreement.

In the U.S. judicial system, either a judge or a jury hears the arguments and reaches a decision. Because of the extensive rules of engagement, the long time it takes to implement them, and the involvement of lawyers as advocates, the judicial process is very costly and time consuming. As a result, many outsourcing contracts call for mediation or arbitration as a preliminary process.

Agreement can be reached through any of these interventions, but at a cost to the relationship. The losing side is seldom happy and is likely to terminate the relationship.

Termination

The existing provider relationship is generally terminated:

- At contract expiration
- For cause
- For convenience

If the contract is not renegotiated it expires. This could occur because either party wants to discontinue the relationship or because they could not agree on new contract terms. Termination for cause indicates that the contract is not at the expiration, one or both of the parties have not performed in accordance with the contract's provisions, and one or both want to end the relationship. Termination for convenience indicates that the contract is not at the expiration and there is a reason to terminate the relationship other than for cause.

If the contract will end at expiration, conventional wisdom has suggested that the provider should instigate renegotiations. Unfortunately, this could backfire on the organization. The later the renegotiations begin, the higher the probability that the provider will be retained, because there is insufficient time to begin the search for a new provider. Instead, the organization should decide whether it wants to consider the provider for further service at least one year prior to contract expiration. If contract renegotiations begin then, a goal should be set to have this wrapped up nine months in advance of the contract expiration.

If either the provider will not be considered for further service or there will be an open market for the new contract, then the search for a new provider should begin at least nine months in advance of the contract expiration. This will allow time for the search and the transition prior to expiration. For complex transactions, a transition of three to six months or longer may be required.

If the contract will be terminated prior to the expiration date (for cause or convenience), then the new termination date should be set to allow time for a new provider to be identified and make preparations to take over the operations. Once a decision is made to no longer engage the provider, the transition planning should begin. The options are to either insource the operations or transfer them to another provider.

In the unlikely event that the organization wants to insource this operation, it will take even longer to rebuild the operation to be successful when the transition occurs. This may be the desired action, because somewhat twisted logic might conclude that if one provider couldn't succeed, maybe the others can't do better. However, serious soul searching should be done before this decision is made.

First, if the decision to outsource was correct, what has changed? If an area was not core to the organization, is it core now? Just because one provider failed does not mean that outsourcing was the wrong decision, only that a poor provider choice was made. Also, as hard as it is to accept, the organization may have contributed to the provider's failure. Second, the problems that caused the termination have made the operation unstable, so this is no time to try to reassume responsibility for it. A failed outsourcing is not the end of the world, but following that with a failed insourcing would be traumatic and could diminish the opportunity for future outsourcing. Third, there are real risks to insourcing that cannot be adequately evaluated in the short term

The reasons to terminate the relationship as soon as possible may be overwhelming, but unless the business will be threatened, it is better to take the time to pick the right provider. Otherwise, as with divorce, you can get caught on the rebound and pick the best-looking provider that crosses the threshold, only to find that this provider is either no better or only marginally better than the last one. There are many capable providers who have smooth-running operations. With careful thought about what went wrong, new criteria can be set up to choose the best provider.

If the business is threatened by continuing the relationship for even several months, the organization should call in the second-ranked candidate from the original outsourcing initiative and determine if a short-term contract can be worked out to carry the organization through the next one to two years, until the situation can be stabilized. The organization will have very little leverage, and the provider will understand this. The provider's price for this service will be higher than normal, probably on a cost plus basis, which is not unreasonable given that the provider must reconfigure its operations to meet the organization's emergency needs with little time to assess the risks. Any promise made to the provider that they will be given first consideration for a long-term agreement if their service is good may lessen these extra charges.

In the contract, how the relationship will be unwound was determined, including the provider's termination assistance. The provider is responsible for a smooth transition of its operations, either to the organization or another provider. The transition will continue at least several months past the termination date until the new provider is operating smoothly.

The relationship team should revisit the contract to see:

- What assistance will be given
- Who will deliver the assistance
- When the assistance will be given (for example, start and end points)
- What the provider's compensation will be for such assistance
- What factors of production will be transferred, at what cost
- What the payment terms will be for such compensation and the cost of any transferred factors of production

The assistance given will be that described in the contract, but in effect should be "whatever it takes." The most knowledgeable provider staff member for each activity should deliver the assistance. Normally, the assistance will begin as soon as the new contract is awarded and end on a set date, generally several months after contract termination. If the organization is paying for the assistance on an hourly rate, based upon usage, it must make sure the new provider is not wasting money with long, unfocused discussions. The organization may want to set a maximum on the amount of assistance it will pay for, and the new provider can pay for the remainder.

The provider's assistance should include the option for the new provider to acquire the factors of production. For example, the organization or the new provider should have the right to interview and offer positions to key provider operating personnel on the account. They should also be able to license key provider operating software and purchase the equipment necessary to continue the service.

Provider Issues in a Recompetition

In each of the termination reasons (at expiration, for cause, and for convenience), the organization may choose to open the contract for other providers to bid on. This is a recompetition. Obviously, if the termination was for cause (for example, the provider had not performed satisfactorily) or if the termination was for the provider's convenience (they were exiting this line of business), the existing provider would not be a part of the recompetition. In each of these cases, the other potential bidders will willingly participate in the recompetition because they know it is real.

On the other hand, if the existing provider will be involved in the recompetition (for example, the contract is approaching the expiration date) and the organization sends out requests for proposals (RFPs), how will the bidding providers react? They understand that in most cases the current relationship and contract could still be restructured and that a change in providers is unlikely. The following are some examples of the questions that will run through the bidding providers' minds:

- Why couldn't the organization and the existing provider reach a new agreement to continue the relationship?
- Does the RFP represent a real competition or is the organization just "kicking the tires" to see what the market is?

- Is the organization just trying to get the provider's attention in the renegotiations?
- Did the existing provider not meet the organization's needs, and if not, could the bidding providers meet their needs?
- Was the organization too difficult to work with, so the bidding providers would likely suffer as well?

The bidding providers will want to get a clear understanding of why the organization and existing provider cannot reach a new agreement. It is normally in each party's best interest to continue the relationship, so what has gone wrong? The existing provider should want a long-term relationship because stable operations, with long-term revenue streams, are where the provider can be most profitable. The higher risks and heavy investment (in transition costs), learning curves, and relationship building needed to start up outsourcing contracts takes several years to recoup. Bidding providers generally don't want to make that investment unless they feel a long-term relationship is possible.

Unless the service is a commodity service, which is well understood in the market and has fairly standard pricing structures and amounts, the bidding providers will evaluate the costs/benefits of responding to the RFP. For RFPs relating to more complex transactions and customized services, as was pointed out in Chapter 14, the provider:

- Has limited resources.
- Will make heavy investments in time and money to prepare the proposal, make presentations and negotiate.
- Will face stiff competition, due to the open market competition.
- Will have tight margins, due to the open market competition.

This environment creates a real business risk for providers and forces them to assess carefully which RFPs to respond to. They cannot afford to perform a market evaluation service (e.g., through the RFP process) without charge, and it is not their business to deliver such services for a fee because outsourcing consultants perform this service. There must be a reasonable probability of success in winning the competition or the bidding providers won't play. Bidding providers cannot and will not waste their precious resources on an organization that is just tire kicking.

Sometimes outsourcing customers feel they are being taken for granted. This can happen even though the service is satisfactory and the relationship is stable. Perhaps the provider's bursts of creativity and gains in performance have become less frequent. As can happen in some long-term marriages, the original sizzle has faded somewhat. Customers might try to jolt the relationship by introducing the fear of losing the contract. The bidding providers will look for this in their review of the RFP and due diligence discussions. They cannot and will not waste their resources on an organization that is just trying to get the existing provider's attention.

They will want to know the specifics of why the organization is so dissatisfied with the existing provider that it would go out for proposal. Was the original contract unfair? Did the existing provider not perform satisfactorily (e.g., poor quality, slow cycle times, or unsatisfactory timeliness)? Did the existing provider not follow through on promises made? Were their prices too high? Did their people not get along with the organization's people? If so, why are these issues not being restructured in the new contract? These are just a few of the questions that will be asked. The bidding provider's outsourcing professionals in any industry will have a fairly good feel for the existing provider's capabilities and how theirs compare. The bidding providers will want to know the specifics in order to determine if they can do a better job of satisfying the organization's needs.

The bidding providers will try to determine what type of people the organization's people are, to see if they can work with them. What was the cultural fit? Did the existing provider have trouble with the organization as a customer? Are they responsive when issues are laid on the table, or do they drag their feet in addressing them or making decisions? Was the provider wrongly blamed for everything that went wrong? Do they constantly want to beat their existing providers down on price, or are the willing to pay for differentiated service? These and many other questions will be asked. In any given industry, for a particular function, the outsourcing world is a small world. The provider can get good intelligence information through their contacts.

If the contract is not near its expiration date, the issues will be even more intensively reviewed. While this situation indicates probable dissatisfaction with the existing provider, if the existing provider has not been excluded from further consideration, the bidding providers will be unlikely to take the RFP seriously. The economics of early termination, with its termination charges, make it unlikely, in the bidding providers' minds, that an organization will actually go through with a change in providers.

Having said this, recompetitions are a valid exercise to consider new providers, with a goal of changing providers. This will become much more prevalent as the early outsourcing contracts near expiration. For example, the early lengthy (often ten-year) contracts of the late 1980s and early 1990s for information systems and technology outsourcing services are or will be expiring in the next several years. Recently, General Motors' Locomotive Division recompeted its IS and IT contract. With GM's spin off of its former subsidiary and existing provider, EDS, the bidding providers took the RFP seriously, and CSC was awarded the new contract.

Organization Issues in a Recompetition

The organization will have a number of issues that it should consider in conducting the recompetition:

- What is the purpose of the recompetition—is it serious about changing providers?
- How will it answer the providers' issues and questions about the existing relationship and provider?
- Who will lead and serve on the recompetition project team—is the relationship manager the best person to lead the team, or are others more capable?
- How should the recompetition be different from the original outsourcing initiative—are there ways to shorten the process?

If the existing provider is allowed to participate in the recompetition, its purpose will seem unclear to the providers who were sent an RFP. Is the organization serious about changing providers? If so, then all of the communications with the bidding providers should be clear on this point. On the other hand, if it is more about tire kicking, the decision to hold a recompetition should be reconsidered. There are other ways in which to test the market, as described in the following section.

The providers will aggressively pursue the answers to their issues and questions including those discussed in the previous section. In the bidders' conference and each subsequent communication, candid answers should be given as to what happened in the relationship and how the provider performed. The providers will be seeking to confirm the organization's answers through their other sources, so candor is the only path to take.

The recompetition team should have a composition similar to the original outsourcing initiative project team and should include the inter-

nal customers who will be served by the provider. The relationship manager should be on the team but should probably not be its leader. First, the
project leader should bring a fresh perspective, and the relationship manager will have some clear biases, at least toward the existing provider. This
is also particularly important in the negotiation, when the "people" should
be separated from the "problems" that the relationship manager has been
living with for years. Second, it may be hard to convince the bidding
providers that the relationship manager can be candid in discussing the
existing relationship and the existing provider. They could see the relationship manager and team as part of the problem but be unable to effectively satisfy their doubts if that is the key person they are communicating
with and could be working with in the future. Third, the project leadership role will be a full-time job for quite some time, and it is unlikely that
the relationship manager can spare the time. Serving in this capacity would
make it very difficult to manage the existing provider relationship through
the contract termination and prepare the transition plan.

Streamlining the Recompetition Process

The organization may embrace a full recompetition or may seek alternatives to the standard RFP, proposal, and vendor selection techniques. If the
later approach is taken, the organization is effectively saying that there are
ways of testing the market that are equally effective and much less costly.
This would include, in the order of quality results, engaging outside advisers who are close to the market, benchmarking other similar organizations
that have completed more recent transactions for similar services, or simply talking with representatives from a few potential providers.

First, outside advisers can streamline the recompetition by adding
their knowledge of the market, the players in it, the current pricing, and
other factors. With input from the relationship manager, internal customers
and other stakeholders (recompetition team), they can compare the old
contract and provider to what is now available in the market. In effect, the
entire process of selecting the vendors could be shortened to formal presentations to the recompetition team from the top two or three adviser-
recommended providers before returning to the standard negotiation
methodology. Of course, the challenge is that this places great responsibility on the adviser. A variation on this is to follow the standard methodology, but have the outside adviser reduce the burden on internal personal

by performing many of the activities instead of using the team approach. This alternative was described in Chapter 13 under "Decision Time."

A second streamlining technique is to benchmark with other organizations that have recently outsourced or held recompetitions for similar functions or processes. The benchmarking concepts were discussed in Chapters 10 and 11 and would be similar to what would be applied here. This would substitute benchmarking for the entire section in the methodology on selecting the vendors. Then the recompetition team would hear formal presentations from the top two or three providers that appear, from the benchmark partner research, to be the most qualified and cost-effective before returning to the standard negotiation methodology. The problem with this approach is that no two organizations are alike. Where benchmarking for performance improvement can be quite effective, because you are looking for ideas that you can apply, benchmarking outsourcing contracts requires more effort in reviewing the details of comparability. Further, benchmarking efforts can be time-consuming in and of themselves.

A third streamlining technique is to meet individually with each of the providers who was involved in the original competition, describe what has occurred in the contract period, and get a reading from them on how their proposals might differ today. In this way, the organization can get more current market data from providers who were familiar with the original unit prior to outsourcing. Then if one provider who was originally qualified promises significant improvement over the existing contract and the others' promises, this provider might make a presentation to the team and negotiations could begin.

There are several challenges with this approach: (1) those involved must be able to cut through salesmanship and rhetoric; (2) those involved must be able to effectively communicate to the providers what has changed since the original competition; (3) the providers may have understood the internal unit several years ago, but they may not remember enough to meaningfully participate (other than just sell); (4) providers' qualifications may have changed since the original competition; and (5) there may be more qualified, cost-effective providers who didn't participate in the original competition and will not get to participate this time either.

Another Reason to Outsource:
Increase Product and Service Value,
Customer Satisfaction, and Shareholder Value

Many of the reasons to outsource (see Appendix 1) will, upon further study, be justified enough to allow outsourcing to proceed. These reasons may be used individually or in combinations. Focus can be enhanced, flexibility can be increased, unavailable expertise can be obtained, performance can be improved, costs can be reduced, the organization's culture can be changed, and other benefits can be gained through outsourcing.

The ultimate reason to outsource, however, is that outsourcing leads to meeting more important long-range objectives: increased product/service value, customer satisfaction, and shareholder value — three qualities that create long-term success. These objectives raise the organization, its managers, and its employees to new levels. Levels that encourage customer loyalty and almost assure financial success. Levels that attract capital for acquisitions and other accelerated organizational growth transactions that simultaneously create individual growth opportunities. Levels that encourage the board of directors to recognize and reward performance: promotions from within, healthy salary increases, bonuses, stock option programs, and other wealth-creating programs. Levels that encourage cutting-edge companies to recruit senior executives for CEO roles in their organizations from the outsourcing organizations. Outsourcing is a powerful transformation tool.

Appendix 1

Reasons to Outsource: Examples

Organizationally Driven

- Enhance effectiveness by focusing on what you do best.   69
- Increase flexibility to meet changing business conditions, demand for products/services, and technologies.   33
- Transform the organization.   85
- Increase product and service value, customer satisfaction, and shareholder value.   294

Improvement-Driven

- Improve operating performance.   46
- Obtain expertise, skills, and technologies that would not otherwise be available.   16
- Improve management and control.   142
- Improve risk management.   112
- Acquire innovative ideas.   209
- Improve credibility and image by associating with superior providers.   154

Financially Driven

- Reduce investments in assets, freeing up these resources for other purposes.   99
- Generate cash by transferring assets to the provider.   264

Revenue-Driven

- Gain market access and business opportunities through the provider's network.   125
- Accelerate expansion by tapping into the provider's capacity, processes, and systems.   281
- Expand sales and production capacity during periods when such expansion could not be financed.   168
- Commercially exploit existing skills.   196

Cost-Driven

- Reduce costs through superior provider performance and the provider's lower cost structure.   57
- Turn fixed costs into variable costs.   183

Employee-Driven

- Give employees a stronger career path.   220
- Increase commitment and energy in noncore areas.   235

Appendix 2

Excuses Not to Outsource: Examples

Uncertainty

- Significant uncertainties exist.
- Existing costs are not well understood.
- Anticipated savings will never materialize.
- Providers' excellent reputations are undeserved.
- Superior providers to the existing internal unit do not exist.

Loss of Control

- Will lose control over provider.
- Will become dependent on providers.
- Will lose cross-functional skills, informal networks, and corporate learning.

Conflict

- Will lose core competencies.
- Will lose confidentiality.
- The conflicting interests between the parties will never work.
- Providers could expand into our business.

Employee Unhappiness

- Will fail to fulfill corporate responsibility to preserve jobs.
- May undermine employee loyalty (what kind of message will this send to the rest of the employees?).

- Will lessen commitment to our community.
- Will damage morale of all employees, not just those outsourced.

Financial

- Providers cannot do these same activities, earn a profit, and give a price that is less than the internal unit.
- Will lose economies of scale.

Excuses

- It needs more study.
- We're too busy to study that now.
- It's a good idea, but the timing is bad.
- Several pilot projects need to be successful first to prove it works.
- Customers will hate this.
- There are too many hidden costs to outsourcing.
- We would never actually terminate employees who would not transfer to the provider.

Appendix 3

Outsourcing: The AMA Survey

OUTSOURCING

Outsourcing, the practice of contracting work to vendors and suppliers, is by no means a new business phenomenon, but a decade of downsizing and restructuring has brought it a higher level of attention. The American Management Association's latest annual survey on job elimination found that 23 percent of job cuts were ascribed, in whole or in part, to outsourcing, up from 21% in 1995.

This finding led AMA Research to the survey herein reported. Our questionnaire listed more than three dozen distinct activities in seven functional categories, and asked if these activities had been outsourced, in whole or in part, to single or multiple providers; and, also, if the outsourcing was long-term (prior to 1994) or recent, or planned for the future.

Charts on the following pages give the responses in detail. Here is a graphic overview for the seven functional categories:

RESPONDENTS CURRENTLY OUTSOURCING ONE OR MORE ACTIVITIES IN EACH FUNCTION

Long-Term   Recent

Function		Total
Finance & Accounting	9% 9%	Total 18%
General & Administrative	68% 10%	Total 78%
Human Resources	60% 17%	Total 77%
Information Systems	45% 18%	Total 63%
Marketing	38% 13%	Total 51%
Transportation & Distribution	56% 10%	Total 66%
Manufacturing (Pct of manufacturing firms only)	44% 12%	Total 56%

Some key findings from the overview:

► 94% of respondent firms outsource at least one listed activity, and the average number of activities outsourced is nine.

► Outsourcing is growing most rapidly in accounting and finance activities, where it has doubled in the past three years. Other important growth areas: information systems (a 40% increase since 1994) and marketing (a 35% increase).

► Cost reductions are the most frequently cited rationales for outsourcing, followed by time reductions and quality improvement. But outcomes fall short of expectations: in most cases, fewer than 25% of respondent firms say those goals have been fully realized.

► For that reason, more than half (51%) of respondent firms report that they have brought at least one previously outsourced activity back in-house.

While it is generally true that companies that have downsized in the '90s are more likely to report outsourced activities than companies that have increased their workforce, the difference is slim (97% vs. 93%), and in all functional categories it is within the sample's margin of error.

FINANCE & ACCOUNTING FUNCTIONS

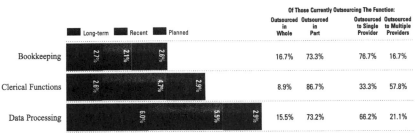

			Of Those Currently Outsourcing The Function:			
			Outsourced in Whole	Outsourced in Part	Outsourced to Single Provider	Outsourced to Multiple Providers
Bookkeeping			16.7%	73.3%	76.7%	16.7%
Clerical Functions			8.9%	86.7%	33.3%	57.8%
Data Processing			15.5%	73.2%	66.2%	21.1%

OF THOSE CURRENTLY OUTSOURCING
ANY FINANCE & ACCOUNTING FUNCTIONS

Goals Intended:

		Total
Cost Reduction		Total 76.1%
Time Reduction		Total 61.5%
Quality Improvement		Total 49.5%

Goals Realized: ■ In Full ■ In Part ■ Not at All ▨ No Answer

Although outsourcing is less common in this function than in other listed categories, it is growing fastest here. Large companies (employing 10,000 or more workers) are twice as likely to outsource one or more financial and accounting activities than smaller ones (34% vs. 17%).

In this function, the typical length of an outsourced vendor contract is just as likely to run for one year (38%) as three or more years (38%). The latter is an unusually high figure; in other functional categories, an average 23% of respondents report contracts of three or more years, while half prefer one-year deals.

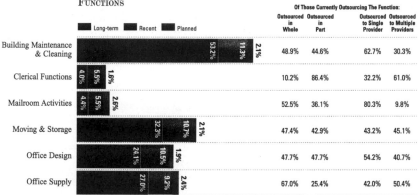

GENERAL & ADMINISTRATIVE
FUNCTIONS

Of Those Currently Outsourcing The Function:

	Outsourced in Whole	Outsourced in Part	Outsourced to Single Provider	Outsourced to Multiple Providers
Building Maintenance & Cleaning	48.9%	44.6%	62.7%	30.3%
Clerical Functions	10.2%	86.4%	32.2%	61.0%
Mailroom Activities	52.5%	36.1%	80.3%	9.8%
Moving & Storage	47.4%	42.9%	43.2%	45.1%
Office Design	47.7%	47.7%	54.2%	40.7%
Office Supply	67.0%	25.4%	42.0%	50.4%

OF THOSE CURRENTLY OUTSOURCING
ANY GENERAL & ADMINISTRATIVE FUNCTIONS

Goals Intended:
Cost Reduction — Total 76.4%
Time Reduction — Total 66.5%
Quality Improvement — Total 53.2%

More companies (78%) outsource one or more general and administrative activities than any other category. Building maintenance and cleaning is the single activity listed in the questionnaire that is most likely to be outsourced, and the one in which companies are least likely to be disappointed in the outcomes. Of all respondent firms, 64% own their worksites, 33% lease them.

Half (50%) of general and administrative outsourcing contracts are drawn for a one-year term; 25% run three years or more.

HUMAN RESOURCES FUNCTIONS

					Of Those Currently Outsourcing The Function:			
	Long-term	Recent	Planned		Outsourced in Whole	Outsourced in Part	Outsourced to Single Provider	Outsourced to Multiple Providers
Benefits Administration	16.8%	5.0%	3.7%		35.6%	60.7%	57.0%	37.0%
Payroll	27.9%	10.5%	4.2%		49.6%	45.0%	88.2%	1.3%
Recruiting	16.6%	9.5%	3.2%		9.3%	84.6%	14.2%	77.8%
Regular Staffing (employee leasing)	8.6%	7.3%	2.1%		13.3%	75.5%	24.5%	64.3%
Temporary Staffing	39.7%	17.6%	1.8%		41.1%	50.4%	21.4%	58.2%
Training – Functional	19.4%	11.8%	2.9%		7.3%	85.5%	11.4%	77.2%
Training – Management & Supervision	20.4%	12.0%	2.1%		17.5%	76.0%	8.5%	82.0%

OF THOSE CURRENTLY OUTSOURCING ANY HUMAN RESOURCE FUNCTIONS

Goals Intended:

Goals Intended:		Total
Cost Reduction	18.7% / 44.6% / 4.9% / 1.9%	Total 70.1%
Time Reduction	24.4% / 41.6% / 4.5% / 1.7%	Total 72.2%
Quality Improvement	16.6% / 42.6% / 4.8% / 2.3%	Total 65.0%

Goals Realized: ■ In Full ▨ In Part ■ Not at All ▨ No Answer

Three-quarters of respondent firms outsource at one or more human resources activities. Unlike the case in most other categories, smaller firms are more likely to do so than larger ones (81% of companies employing fewer than 500 workers, compared with 69% of all others).

Contracts are generally short-term: 58% report that one-year deals are typical in this category, with only 20% reporting a standard of three or more years.

INFORMATION SYSTEMS FUNCTIONS

Legend: ■ Long-term ■ Recent ■ Planned

	Long-term	Recent	Planned	Of Those Currently Outsourcing The Function:			
				Outsourced in Whole	Outsourced in Part	Outsourced to Single Provider	Outsourced to Multiple Providers
Batch Processing	4.8%	3.4%	1.8%	37.3%	54.9%	70.6%	17.6%
Data Communication	10.0%	7.1%	2.3%	39.6%	56.6%	61.3%	31.1%
Voice Communications	14.1%	8.1%	2.4%	50.4%	44.5%	65.0%	26.3%
Installation/Maintenance	28.4%	15.3%	4.2%	31.4%	65.3%	52.4%	42.1%
PC Supply/Maintenance	27.8%	18.3%	3.1%	33.0%	62.8%	47.4%	45.6%
Photocopying	14.4%	5.5%	2.6%	39.0%	50.4%	53.7%	33.3%
Systems Design	14.1%	10.5%	4.0%	28.3%	68.4%	38.2%	48.0%

OF THOSE CURRENTLY OUTSOURCING
ANY INFORMATION SYSTEMS FUNCTIONS

Goals Intended:

	In Full	In Part	Not at All	No Answer	
Cost Reduction	16.0%	51.1%	5.9%	2.0%	Total 75.1%
Time Reduction	20.9%	44.8%	3.6%	0.8%	Total 70.0%
Quality Improvement	21.4%	45.3%	4.3%	1.5%	Total 72.5%

Goals Realized: ■ In Full ■ In Part ■ Not at All ▨ No Answer

Nearly three-quarters (73%) of the mega-firms (employing 10,000 or more workers) outsource at least one information systems activity, compared with 62% of those employing fewer than 500. Supply and maintenance of microcomputers ranks fourth in outsourcing among all listed activities in any category, and installation and maintenance of other information technology ranks fifth. Despite this reliance, typical contracts are twice as likely to be short term (51%) than long-term (24%).

MARKETING FUNCTIONS

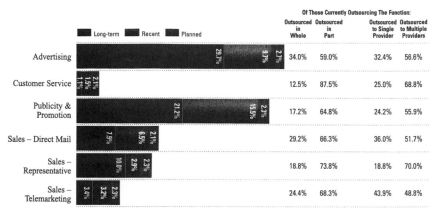

	Outsourced in Whole	Outsourced in Part	Outsourced to Single Provider	Outsourced to Multiple Providers
	Of Those Currently Outsourcing The Function:			
Advertising	34.0%	59.0%	32.4%	56.6%
Customer Service	12.5%	87.5%	25.0%	68.8%
Publicity & Promotion	17.2%	64.8%	24.2%	55.9%
Sales – Direct Mail	29.2%	66.3%	36.0%	51.7%
Sales – Representative	18.8%	73.8%	18.8%	70.0%
Sales – Telemarketing	24.4%	68.3%	43.9%	48.8%

OF THOSE CURRENTLY OUTSOURCING ANY MARKETING FUNCTIONS

Goals Intended:

		Total
Cost Reduction	12.0% ... 40.2% 7.3% 0.6%	Total 60.1%
Time Reduction	20.9% ... 39.6% 2.2% 0.6%	Total 63.3%
Quality Improvement	25.3% ... 47.5% 2.2% 0.6%	Total 75.6%

Goals Realized: ■ In Full ■ In Part ■ Not at All ▨ No Answer

By and large a small-company option: 62% of the sample's smallest firms (fewer than 100 workers) outsource one or more marketing activities, compared with just 39% of those employing 10,000 or more. Marketing is unique in that quality improvement is the leading rationale for outsourcing (cost reduction leads in other categories), and those that outsource marketing activities are most likely to report that their goals have been realized "in full." Annual reviews are the rule: 58% of respondents report a typical contract term of one year, compared with 22% reporting terms of three or more years.

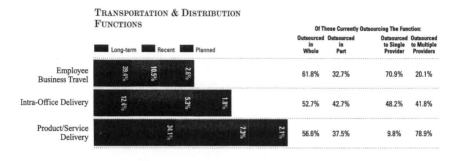

TRANSPORTATION & DISTRIBUTION FUNCTIONS

	Long-term	Recent	Planned	Of Those Currently Outsourcing The Function:			
				Outsourced in Whole	Outsourced in Part	Outsourced to Single Provider	Outsourced to Multiple Providers
Employee Business Travel	39.4%	10.5%	2.6%	61.8%	32.7%	70.9%	20.1%
Intra-Office Delivery	12.4%	5.3%	1.8%	52.7%	42.7%	48.2%	41.8%
Product/Service Delivery	34.1%	7.3%	2.1%	56.6%	37.5%	9.8%	78.9%

OF THOSE CURRENTLY OUTSOURCING ANY TRANSPORTATION & DISTRIBUTION FUNCTIONS

Goals Intended:

	In Full	In Part	Not at All	No Answer	Total
Cost Reduction	35.0%	45.7%	2.7%	1.5%	Total 84.8%
Time Reduction	35.9%	34.7%	3.4%	1.0%	Total 75.1%
Quality Improvement	20.8%	36.9%	2.7%	1.0%	Total 61.4%

Goals Realized: ■ In Full ■ In Part ■ Not at All ▒ No Answer

Employee business travel ranks third among all listed activities outsourced. Comparing all categories, transportation and distribution is by far the winner in fully realizing the goals of cost savings and time reduction. One-year contracts are less frequent than in other categories (46%), and three or more year terms more typical (29%).

MANUFACTURING FIRMS ONLY:
MANUFACTURING FUNCTIONS

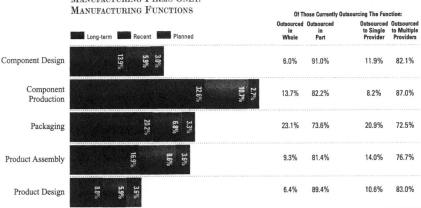

	Of Those Currently Outsourcing The Function:			
	Outsourced in Whole	Outsourced in Part	Outsourced to Single Provider	Outsourced to Multiple Providers
Component Design	6.0%	91.0%	11.9%	82.1%
Component Production	13.7%	82.2%	8.2%	87.0%
Packaging	23.1%	73.6%	20.9%	72.5%
Product Assembly	9.3%	81.4%	14.0%	76.7%
Product Design	6.4%	89.4%	10.6%	83.0%

OF THOSE CURRENTLY OUTSOURCING
ANY MANUFACTURING FUNCTIONS

Activities in the manufacturing function are far more likely to be outsourced to multiple providers than is the case in other categories; such is the nature of the business. Cost savings and time reduction are more likely to be cited as rationales, and the goals are more likely to be met "in full," than is typical in other categories. More than half (55%) of all manufacturers report bringing one or more previously outsourced activities back to home production, but only 35% report bringing a *manufacturing* activity back in-house.

Annual contracts are more the rule here than in any other function: 60% of manufacturers report a typical contract term of one year, while only 13% report a norm of three years or more, the lowest figure for long-term contracts in any category.

Overall Ranking: Listed here are all 37 activities presented in the AMA questionnaire. The first set of columns gives the percentage of respondent firms that *currently* outsource the activity, with its current rank. The next shows the *percentage of increase* reported from 1994 to 1996 in the share of companies that outsource the activity, and its rank in that regard. The third set of columns shows the percentage of increase *planned* for that activity over the next three years, and its rank in that regard. The fourth shows the *total* percentage of respondent firms that will outsource the activity three years from now, and its rank.

Bear in mind that the *percentage of increase* is a relative, not an absolute, number. For example, if 25% of companies outsourced an activity three years ago, and 50% outsource the activity now, the 1994-96 percentage of increase is not 25% but 100% — the share of companies outsourcing the activity has doubled, a 100% increase.

Percentages given for manufacturing activities are percentages of the 337 manufacturing concerns in the sample, not of the 619 companies in the entire sample. The category codes in the left-hand column should be read as follows: FA=Financial & Accounting; GA=General & Administrative Services; HR=Human Resources; IST=Information Systems; MFG=Manufacturing; MKT=Marketing; TD=Transportation and Distribution.

Cat	Activity	Current	Rank	1994-96 Pct of Incr.	Rank	Planned Pct of Incr.	Rank	Total Current and Planned	Rank
GA	Building maintenance & cleaning	64.5%	1	21.3%	37	3.3%	36	66.6%	1
HR	Temporary staffing	57.4%	2	44.3%	22	1.8%	37	59.1%	2
TD	Employee business travel	49.9%	3	26.6%	35	5.2%	33	52.5%	3
IST	PC supply/maintenance	46.0%	4	65.7%	15	6.7%	28	49.1%	4
IST	Installation/maintenance	43.8%	5	54.0%	20	9.6%	24	48.0%	5
MFG	Component production	43.3%	6	32.7%	31	6.2%	31	46.0%	6
GA	Moving & storage	43.0%	7	33.0%	30	4.9%	35	45.1%	7
TD	Product/service delivery	41.4%	8	21.3%	36	5.1%	34	43.5%	8
MKT	Advertising	39.4%	9	23.6%	32	7.0%	26	42.2%	10
HR	Payroll	38.4%	10	37.6%	27	10.9%	22	42.6%	9
MKT	Publicity & promotion	36.7%	11	73.3%	12	6.2%	30	38.9%	11
GA	Office supply	36.2%	12	34.1%	28	6.7%	27	38.6%	12
GA	Office design	34.6%	13	43.6%	23	5.6%	32	36.5%	13
HR	Training (management/supervision)	32.3%	14	58.7%	17	6.5%	29	34.4%	14
HR	Training (functional)	31.2%	15	60.8%	16	9.3%	25	34.1%	15
MFG	Packaging	27.0%	16	33.8%	29	12.1%	20	30.3%	16
HR	Recruiting	26.2%	17	57.3%	19	12.3%	19	29.4%	17
MFG	Product assembly	25.5%	18	50.9%	21	14.0%	15	29.1%	18
IS	Systems design	24.6%	19	74.7%	10	16.4%	12	28.6%	19
IS	Voice communication	22.1%	20	57.5%	18	10.9%	21	24.6%	21
HR	Benefits administration	21.8%	21	29.8%	33	17.0%	10	25.5%	20
MFG	Component design	19.9%	22	42.6%	25	14.9%	13	22.8%	22
IS	Photocopying	19.9%	23	38.2%	26	13.0%	18	22.5%	23
TD	Intra-office delivery	17.8%	24	42.9%	24	10.0%	23	19.5%	24
IS	Data communication	17.1%	25	71.0%	13	13.2%	17	19.4%	25
HR	Regular staffing (empl. leasing)	15.8%	26	84.9%	7	13.3%	16	17.9%	26
MKT	Sales - direct mail	14.4%	27	81.6%	8	14.6%	14	16.5%	28
MFG	Product design	13.9%	28	74.1%	11	25.5%	6	17.5%	27
MKT	Sales - representative	12.9%	29	29.0%	34	17.5%	9	15.2%	29
FA	Data processing	11.5%	30	91.9%	6	25.4%	7	14.4%	30
GA	Mailroom functions	9.9%	31	125.9%	4	26.2%	5	12.4%	31
GA	Clerical functions	9.5%	32	136.0%	2	16.9%	11	11.1%	32
IS	Batch processing	8.2%	33	70.0%	14	21.6%	8	10.0%	34
FA	Clerical functions	7.3%	34	181.2%	1	40.0%	3	10.2%	33
MKT	Sales - telemarketing	6.6%	35	91.9%	5	34.1%	4	8.9%	35
FA	Bookkeeping	4.8%	36	76.5%	9	53.3%	2	7.4%	36
MKT	Customer service	2.6%	37	128.6%	3	81.3%	1	4.7%	37

Index